Gerard O'Brien

ANGLO-IRISH POLITICS IN THE
AGE OF GRATTAN AND PITT

GERARD O'BRIEN

Anglo-Irish Politics
in the Age of
Grattan and Pitt

IRISH ACADEMIC PRESS

The typesetting of this book
was output by Computer Graphics Ltd, Dublin
for Irish Academic Press Ltd, Kill Lane,
Blackrock, Co. Dublin.

BRITISH LIBRARY CATALOGUING IN PUBLICATION DATA

O'Brien, Gerard
Anglo-Irish politics: in the age of Grattan and Pitt.
1. Ireland — Politics and government — 18th century.
I. Title
320.9415   JN1411

ISBN 0-7165-2377-9

Printed in Great Britain by
Antony Rowe Ltd, Chippenham, Wiltshire

Contents

Contents

To the memory of
Matthew Francis O'Brien
(1916-1975)

Acknowledgments

In the course of writing this book numerous debts of gratitude have been incurred: Brendan Bradshaw who so benevolently supervised the doctoral dissertation on which it is based; Anthony Malcomson who provided unstinting help at all stages and hospitality at several; Jim and Una O'Donovan, Gerry Kelleher and Tony O'Brien who forebore the mercurial personality of the author at many moments; Joe Lee whose advice was important at both the opening and closing stages; the Master and Fellows of Peterhouse, Cambridge, but more especially Martin Golding and Philip Pattenden who at various times smoothened a strained atmosphere; David Cannadine of Christ's College, Cambridge, who was positive at moments of great negativity; Michael Ryder, now of H.M. Foreign Office, who set the standard. In addition, relief and sustenance was provided from time to time by Gearoid and Marian Ó Tuathaigh, Tom Dunne, Michael Cullinan, Eunan and Rosemary O'Halpin, John Sansom, R.J. Hunter, Peter Roebuck, Tony Hepburn, Frank D'Arcy and Peter Jupp. Frank Cassidy of Magee College gave crucial guidance with the transformation of typescript into floppy disk. Michael Adams of Irish Academic Press adopted a patient and positive approach throughout. Formal thanks must also be offered to the owners of the several manuscript collections listed in the bibliography, to the staffs of the various record offices and libraries in which I worked, to the authors of the unpublished theses which I was permitted to read, and in particular to the University of Ulster for a generous grant in aid of publication.

Aside from such formal and informal plaudits, acknowledgment must be made to my mother whose assistance and support throughout was unfailing and unrewarded but, despite appearances, never unappreciated.

Introduction

It has now been over twenty years since J.C. Beckett drew attention to the profusion of writings on late eighteenth-century Irish political history "a mere list of which", he asserted, "would make up a moderate-sized volume".[1] However, it is clear from a glance at this list that it is largely composed of near-contemporary memoirs by participants and eye-witnesses, or of their correspondence, published by proud and selectively-minded descendants. In fact between the classic narrative histories by Froude and Lecky in the nineteenth century and the work of E.M. Johnston and Beckett in the 1960s, the scholastic coverage of the period 1782 to 1800 has been spasmodic, limited in terms of research, and narrow in its general outlook.

The nationalist political movement of the late nineteenth and early twentieth centuries gave rise to a formidable but carefully slanted rash of political studies of the late eighteenth century. All of these were designed to justify the proposed overthrow of the union by portraying the supposedly immoral manner in which that union had been brought about.[2] The growing stability which accompanied the establishment of the Catholic nationalist Irish State in the 1930s and '40s saw the rise of two simultaneous and interconnected phenomena. The need to justify the revolution by which the State had been established had now given way to the need to furnish the State with pre-revolutionary foundations of a type which would reflect the credibility and righteousness of its people's national pride. Hence it was that several skilled and relatively unbiassed authors turned their attentions to the study of the United Irishmen who were regarded as the ancestral founders of the modern Irish State, and to the struggle for Catholic Emancipation which was believed to represent the essence of the Irish spirit.[3] The two strands tended to complement each other and suggested a type of identity to which twentieth-century Irishmen could relate without doubt or qualm. Both strands represented a collective tale of suffering and triumph, of temporary defeat and ultimate victory, of crucifixion and resurrection.

The second phenomenon was the rise of a generation of post-revolutionary scholars who scrutinised the now-neglected field of the Anglo-Irish gentry and their politics. Perhaps not too surprisingly, the work of the former scholars saw publication while that of the latter group remained (and still remains) in the form of unpublished M.A. theses.[4] Only the most successful of these works, that of R.B. McDowell, became commonly available.[5] The restrained publishing industry of pre-war Ireland had little interest in sophisticated studies of traditions and characters who seemed irrelevant to the modern Irishman. Beyond irrelevance was the race-memory that the Anglo-Irish of the 1790s had been the enemies both of United Irishmen and Catholic Emancipation. Moreover, the process of re-Gaelicization (then in progress) could scarcely be combined with in-depth study of the ancient enemy without risk of purposeless distraction.[6]

Although thorough in their treatment of printed sources, few of the authors of the M.A. theses of the 1930s were able or willing to make use of the indispensable manuscript material which even then lay in abundance in Irish and British repositories. But aside from the limitations imposed by the neglect of manuscript sources the real failure of the post-revolutionary generation was one of imagination. No attempt was made to depart substantially from the uncritical and somewhat sympathetic narrative set down by Lecky. With the exception of McDowell whose work on the rise of democratic thought between 1750 and 1800 remains one of the more positive contributions of the period, none of the later works did other than to "fill out" Lecky's treatment in point of detail.

With the exception of a carefully-researched study of the Irish militia and of Edmund Burke's attitude(s) to Irish affairs the years 1945-63 comprised a singularly uninspired period which saw few unpublished works on the late eighteenth century and none of which was prepared to revise the Leckian view on the basis of comprehensive research.[7] One of the many tragedies of eighteenth-century Ireland was that the divisions between its several communities were so acute as to make it possible for later generations of scholars to concentrate exclusively upon one community with no more than passing reference being made to other sectors of the same society.

The view of eighteenth-century Ireland presented in published and unpublished works until the 1960s failed to differ significantly from the whiggish interpretation set down by Lecky. The identification of the patriot members with the promotion of enlightened reform, with the winning of the 1782 constitution, and with the efforts to defend that constitution from encroachment and union became embedded in Irish mythology with unfortunate consequences. Firstly, the integrity and cohesiveness of the patriots, although never fully investigated, became not objects of critical scrutiny but rather accepted facts to be added to and consolidated. Secondly, the attention afforded the patriots and their various activities led to scholarly neglect of the other groups and members of the Irish parliament, an imbalance which has not yet been properly redressed. But the most damaging

12

aspect of the Lecky inheritance has been the concept of the Irish and British administrations not as rational and responsible governing entities but rather as misguided reactionary bodies obstructing the inevitable advance of progress. Despite McDowell's efforts to present a more balanced analysis, this understatement and distortion of the role of government in Irish affairs was reproduced undiluted in a major study of the period in 1965.[8]

The application of Namierite techniques to Irish politics by E.M. Johnston in 1963 represented the first effort to break the familiar succession of uncritical narratives.[9] Although primarily descriptive due to the amount of material to be covered, the book laid the foundations for future specialised studies of the Anglo-Irish political machinery. A year later in a short but brilliant reappraisal of the period Beckett drew attention to the absence of any "alternative" assessment of later eighteenth-century Ireland.[10] But aside from G.C. Bolton's specialised account of the passing of the Act of Union, the only serious attempt to examine the attitudes and motivation of those who composed the administrations has been the study of John Foster, the last Speaker of the Irish Commons.[11] Although necessarily a mainly Foster-related book, the depth with which Malcomson has treated his subject has provided much encouragement for further work on the roles of both governments.

The nature of the 1782 settlement was such that the balance of power which had existed throughout the century between the Irish parliament and the administrations in Dublin and London shifted dramatically in favour of the Irish parliament. The essence of the settlement had been the effective abolition of the power possessed by the two administrations to restrict and control the passage of legislation through parliament. The overall effect of this abolition was to standardise the existing power of legislative veto possessed by both parliaments in order that each could defend itself on equal terms from incursions by the other. The policies, wishes and actions of the non-government members of parliament, which hitherto (because they were at the mercy of the veto possessed solely by government) had been merely of academic consequence, were now invested with a very real significance. The Irish "opposition", whether patriot or venal, had acquired a share in the exercise of legislative power in Ireland. A situation had come into being which had never before existed and which after 1800 was never to exist again. "Grattan's Parliament" was a unique institution. Its uniqueness lay not less in its lack of precedence and sequel than in the degree of complexity which the conditions governing its existence lent to the decision-making process in Irish affairs. Since the London and Dublin administrations were now obliged to share their mandate for the making of Irish policy with the elected members of the Irish parliament legislative power over Ireland rested not only between London and Dublin (as it had done at least since 1720) but rather between those two administrations and that parliament. In short, an experiment in power-sharing between the British government and the Anglo-Irish community had come into being. This book is an exposition and an analysis of the manner in which that experiment was conducted.

The scope and content of the book have been determined as much by the limitations of source material as by the nature of the problem. One of the reasons underlying the failure of past commentators to give balanced consideration to Irish opposition members and groups was the loss of relevant family papers. The fact that Grattan near the end of his life rewrote his earlier speeches[12] suggests that he may also have destroyed his earlier papers in the vain effort to create an illusion of consistency. None of Corry's papers and only a tantalising few of Forbes's letters have survived. Since the heydays of Lecky and McDowell the papers of "great interests" such as the Shannons and Leinsters have been added to the corpus of available sources but, somewhat surprisingly, were of disappointing quality.

Like historians who preceded me in this area I was forced back to the well-thumbed *Parliamentary Register* for guidance as to opposition politics and attitudes. But the *Register* is by no means a questionable or necessarily unreliable source. It is unlikely that the public arguments employed by the vocal sector of the opposition were a false representation of their private views because no conglomerate as diverse as that which at any given moment composed the Irish opposition could have survived long in the face of such machiavellianism; true conspiracy demands a much higher level of commitment.

However, it is in this very area — that of members' allegiance — that the real potential of the *Register* has never been appreciated. It is true that no more than a fraction of the Irish Commons ever gave utterance. But even in a period when party could still be overshadowed by the accusation of "faction", and group membership was a creature as fluid as circumstance, one member could still speak for many. In the past the *Register* has been used to illustrate the views of opposition members — to fill the gaps left by the absence of family papers. In this work it is being used to trace, through the speaking patterns of members, the ebb and flow of the anti-government phalanx and the development of an "alternative" government on the opposition benches. Little attention has been paid to opposition members' role as philosophers or as purveyors of a social doctrine except where these sentiments can be shown to have been profitable in terms of obtaining further support. The opposition are depicted in Chapter 4 rather as practical-minded politicians whose object was the achievement of

14

their policies either in a piecemeal fashion by passing relevent bills or *en masse* by the defeat and downfall of the government and the establishment of their own policy-makers in the Castle.

Certain presumptions have been made. However fluid was the concept of group loyalty in the later eighteenth century it has never at any time been other than inimical to even the most elementary form of group achievement for members of the same group to speak against each other. Therefore, whenever this has occurred I have (rightly or wrongly) considered it to indicate a shift in members' political alignment or, where the evidence allows, as a struggle between individual members for personal dominance within the group or alliance of groups which at a given moment made up the anti-government section of the House.

Manuscript letters which might have cast much-needed light on the internal politics of the Dublin Castle administration appear to have been lost. In an effort to repair this defect (to whatever limited extent possible) the papers of individual lords lieutenant and chief secretaries were pillaged for originals or copies of letters from leading Castle figures such as John Beresford, John Foster, John FitzGibbon and others. My astonishing lack of success in this endeavour, together with the fact that Foster's own voluminous papers are not particularly informative in the realm of Castle politics, leads me to the tentative conclusion that such evidence may never have existed. It is true that in several instances letters of leading politicians (FitzGibbon and Henry Flood for instance) were deliberately destroyed. It is conceivable that the originals of letters to a small number of confidants and friends were purged at the behest of the dying politician or of his immediate relatives. But it is scarcely possible that such a purge could have been extended to the papers of several lords lieutenant and chief secretaries, some of whom would not have been on intimate terms with Castle administrators and virtually all of whom left Ireland at the close of their terms of office. Members of the opposition were often in the position of having to communicate with each other from their respective constituencies — the few collections which have survived the no less energetic purging of their papers testifies to this. But the Castle administrators, even between sessions, worked in close proximity to each other and to the chief secretary within the confines of the Castle itself. They would have had no occasion to write to each other unless one of their number was in London or in the provinces — the fact that the bulk of the surviving original letters from the Castle mandarins falls into these latter categories would appear to support the theory. Further corroboration is provided by the fact that it proved possible in many instances to identify the views of the Castle administrators from the dispatches of the viceroys and chief secretaries, even in the absence of personal letters.

The loss of virtually all of the proceedings of the Irish House of Lords would have been a matter of devastating consequence but for the strange balance of power which prevailed in Ireland. Despite the fact that several members of the upper House were regarded as leading parliamentary "interests" they as individuals were evidently regarded by the government as posing no threat. Throughout the hundred or so volumes of dispatches and letters which reflect the fears, joys and general views of the Irish viceroys for this period, the Irish Lords scarcely merit a mention except as "controllers" of members of the lower House. Their appearance in official correspondence almost invariably related to patronage, and their political influence seems to have operated by proxy through "their" members in the Commons. The few printers who sought to exploit the commercial value of parliamentary debates confined their publications to the proceedings of the lower House. This happy combination of circumstances has enabled me largely to ignore the upper House except when its perambulations in some way affected the overall course of events.

Finally, this study is not concerned with constituency politics. The minutiae of inter-changing interests in the Irish provinces undoubtedly had some effect on the ebb and flow of events in the larger arena of parliament, but any attempt to give coherence to them would necessitate at least three further books. Moreover, for more salient reasons which emerged in the course of the enquiry and which are outlined in the Conclusion a Namierite analysis of constituency matters was felt to be inappropriate.

1

Government and Opposition in Ireland, 1692-1780

The rather exclusive nature of the Irish parliament in the eighteenth century was not as uncharacteristic as was once suggested. It was true that Catholics were excluded by law, but this was also the case in England. In terms of genuine representativeness the Irish parliament was no less a misnomer than its English counterpart. The ideology which governed parliamentary institutions for much of the eighteenth century was grounded in the notion of "virtual" rather than direct representation with social and economic status as the criteria for a share in the franchise. This system operated to exclude the bulk of Englishmen from their parliament and from choosing its members, as much as it did Irishmen from their legislature.

The difference between the situations lay not in superficial structures but in dissimilar social contexts. At the root of conscious exclusivity lay fears which themselves grew from the circumstances of the political system's foundation. The victors in both kingdoms feared the postponed wrath of their erstwhile foes. The fear of a Jacobite resurgence which pervaded England for the first quarter or more of the century faded gradually as some enemies became reconciled to the Hanoverian State and others failed to pass their spleen to the succeeding generation.

In Ireland, however, the Jacobites who had been defeated at the Boyne were regarded as enemies of the State less because of their politics than because of their religion. The war in Ireland at the end of the 1680s, as well as being bloodier and more desperate, was also more openly sectarian in character than had been the case in England. In England a political coup with religious undertones had taken place; in Ireland a colonist minority had engaged in a struggle to retain its property and social standing against an indigenous people who regarded the property as theirs and the colonists as heretics and invaders. In England the war was primarily political; in Ireland it was primarily sectarian. Both Protestants and Catholics in Ireland then and now, agree in their interpretation of the events of 1690: It was the year that William of Orange came to defeat the Catholics. The reality — that William had come to defeat Jacobites — has never been thought relevant in Irish history.

Because a week was no shorter in eighteenth-century politics than it is now, it was possible for the English Jacobites to change sides or fade away. But the failure to extend olive branches or inducements to the defeated Irish Catholics had the effect of transforming the victory into a permanent truce. The fragility of this truce was to remain a matter of guesswork for both government and opposition for the whole of the eighteenth century. But even had the passage of time led to trust, and trust to reconciliation, between the Irish Catholics and Protestants it is certain that such harmony would not have altered the material realities of the Williamite settlement. For many reasons Catholicism remained the *bete noir* of a vocal and powerful (if decreasing) minority of Englishmen until 1829 and even later. Irish Protestants could not realistically have shared landed property with Irish Catholics without the permission of the monarch of both kingdoms (who was sworn at his coronation to uphold a Protestant establishment) and of the English parliamentarians whose fears were grounded in history but real enough.

Thus it was that the Boyne marked not the end of sectarian conflict in Ireland but rather a stage in its development. The membership and legislation of the Irish parliament in the eighteenth century were from the beginning circumscribed by fear of the Catholic population and the members themselves preoccupied with the need to secure Protestant persons and property against the long-awaited renewal of the war. The principal side-effect of these circumstances was to poison the relationship between the Irish parliamentarians and the English government. The English ministers, presiding as they did over a country in which Catholics were too few in number to present any threat to the State, displayed from an early stage in their dealings with the Irish parliament an indifference to the anxieties of Irish Protestants. The terms of the Treaty of Limerick were regarded by the Protestants as too lenient to allow them to live securely in Ireland. The five-year dispute which followed the signing of the Treaty in October 1691 reinforced their hostility towards the defeated Catholics and created the contentious relationship between government and colonists which was to characterise the Irish legislative processes for the whole of the eighteenth century. The second civil article of the Treaty guaranteed to those Irish Jacobites who were still in arms continued possession of their estates in return for submission. The original draft of the second civil article may have included the Jacobites in the five western counties of Limerick, Kerry, Clare, Mayo, and also Cork. But in the signed copy of the Treaty, on its arrival in England, the crucial words signifying the inclusion of the above counties were omitted. William in his privy council accepted the evidence of his leading negotiator that the omission was a clerical error and ordered that the "missing clause" should be restored. In 1697 the civil articles in the form of a bill were transmitted to London

18

by the Irish government in accordance with Poynings' Law procedure, for the approbation of William and the English privy council. The contentious clause was again omitted. The bill was submitted to William (in Holland) and without apparent explanation he gave his approval to the bill regardless of the omission. The bill was then accepted by the Irish Commons but was less easily accepted by the Irish Lords, a number of whom protested vigorously against the omission of the celebrated clause. The Lords' protestations were viewed as "surprising" by contemporaries and as "remarkable" by historians[1], but explanations of the phenomenon have been less than adequate. It is plausible that "public opinion" was by 1697 "so favourable to the Catholics" as to permit the inclusion of the clause.[2] If so, the fact was ignored by the surely more sensitive Commons. It is probable that the attitude of the Lords concerned stemmed from party politics. It is even possible that the "recent Protestants" amongst the protesting peers metaphorically bled a little for the Catholics.[3] But it is also likely that the Lords' indignation related to the fact that the arbitrary omission of the clause from the bill was undertaken by the lords justices and without the sanction of the Irish parliament. The lords justices ran the Irish government in the absence of a lord lieutenant or lord deputy. Together with their few administrative assistants, the lords justices of 1697 formed the nucleus of the Irish privy council. Conclusive evidence for the latter theory is of course no more plentiful than for the others. In the succeeding century it was the Commons rather than the Lords which led the campaign against the Irish privy council's practice of interfering with Irish measures before transmitting them to London. But the Commons of 1697, having delayed the introduction of the bill for over five years, may well have taken the line of least resistance rather than risk the subsequent appearance of an alternative and perhaps even less favourable bill. We do not as yet know the extent to which Irish measures were altered or suppressed by the Irish privy council during the first half of the eighteenth century, but by 1750 such interference had become an annual practice and by 1779 a major constitutional grievance.

A further historical mystery is the failure of the English government of the 1690s to appreciate the reasons which underlay Irish Protestant fears. It is true that for William Ireland was an unwelcome distraction in a time of European uncertainties, but even he could not have been unaware that the sheer number of Catholics in Ireland lent a disagreeable reality to the colonists' fears.[4] An explanation of sorts may lie in the possible failure of the English government to grasp the implications of Irish history. The social stability which played such a major part in the relatively bloodless victory of William in England and the transfer of power to his ministers did not exist in

Ireland. Stability in England at this time rested on the popular belief in Protestantism and the acceptance of the deference relationship. The fearful murmurings of the Irish Protestant parliamentarians do not give the impression that respect for and obedience to one's patriarchal overlord had survived the Jacobite war — if indeed they had ever existed. The Protestants' anxiety at the supposed "leniency" of the Treaty of Limerick is credible evidence that the Catholic populace regarded them as land-thieves, foreigners and heretics. The more notorious proceedings of the "Patriot Parliament" of 1689 seemed to corroborate the Protestant fears. The roles played by common nationality and common religion in sustaining the deference relationship in England have not been the subject of much research. It may have been that the English ministers of William's time and later were simply unable to comprehend the implications of a society (even an Irish one) without deference.

But long before the Treaty of Limerick became a point of parliamentary discussion the sense of insecurity it created amongst the colonists had spilled over into the Irish parliament. Until the construction (begun in 1729) of the imposing edifice which still stands on College Green the Irish parliament met in Chichester House, a decrepit mansion on the same site.[5] The parliament of 1692 lasted but a few weeks, the lord lieutenant of the day (Lord Sydney) being forced to quickly prorogue what he termed "a company of madmen".[6] Three issues bedevilled Sydney's efforts to orchestrate a smooth session. Firstly, the colonists were unmoved by the government's attempt to reconcile William's treaty concessions to Catholics with their own insecurities. Their clear opinion that for them the war went on was demonstrated by their refusal to countenance the burning of the records of the "Patriot Parliament". The second main strand of the government's legislation, the Militia and Mutiny bills, was rejected because, among other reasons, it "gave too much power to the executive".[7] Two leading members of the executive of 1692, Sir Charles Porter and Lord Coningsby, were among the signatories of the Treaty of Limerick. This leaves it unclear whether the colonists' hostility was directed toward them as individuals or as interfering ministers. But the third issue focussed quite clearly on the extent to which the Irish parliament was expected to share legislative power with the Dublin and London administrations. Sydney, in accordance with Poynings' Law procedure, had three supply bills drawn up by the Irish privy council and transmitted to the English council for approval. On their return (two of them initially) they were rejected by the Irish Commons on the grounds that the House had not been consulted in their preparation. This was to be the beginning of a long-running dispute in which the Commons was to assert that it had the "sole right" to bring money bills before parliament. The latter practice had become common in the parliament of the 1660s.[8] The stance taken by the House in 1692 was both a defence of this privilege and an effort to curtail insofar as possible any seepage of power to the Dublin and London executives, both of which were composed of persons seemingly indifferent to the anxieties and interests of the Irish Protestants. Of the ten government bills laid before the 1692 parliament only four innocuous administrative measures were accepted. Sydney ignominiously brought down the curtain amid a welter of sordid allegations that certain members of the administration had profited illegally from the arrangements surrounding the forfeiture of landed estates.

Sydney's failure in subsequent political developments in England led to his replacement by Lord Capel who dealt with the Irish parliament more successfully on its next meeting in 1695. Two novel but ingenious measures were resorted to in order to break the impasse between the executives and the parliamentarians. Firstly, there was the material device of purchasing the support of those members who had been prominent in orchestrating the opposition to government measures in 1692. The Brodricks, brothers Alan and Thomas, were enrolled as the first "undertakers" — members who agreed to secure the passage of supply bills in exchange for a significant share of government patronage and a say in the type of legislation placed before parliament.[9] Secondly, an effort was made to restore some vestige of the government's rather tarnished authority in the matter of Poynings' Law. After the 1692 embarrassments Sydney had sought legal succour from the Irish judges who had agreeably declared that the Commons had no "sole right" in the matter of supply bills.[10] By judicious use of carrot and stick Capel managed to pass a government-inspired supply measure involving a small sum of money. The parliament was allowed to prepare and introduce the bulk of the supply bills. This strange compromise could only have been possible if some doubt existed as to the precise point of principle at stake in the issue of "sole right". The Commons was unlikely to be impressed by the pronouncements of the Irish judges, particularly in view of the fact that they had been knighted thereafter.[11] It does seem that, at this stage at least, the "sole right" issue was not primarily one of political principle or legality but rather one of power — the real raw power possessed by those who control substantial amounts of money.

Events in England led to the formation of ephemeral Court and Country groups in the Irish parliament of 1697. The lords justices, ruling since 1696 in the absence of a viceroy, recognised the wisdom of encouraging the split but were also wise enough to purchase sufficient support from both sides to safeguard the supply bills. The

Commons having been brought into a state of quiescence, it was from the Lords that the government was next attacked. A government measure "for the security of the king's person", and a supply bill returned in an altered state by the English privy council were thrown out by the Lords, a prominent part being taken (as in 1692) by Bishop William King. The issue at stake in regard to both measures was the amount of legislative power in the hands of the executive.[12]

Typical of the English government's inability to comprehend Irish affairs was the debacle over the woollen bill. The government, responding to the demands of English merchants, intended to substitute linen for woollens in the hierarchy of Irish cloth manufactures. Apparently unknown to William's ministers, the Irish woollen industry was largely in the hands of the Church of Ireland or its members, and linen production was viewed by the latter "as a Presbyterian interest". The Irish Lords, again led by Bishop King, threw out the bill to encourage the linen industry, but accepted the imposition of export duties on woollens in the belief that rejection of the latter measure would provoke Westminster into banning Irish wool exports altogether.[13] The government's disastrous failure in 1699 to prevent the prohibition of all Irish woollen exports (except to England) was not mitigated by the parallel encouragement offered to the linen industry and to other Irish cloth manufacturers.[14] In Protestant eyes the implicit encouragement given to the already-strong Presbyterian community in Ireland was compounded by government manipulation of Irish commercial interests to suit those of English merchants. The interests of Ireland were now seen clearly as being, in government eyes, of secondary importance to those of England.

Opposition in the Irish parliament in the reign of Queen Anne was governed primarily by the shifting sands of party politics in England (which saw the frequent alternation of viceroys in Ireland) and the broadening spectrums of constitutional grievances. Following an exhaustive enquiry into the administration of estates forfeited during the previous decade, the English Commons rescinded virtually all of the land grants made under William. The ensuing resumption bill in 1700 was forced through the Irish parliament only due to its being written into a supply bill. An unsuccessful campaign was waged against it by the leading undertakers Alan Brodrick and William Conolly, both being dismayed at the unsolicited manipulation of Irish property by the English legislature.

Despite the sinister use of the supply bill for the ulterior purpose of the resumption measure, the 1695 compromise invented by Capel continued to operate. Supply bills were hotly debated during the 1700s and the opposition elected the Speaker in four of the sessions,[15] but the issue of "sole right" was left in abeyance. The entry of English party politics into the Irish legislature had the effect of confining the agitation of constitutional grievances to whichever group happened to be out of favour. The undertakers began to "play politics" with the grievances, thus involuntarily taking the sting out of some of them. Such games may also have de-focussed the discussions on the desirability of an union which both preceded and followed the Anglo-Scottish agreement of 1707. Despite the considerable amount of debate generated both for and against such a measure, conclusiveness was lacking. The long-term effects of the woollens legislation can, however, be seen in the Irish rejection of an altered supply bill in 1709 and of an altered tillage bill two years later. In the latter case the issue was again that of preventing a seepage of power to the Irish privy council.[16]

The attention of the Irish Lords, who did not so readily respond to the lure of English party divisions, was for much of the period distracted by the matter of their status in relation to the upper House in London. In the course of a dispute over land and fishing rights between the Irish Society of London and Bishop King both parties appealed to the upper Houses for a decision, the Irish Society to Westminster and the bishop to College Green. The two Houses gave contrary decisions, a situation rendered even more ominous by the fact that the British Lords supported the Irish Society. The Irish Society eventually secured the disputed land but the Irish Lords proceeded in later cases to ignore the implied superiority of the British House.[17]

The gradual stabilising of the British political scene following the accession of George I was mirrored in Ireland by the firm re-establishment of Alan Brodrick in Castle favour. Part of the political stability which came to prevail in Ireland resulted from the consolidation of the undertaker system. The spirilling of the Irish national debt during the succeeding years gave a degree of permanence to the horse-trading of supply bills and Commons-born bills.[18] For much of the reign of George I the energy of the Commons was directed away from the Irish privy council (with which a truce based on mutual largesse had of course been agreed) and into personal rivalry between undertakers William Conolly and Alan Brodrick (now Lord Midleton).[19]

But conflict between the Irish legislature and the British government, when it occurred, was of major proportions and far reaching in its consequences. The long-suppressed dispute over the judicial supremacy of the two upper Houses was revived again in 1716. Following a long-running conflict over money and land between one Hester Sherlock and one Maurice Annesley the British Lords in 1720 proceeded to define the subordinate status of the Irish parliament in legislative terms.[20] The Declaratory Act was a symbol of the unequal relationship which had come to exist between the two kingdoms and which was eventually to become a constitutional grievance of exaggerated but significant stature.

The Declaratory Act was a British parliamentary measure and did not therefore become a matter of debate in the Irish Houses. The Wood's Halfpence Affair was different. Since the right to produce the coins, sold to William Wood by the king's mistress, the Duchess of Kendal, was in the form of a royal patent, it never became a piece of legislation. The Irish parliamentarians, faced with the difficulty of opposing a theoretical mark of royal favour, resorted to addresses to the king to represent their disfavour. Like the Bank of Ireland scheme, which had foundered on members' economic misgivings in 1721,[21] Wood's copper coinage became a casualty of the colonists' mistrust of copper coins; it was undoubtedly true that the circulation of any considerable quantity of such coins would create opportunities for counterfeiters. But the greatest single factor at the root of the Irish unrest was that the coins were not being minted by an Irishman for Irish economic needs, but by an Englishman apparently for personal gain. As in the matter of the woollen exports a generation earlier, the colonists interpreted the incident as a further indication that their economy was being treated by the British government as a matter of secondary importance. Much of the pamphlet literature during the coinage dispute referred to the fact that the Irish had not been consulted before the patent was issued. It was but a short step to the view that the patent was a reinforcement in economic terms of the Declaratory Act's political subordination of Ireland. In the end the British government, responding to the unusual degree of opposition solidarity brought about by the dispute, and perhaps also to the reality that the issue simply was not worth the possibly indefinite loss of Irish support, withdrew the patent.[22]

At the close of the 1720s Midleton retired to England, his son St. John (who had managed his interests in the Irish Commons for years), William Conolly and Archbishop King all died, ushering in what has been termed a twenty-year "lull".[23] The initial confusion which followed the disappearance of the leading interests — in particular that of William Conolly — took a few years to resolve itself. When the smoke cleared in 1733 Henry Boyle emerged as the leading undertaker in the Commons. With the demise of Archbishop King, the influence of his fellow-cleric Hugh Boulter thereafter went unchallenged in the upper House — though it should be mentioned that Boulter's own interest in politics was minimal. A staunch believer in the social and political stability which had accompanied the rise of Walpole in England, Boulter succeeded Bishop John Evans in pursuing the appointment of Englishmen to important Irish posts.[24] In the tranquil period between 1730 and 1750 four lord lieutenants and eight chief secretaries came and went, the majority of them hardly

24

ever setting foot in Ireland.[25] The calmness was ruffled in 1749 with the election of the Wilkes-like figure Charles Lucas to the Commons. It seems clear that the "patriotic" theories of Swift and Molyneux, as espoused by Lucas, did have a popular following in Dublin. However, such popularity could not have extended far into the Commons since the lord lieutenant, Lord Harrington, without difficulty had him declared an enemy of the country. In the parliamentary arena the affair signified the first determined attempt by the Ponsonbys, who had begun to rise to prominence at the close of the 1730s, to challenge the pre-eminence of the Boyles. The Ponsonbys, having egged Harrington on to the proscription of Lucas, withdrew their public support once the decisive stage had been reached, leaving the government and its principal supporters isolated before the storm of popular obloquy.

The ultimate collision between undertakers came in 1753 when Boyle struggled to retain his pre-eminence in the face of John Ponsonby and George Stone, both of whom were in Castle favour due to a happy change of viceroys. Two interconnected issues were involved: firstly, whether or not a surplus remaining in the Irish treasury should be applied to the reduction of the Irish national debt; and secondly, the right of the privy councils to alter a bill embodying the above application. Boyle's victory in parliament over the opposing undertakers and the Castle revealed yet again again the unifying potential of the constitutional grievance. It also demonstrated that the undertaker system worked only as long as there was an outright winner amongst the warring magnates. In the absence of such a winner the Castle might find itself on the losing side.[26]

The 1753 affair highlighted some of the more disagreeable limitations of the undertaker system, but it did not lead directly to any change in procedure or to any radical alteration of the balance of legislative power. Money bill crises on a smaller scale occurred in 1757 and 1760 without noticeable long-term effect. The critical changes came with the Townshend viceroyalty in 1767. The failure of a money bill in 1769 on the old pretext of "sole right" was interpreted not as a genuine manifestation of constitutional grievance but rather as a blatant misuse of undertaker power. It has been shown by Dr Bartlett that the large-scale policy changes of the years 1767 to 1772 did not originate with the cabinet in London (although they were implemented with cabinet approval) but with the lord lieutenant — that they were "shaped by his character, connections, political principles and his experiences in Ireland".[27] Townshend's decision to reside in Ireland for his full term of office preceded his decision to smash the undertakers, but it was in fact a corollory of the latter. No viceroy could exercise a sufficient proportion of legislative power *in absentia*. Within the space of a thirteen-month prorogation

Townshend outmanoeuvred the chief undertakers Ponsonby and Shannon and created a "Castle party". A factor of crucial significance was the extension of government control over the Irish revenue board — one of the greatest single sources of undertaker patronage and power.

The importance of 1770 cannot be overstated. It was the first of three major occurrences each of which resulted in a dramatic shift in the balance of legislative power in Ireland. By transferring managerial powers to the Castle Townshend had effectively abolished the undertakers as political middlemen and created a polarity in Irish politics which had not existed since 1692. Henceforth, the ex-undertakers would be resentful and powerful members of the opposition, whose sole aim was to re-establish their former positions by proving to the Castle that it could not succeed without them. The conflict between the government and the Irish opposition, which had for so long been deflected into personal feuds between individual undertakers, was now starkly exposed as a reality of the Anglo-Irish constitutional process. After 1770 the various constitutional grievances which had been chronicled at stressful moments by Molyneux and Swift and articulated crudely by Lucas would find new champions. The appearance of such champions after 1770 was as much a result of the new balance of power as of the stirrings in America.

The death of Lucas in 1771 left Henry Flood (who had pursued a similar line in parliament since the 1760s) to take what advantage he could of the new situation. He quickly discovered that advantage to be slight, since the venal motivation of the ex-undertakers — and of most of the other members — had not changed. Unable to advance the resolution of constitutional grievances Flood in the year of the Boston Tea Party joined the Castle, possibly with a view to changing things from inside the real source of power. The move was mistimed. The rebellion in America soon created a military and political situation which was to be to the advantage of those who could mould a coherent opposition group for an ostensible purpose other than that of occupying Castle office. From the early 1770s an informal group of perhaps a dozen parliamentarians called "The Society of Granby Row" met to discuss constitutional matters.[28] Originally led by Flood, their leadership in parliament later fluctuated in a manner not unlike that which became common in the 1780s. The group's significance increased out of proportion to its numbers as the bulk of non-government members sought to take advantage of the political uncertainties created by the worsening Anglo-American conflict, and needed a ready-made justification for so doing. The influence of the "patriot" members (as they became generally known) reached its zenith in the session of 1779-80 when a number of measures which had forced Irish trade and manufactures into a secondary role to that of Britain were repealed. The struggle which followed for the relief of constitutional grievances was partly a struggle by the patriots to retain the political position they had achieved in 1779. In order to give that position a degree of permanence it would be necessary to keep the support of the majority which had secured their triumph in the free trade dispute. Experience would soon show that such support would fluctuate in response to circumstances not in the control of the patriots. Only the government, the source of patronage, had such control in the long term. The acceptance of venality in Irish politics was from an early stage a feature of the patriot psyche; it was one which the patriots themselves would never lose and which, in the absence of constitutional grievances after 1782, threatened to absorb them into a dubious programme of administrative reform. The object of this reform eventually eroded the distinction between them and the Castle members whom they opposed.

2

The Making of 1782

(1) *The Situation*

Before we examine the conceptions of grievance entertained by those responsible for the legislation of 1782, it may be instructive to ascertain the actual effects of the restrictions complained of. The kernel of the restriction under Poynings' Law was the power of a group of men usually (though not necessarily) members of parliament, who had been appointed advisers to the lord lieutenant, to alter or suppress heads of bills at their own discretion. That the Irish privy council possessed such powers was a fact never denied even by its members.

The reason for the absence of any modern attempt to assess the extent to which these powers were exercised lies in all probability in the fact that the Irish privy council papers were destroyed earlier in this century. The papers of the British privy council which relate to Irish affairs are for the most part fragmentary. While these circumstances render it difficult to determine which heads of bills were suppressed by the Irish privy council, such an enquiry has not proved impossible. A heads of bill could be introduced into either house of the Irish parliament by any one of its members. It would be read three times before being transmitted to the other house. It would then be given three further readings and, if successful at the third of these readings, it would be sent to the lord lieutenant and his privy councillors for transmission, at their discretion, to the king who would duly consider it in his privy council in London. The ministers in London would, at their discretion, then return the heads for acceptance or rejection by the Irish parliament. The point at which Irish heads are referred to in the *Irish Commons Journals* as having been "sent to his Excellency" indicates that they had been given into the hands first of the Irish and then of the British privy councillors. Normally they would reappear later in the *Journal* in the form of a bill for passage through both houses. But if the heads were suppressed by either privy council they would not of course reappear in any form. By using the British privy council papers for the years for which it is known which Irish heads were suppressed, and by tracing for these same years in the *Journal* those heads which cannot be traced beyond their transmission to the lord lieutenant, it was possible to isolate the heads which were suppressed by the Irish privy council.[1]

The British privy council papers relating to Irish affairs before 1782 are complete only for the years 1773 to 1782. In analysis the bills stopped by the Irish privy council during these years were found to outnumber those stopped by its British counterpart. But while in each of these sessions the number of bills stopped by both councils amounted to a steadily-decreasing proportion of the total number dealt with, that proportion (slightly less than one-third in 1775-6) was considerable enough to validate the demand for the removal of the privy councils' power.[2] Sadly, neither the *Journals* nor the British privy council papers provide any quantifyable indications as to the extent to which the councils exercised their power of altering heads of bills. However, it was apparently not unusual for altered heads to be rejected out of hand on their return to the Irish Commons and to be reintroduced in their original form. The fact that these reintroduced heads were invariably carried suggests that some mutually-acceptable compromise had been reached between government and opposition.[3] Bills stopped by either privy council were sometimes successfully reintroduced in later sessions.[4]

Left untouched by the 1782 legislation, for reasons which we shall see, was the power of the British privy council to suppress heads of bills. It is clear from the extant British privy council papers that by the second half of the eighteenth century the practices of alteration and suppression had become well established. There were two methods of suppression — heads of bills could be either postponed or respited. The careful separation of the two terms on the lists of bills which exist for the 1770s indicates that a distinction had at one time been made between the temporary and permanent suppression of a heads of bill. (I have decided to substitute hereinafter the word "bill" for the more clumsy term "heads of bill".) However, by 1758 the two had evidently become confused. In that year the lord lieutenant was informed that a bill "for limiting the sitting of parliaments" had been "respited which in other words is laying it aside and will not therefore be returned".[5] Several weeks later bills for improving unreclaimed land and for regulating the giving of credit on purchases of alcohol "have been looked upon here, as not proper to be passed into laws, and are therefore ordered to be postponed".[6] Similarly the postponement was ordered of a bill concerning one James Neville "which your Grace did not wish to see again".[7] In the margin to a draft letter informing the Duke of Bedford of the postponement of three bills and of the failure of the attorney and solicitor generals to report on the suitability of a fourth, it was cryptically noted that four bills had been "dropt".[8] Several years later a bill for limiting the duration of parliament was "ordered to be postponed *sine die*".[9]

The reasons for respiting and postponing individual bills were not invariably stated even to the lord lieutenant, but their constitutionality was always a matter for concern and many bills were halted on the advice of the attorney and solicitor generals. While it does not seem probable that these bills were ever read in public, it seems clear that their content was made known to members of the British parliament who apparently had the right to request their suppression on behalf of themselves or of their constituents. The law officers experienced considerable difficulty in respect of a bakers bill in 1760 — "a *caveat agat* it had been entered with them and council is to be heard thereupon".[10] In that same year the law officers were unable to report on the suitability of a turnpike bill "as nobody appeared before them about it".[11] Similarly, several private bills were returned in 1762, "no opposition having been made" (except to one involving Limerick Corporation).[12] In 1766 the name of Theobald Wolfe was removed from an insolvent debtors bill in response to a petition from one of his creditors.[13]

But a more common reason for suppression, and even more common for alteration, was the economic factor. In 1766 Lord Hertford was informed:[14]

The book of rates annexed to the revenue act is ordered to be laid aside, and consequently all the clauses in the act relative thereto are omitted, but this is not the first time the book has met with this fate, the like having happened when annexed to the revenue bills, in the years 1762 and 1764, and the same reasons still subsist or are rather stronger against the present bill than the former, as laying higher duties upon the manufactures of Great Britain.

Some measures such as the distillery bill of 1771 were thought "inexpedient to return"; others such as the 1766 bill for better securing the liberty of the subject were judged to be "of a very nice, tender and delicate nature", and were suppressed accordingly.[15]

It is notable, however, that the suppression of a bill was conducted in terms of regret. Bills transmitted to London were in theory sent with the blessing of the lord lieutenant; the outright rejection of a bill by the British privy council would seem to imply mismanagement or lack of judgment on his part and would moreover be a potential source of difficulty for him in the Irish parliament when the bill was not returned. The alteration of a bill was a much more common process and far less a potential flashpoint.

Although the lists of bills for the 1770s yield no clues as to the precise extent of this practice, scattered references in the drafts of letters which accompanied bills on their return to Dublin show it to have been probably annual in occurrance. Again reasons were not always stated, but matters of economics and expediency were in evidence. "The only material alteration" in two bills prohibiting corn exports and grain distilling in 1765 "is a power given . . . to the king and privy council of Great Britain, reciprocal with that vested in the said bill in the lord lieutenant and privy council of Ireland to permit the exportation of corn from that kingdom".[16] The penalties imposed as part of a bill of the following year to more effectually amend the public roads were felt to be over-harsh "and in some instances to have a tendency to intimidate and discredit the subordinate officers of the peace in the execution of their duty". The bill was adjusted accordingly.[17] In at least one instance the alterations made were those suggested by the lord lieutenant himself.[18]

One rather ominous reason for alteration, however, was stated repeatedly. Two or three "litteral" amendments were made in bills in 1759, 1761 and 1765, "such as are usually made for preserving the right of amending those bills".[19] In the 1765 example this right of amendment was specifically referred to in relation to money bills, and the adjustments in question were stated to be "only verbal".[20] Despite the insignificant character of this type of adjustment it is clear that the British government of the period considered it a point of some importance that the Irish parliament should be *seen* to be subordinate to its counterpart at Westminster.

A detailed examination of the operation of the 1720 Declaratory Act in the period to 1782 has shown it to have been more a potential than an actual restriction upon Irish legislative freedom. There were in fact only 42 acts passed by the British parliament intended specifically to bind Ireland, and some ten of these merely confirmed or continued earlier legislation. Further excisions from this list can be made when it is considered that two other acts merely extended existing British legislation to Ireland and that yet other acts were a source of benefit to Ireland: "When allowances have been made on all these grounds there remain only about a dozen acts which can be regarded as new special legislation imposed on Ireland in the interests of Britain".[21] There was also passed in Great Britain a number of acts (107 in fact) which applied to both kingdoms irrespective of the wishes of the Irish parliament. A further 86 acts which regulated mutiny laws for the army and navy were also binding on Ireland, and sixteen other acts included the word "Ireland" "incidentally or for administrative purposes".[22] What was largely ignored by the Irish parliamentarians of 1782 who framed the destruction of the Declaratory Act was that the acts enumerated above did not begin in 1720 but represented merely the continuation of a pattern of legislation which had its origins in the distant past. The pattern of legislation between 1720 and 1782 did not differ from that pursued in the reigns of Anne, William III, James II and Charles II.[23] In fact the most striking aspect of the history of the Declaratory Act is that it seems not to have been explicitly used.

Despite the several disputes with the Irish parliament in the period before 1780 (1753, 1757, 1760 and 1770) the British government preferred to rely on the usual means of parliamentary management rather than use the sweeping powers available under the Declaratory Act. For this there are two interrelated reasons. Firstly, the prevalence of such disputes testifies to the development and continuation of a belief amongst Irish politicians that their interests were being treated by the mother country as a matter of secondary consideration. Secondly, the obvious reluctance of the British government to bring the full weight of its authority to bear when faced with Irish opposition suggests that the acceptance of Irish interests as a secondary matter was a phenomenon of more gradual development. The Declaratory Act, however general were its terms, was designed as a response to a specific problem.[24] Its designation as an attack on the rights of the Irish parliament and as an imposed badge of subordination was a product of the years 1780-82.

(2) *The Opposition*

Having examined the realities behind the grievances complained of in 1780-82 we may now turn to the expression of those grievances. It is important to make this distinction, for the changes made in 1782-83 which affected the realities with which we have been dealing were not designed with this end. They were intended rather to provide a response to the conception of those realities which was expressed in terms of grievance.

The assertion of constitutional grievances which led directly to the settlement of 1782 arose from a dispute that was economic in substance, however political were its overtones. The political campaign appears to have begun in November 1779 and was directed initially against the Declaratory Act. The Act was to be assaulted, wrote an astute (though admittedly hostile) observer, because it "takes away the jurisdiction of the House of Lords of Ireland". This point of constitutional law was to be advanced by a lawyer and a member of parliament, Barry Yelverton.[25] This attempt, though still expected in early December, did not materialise.[26] But within those few weeks the objectives of the attack appeared to have expanded. An under-secretary at the Castle fully expected "to see attempts made to abolish Poynings' Law, to deny the power of the British parliament to bind us by British laws in any case, and to set up a claim in the House of Lords here to hear appeals from the Four Courts".[27]

Although Yelverton's name was not explicitly connected with the latter aims, his leading role in the modification of Poynings' Law would seem to suggest that he was closely associated from the outset with both parts of the eventual settlement reached in 1782.

An examination of the debate in the Irish Commons on 20 December 1779, the day which saw the settlement of the free trade dispute, suggests that Yelverton may well have been the originator of the campaign for legislative independence. The two members closely associated with that campaign who spoke on 20 December, Grattan and Denis Daly, ignored the opportunity to link the trade issue in that moment of constitutional triumph with constitutional grievances. They also expressed themselves satisfied with the outcome in terms which signified their belief that all controversy was at an end.

Daly: I do not look upon a free trade as being free from all restrictions, but as free from all such restrictions as are injurious, or useless; what we are to receive from England will give it to us completely ... It is now incumbent upon us to declare to the world we are satisfied.

Grattan thought: the three resolutions ... in substance to be adequate to the wishes, and adequate to the distresses of the kingdom. I conceive the repeal of the prohibitions on our exports, a reparation to an injured constitution; as I conceive the plantation trade an act of kindness, and justice on the part of England ... I consider both together ... to be a cause of immediate satisfaction, a foundation of future prosperity, and of indissoluble affection.

The only insinuation that the dispute was not over came from Gervase Bushe who felt "that in a commercial view, every thing is promised that can reasonably be expected", and who had "no apprehension any thing will be retracted". But even these mild reservations were buried in blancmange.[28]

By the new year the Yelverton programme had expanded still further. In addition to a "total or partial repeal of Poynings' Law" and the challenge to the supremacy of the British Lords, an informant told Lord North of a "bill for rendering the tenure of the office of the judges *quamdiu se bene gesserint*, as in England", a tax on absentee landlords, and an Irish mutiny bill. As a means to these ends a short (twelve-month) money bill was planned "in order to secure annual meetings of parliament".[29] The members involved in these plans did not identify themselves until 9 February 1780, when Grattan "touched upon Poynings' Law, and other constitutional points, he said a free trade without a free constitution was an abuse of language". The question of the day was the government proposal that a committee of the whole House should meet to put in hand the new commercial arrangements decided upon before the Christmas recess. Grattan "suspected from the late adjournment, and from the suddenness of

33

the present motion something was meant that was not expressed". Moreover, many members were necessarily absent at the assizes. In a display of unity which was to be wanting in the months ahead, Daly, Bushe, Metge, Sir Lucius O'Brien, Forbes, Ogle and Sir Henry Cavendish supported Grattan's demand for details of the proposed agenda of the committee. The dispute centred around Grattan's clear determination that the supply bill should not be discussed in the absence of a full House. The short money bill of which North had been warned was clearly in the offing. At the Castle it was thought that the opposition attempt to postpone business until after the assizes was made in the hope that by that time addresses and instructions would have arrived to help sway wavering members.[30] In expansion of Grattan's unspecified suspicions, Sir William Osborne claimed that "repealing part of the act of parliament about glass, and leaving the other part unrepealed, was very insidious".[31] While we do not know in what manner Grattan "touched" on Poynings' Law and on the "other constitutional points", later debates make clear the import of these exchanges; namely that a more complete measure of Irish control of Irish legislation was necessary to safeguard the free trade concessions from withdrawal or restriction.

The connection now having been established between the Yelverton programme and those who were to represent it in parliament, we may examine more closely the elements of that programme which did not form part of the 1782 settlement but were rather the means by which it was to be obtained. The most potent of these elements were undoubtedly the short money bill and the Irish mutiny bill, though only the latter of the two was carried into practice. The attainment of an Irish mutiny bill was never an object in itself but was sought as a dual-symbol of British inability to enforce British law in Ireland and of the legislative equality of the Irish parliament. Beneath the simple title of mutiny law were concealed sweeping powers of regulation, pay and quarterage, without which the army in Ireland, as in England, would be effectively ungovernable. The administrative difficulties which would ensue should its renewal not be effective in Ireland gave it an explosive quality equalled only by that of the supply bill. Although no evidence remains as to the origins of its inclusion in Yelverton's programme of January 1780, the mutiny law was a classic example of the British parliament's practice of legislating for Ireland without Irish consent. Ireland had been included in British mutiny acts since 1701, and in the period from the Declaratory Act to 1782 more than 60 such acts had been passed (along with 26 marine mutiny acts).[32] Thus, although this particular grievance did not have its origins in the Declaratory Act, it was one of the several measures over which Ireland was refused any influence. Other such measures included the Habeas Corpus Act cf 1679 and the "good behaviour" tenure of judges (as in the Act of Settlement of 1701).[33] There seem to have been few aspects of its use in the Irish campaign of 1780-82 which related it directly to the standing army dispute from whence mutiny acts had sprung. However, it is worth noting that the standard pamphlet on the subject was reprinted in 1782.[34] Curiously, the fact that standing armies, as well as being a military threat, were held also to represent an objectionable source of patronage, went unnoticed by the Irish politicians.

In the beginning the attainment of an Irish mutiny bill was seen as a means of weakening the British government's theoretical position on British control of Irish internal affairs by revealing its inability to enforce that control. Had this tactic succeeded it would have paved the way for a repeal of the Declaratory Act which could then have been cited as an irrelevant and void statute. Only when the tactic failed did the Patriot members attempt to link the mutiny bill with the modification of Poynings' Law in an all-out assault on British control.

It is not entirely clear why the original Irish mutiny bill was introduced through the House of Lords by Carysfort ("a heavy speaker")[35] but it may have been with a view to diminishing its chances of being interfered with by the Irish privy council should it have been passed.[36] When the bill appeared in the Commons on 18 April 1780 it was Bushe who moved for leave to introduce it in tandem with bills relating to articles of trade.[37] It may well have been the fact that the government on this occasion managed to procure an adjournment by merely thirteen votes that spurred on the famous assault on the Declaratory Act the following day. Even before the issue arose as to whether or not an Irish bill could be passed the effectiveness of the British mutiny act in Ireland was already in doubt. "Many gentlemen who were magistrates" were reported to have said on that day that "they would never execute for the future any part of the British Act of Mutiny".[38]

For several weeks the lord lieutenant had been aware that the reluctance of magistrates in this matter had gone from declaration to practice.[39] He was indeed aware that the point of the proposed bill was "to enforce the independency of the Irish legislature, and the incompetence of a British Act".[40] Buckinghamshire's powers of management held out long enough to obtain a postponement of sufficient duration to enable him to regroup his forces.[41] However, the disunity manifested by the success of the move to postpone was further clarified after Bushe finally introduced the bill on 26 May. Several members, worried by the implications of denying the validity of British acts in Ireland, approached Buckinghamshire with an alternative bill which apparently did not entirely supplant the British mutiny act.[42] This was a further representation of the fear expressed by several members during the debate of 19 April that the invalidating of any one British act binding Ireland would by implication have a corresponding influence on the validity of other such acts relating to the land settlements under which many members held their estates.[43] In July a nervous Lord Carysfort was to privately suggest a bill to reinsure the legitimacy of those settlements.[44] Carried by a small but respectable majority, Bushe's bill was transmitted to London at the end of May diluted only by a face-saving amendment from Foster.[45]

When the bill was returned in August, altered and made perpetual to forestall any possible threat to withhold its renewal, the members' nervousness on the point of property ensured its safe passage.[46] Thus, while the bill's association with the Declaratory Act had not been severed, the manner in which it had been handled after its initial passing in May exposed it to a fresh assault, for it was in one or other of the privy councils that the bill had been altered. When the mutiny act was next debated in parliament it would be as part of a concerted effort to modify Poynings' Law and repeal the Declaratory Act.

In the argument published by Grattan in preparation for the 1781-82 session the imposed perpetuity of the mutiny act was arraigned on traditional grounds: "I conceive ... that a perpetual mutiny bill is beyond the power of parliament inasmuch as it creates in the crown a perpetual legislative authority distinct from, and totally independent of the constitutional legislature of the realm". But this argument was set in a distinctly Irish context — "the encroachments of the Prince" were coupled with "the usurped authority of the British parliament". Grattan warned that the act would allow unlimited numbers of troops for an undefined period to enforce the will of the Westminster parliament. It was pointed out that a mutiny act limited in duration would, in the manner of a limited supply bill, serve as a means of restricting the encroachments of the executive; for the prime minister in London is "not responsible to your parliament" and is "free from the control of an expirable authority". From this lack of popular control have stemmed other evils, such as

the frequent, studious, and almost periodical breach of the privilege of the Irish House of Commons in the alteration of her money bills; the solemn protest imposed ... on the Journals of the Lords against the inherent and exclusive right of the Commons, to originate bills of supply; the tedious, lawless, wanton and successive embargoes frequently laid during the sitting of parliament, and without its consultation. The continuing to pay, by virtue of the King's letter, the very pensions which the House of Commons had repeatedly disallowed; the refusing to give any account of the great sums disbursed by the Privy Council under the denomination of *Concordatum*, and screened from every enquiry under the impudent hypocrisy of an oath.

From this diminution of parliamentary influence will spring further evils: "it entitles parliament to repeal the octennial bill; it entitles parliament to give whatever the treasury will buy or the adventurer part with; it entitles parliament to make the king absolute".[47]

Grattan's last contribution to the argument on 13 November 1781, when he unsuccessfully sought leave to introduce a new mutiny bill, was that the present act left them without the means to give a military response should the free trade concessions be revoked. In the light of the patronage arrangements which were so skilfully prepared by the new chief secretary, William Eden, it was clear that the motion was doomed. The token counter-argument by Langrishe, Crookshank and Carleton that parliament yet retained control over the army by means of the supply bill since the army was materially supported from that source, was almost unnecessary. This seems to have been the last organised attempt by the Yelverton-Grattan group (or "Patriots") to advance their programme by means of a mutiny bill. The efforts by O'Hara and Flood to make use of the issue later that month were clearly dissociated from those of the Patriots.[48]

Other issues used by the Patriots in the same manner as the mutiny bill were the sugar bill dispute and the question of judges' tenure. The sugar bill seemed a promising gambit, particularly since it hinted at interference with the free trade concessions and ultimately took the form of an altered mutiny bill.[49] But the financial complexity of the bill made it unsuitable as a pivot of parliamentary rhetoric and its clarity as a symbol of a violated constitution was in doubt. So despite an initial success in having it re-committed in the face of government disapproval, the matter was quickly allowed to drop.[50]

The attack on the tenure arrangements of Irish judges, who held office "during pleasure" instead of "during good behaviour" as in England seems to have been a personal project of Forbes's. It was a measure which had been repeatedly passed by the Irish Commons and repeatedly rejected by the British privy council.[51] Although eventually carried into legislation it was rarely paraded during the 1781-82 campaign as a distinct national grievance. When it appeared in the Commons on 7 December 1781 Grattan confined his use of it to a pretext to debate public expenditure and pensions. (The office of judge was, of course, part of the patronage system.)[52]

The absentee tax, in whatever form it had been originally proposed, was certain to affect the fortunes of at least some of those members on whose votes the Patriots would depend to carry through their main legislation. Moreover, even as a concept it wore the mantle of an attack on property rights and so was never raised in parliament. An issue which was not part of Yelverton's original programme but which was referred to in the Commons was the British management of the Irish Post Office. This potential flame was extinguished late in 1781 through a timely concession by the cabinet in London.[53]

Thus it remains to consider the legislation which was the kernel of the Patriot programme. While Grattan's interest in asserting the commercial rights of his fellow-countrymen is clear from his performance on the free trade debates, the moment of his decision that internal self-government was the penultimate political right is less easy to identify.[54] His co-operation in the authorship of a set of satirical letters on the Townshend administration shows his early awareness of the unconstitutional behaviour of the Irish privy council: "The privy council is no part of our constitution, any more than the counsel at the bar are of our courts. They have forced themselves upon us like the Decemvirs upon the Romans. They were no part of the original institution".[55] Curiously, he finds no fault with the British privy councillors "who confine themselves within the original design of their institution, by continuing to act only as a council of advice, not of operation".[56] Within four years however, Grattan and his co-authors became aware and critical of the British privy council's power to alter Irish heads of bills. He concedes to the king the right to suppress a bill (this I believe to be an early example of the deliberate fudging of the functions of the king with those of the privy council) but not to alter it.[57]

What then is the privilege? Not, that the Commons should have *barely a negative* to a money-bill, like the king; but that they *alone*, should *propound* and *model* bills of supply; and that a power of *dissenting, only*, should remain with the nobles, and with the crown. Whereas if you give the sovereign a power to *alter*, you give him a power to propound and model; and leave to the Commons, as a security over their *own grants*, a *negative only*: that is, you reverse every principle of the constitution, and confound every maxim of common sense and equity.

Of the early career of Barry Yelverton, who seems to have been the originator, and was certainly the architect of the 1782 settlement, we know very little. By late 1779 the Castle saw him as being "rooted in habits of republicanism, of American opposition, and chained down by strong, coarse, and decided sentiments of faction, besides being a dependant of Lord Donegal's, of obscure origin and slender fortune".[58]

While it would clearly have been good politics to have concealed the constitutional ambitions of certain Irish politicians until the free trade concessions were safely passed, there was no obvious reason why the occasion of their passing could not have been used to launch the constitutional campaign. Thus it may be suggested that the programme which was to be pursued for the following two years was laid down with Grattan's concurrence during the Christmas recess of 1779, and that this was the programme the substance of which was conveyed to Lord North in January 1780.[59] The Patriot plan of action was to withhold all explicit pronouncements on constitutional issues in parliament until a sufficient level of support for their aims had been manifested publicly by their constituents.[60] This was clearly demonstrated on 1 March when Grattan joined the majority of the Commons in quashing efforts to raise such issues by members not associated with the Patriot group.[61] However, the failure on 14 April to carry the short money bill which would have ensured the recall of parliament in the autumn of that year meant that no more time was to be lost. That this defeat was a cause of some disunity among the Patriots is suggested by the fact that Forbes, Bushe, Metge and O'Brien did not support Grattan and Yelverton on 19 April.

Despite its admirably-formulated rhetoric, Grattan's assertion of Irish legislative independence on that day was disappointing in its lack of foundation. His call to the members to respond to their constituents' demands is its most substantial element, but it was not one likely to appeal to eighteenth-century politicians. His insistence that "we are too near the British nation to be less than equal to it" and his attempt to link his demand for Irish legislative freedom with the demand for liberty in 1688 were not elaborated upon but instead were left drifting in a sea of rhetoric. However, the contemporary taste for rhetoric was such that Grattan's rhetoric was evidently more pleasing to his audience than logic or precedents. Although defeated, the fact that the resolution commanded 97 votes (especially in view of the desertion of its strongest supporters) was decidely impressive; it alarmed the lord lieutenant and may have helped to heal the breach in the Patriot ranks.[62]

A motion by Yelverton on 26 April for leave to introduce a bill designed to abolish the alteration and suppression powers of the Irish privy council may have been intended partly to display the renewed unity of the Patriots as well as to test the temperature of the House. The motion was lost by a narrow majority (of 25). Had it succeeded it would perhaps have made unnecessary the campaign for an Irish mutiny act which took place between May and August of that year.[63]

The loss of the papers of individual Patriots increases the difficulty in tracing the development of their views during the long prorogation of September 1780 to October 1781. A close examination of their extant speeches and writings was made by Dr Raymond Barrett a generation ago; it revealed the Patriots as ideologically shallow and deficient in the formulation of "a system of imperial relationship".[64] Of the few pamphlets of the period whose authors can be clearly identified as Patriots, the two by Charles Francis Sheridan merit attention. Dr Barrett refused to consider Sheridan's work as seriously representative of Patriot viewpoints apparently because the second pamphlet seems to repudiate the first.[65] However, despite the apparent insincerity of Sheridan himself, the first pamphlet almost certainly represents the Patriot "case" as it stood at the close of 1779. The second pamphlet, in its efforts to repudiate its predecessor, makes use of the types of argument through which the Patriot cast of mind may well have developed the stance adopted in the autumn of 1781.

Taking a stance on Lockean principles Sheridan in his first pamphlet cites government as a man-made thing: "that *all* the power vested in the government is delegated to them *by* the society, and that consequently, the government can be possessed of none, of which the parties delegating, were not previously possessed themselves". "Nor", it follows, "can the parliament of Great Britain be rightly possessed of *any power whatsoever*, of which the members of the community, were not themselves in their *collective* capacity antecedently possessed".[66] Among the rights identified by Sheridan as deriving from God was an implicit right to "repel by force" any infringement of personal security, property, and "the right of personal freedom, or of regulating our own motions without any foreign control, as long as they do not infringe upon the rights of others". This appears to have been the Patriot definition of liberty — legislative independence expressed in non-parliamentary terms.[67]

Sheridan proceeds to argue that, even as no individual or community of individuals can invade the rights of other individuals, "neither can the government of one community [have power] over that of another. For as the government derives all its powers from the community which established it, it cannot be possessed of more than the community had to give. Hence we may judge how far the power of the parliament of Great Britain can extend itself over (what are called) the dependencies of this kingdom".[68] Sheridan (like Locke) is not prepared to concede the validity of title by right of conquest. However, he is prepared to answer it on its own terms by claiming that if the land of Ireland did belong to the Anglo-Irish by virtue of their ancestors' conquest, by what rights did *Britain* claim the fruits of that inheritance?[69] The sinister feature of the latter two arguments is the extent to which they imply a separation of the two kingdoms. The term "Anglo-Irish", it should be noted, which has been used by several generations of historians of this period as a means of distinguishing between the class represented in the Irish parliament and those of "native" Irish descent, was rarely used by the Anglo-Irish themselves. Since the Anglo-Irish did not recognise the political existence of the "native" Irish, the term "Irish" as used by the Patriots themselves referred exclusively to the Anglo-Irish community. Sheridan's admission that the "Irish" community was one quite distinct from the community in Britain took the concept of separate nationality implied by the duality of the kingdoms a step further and was the nearest the Patriots ever came to a form of nationalism.

In continuation of this theme Sheridan claims that the identity of interest which exists between the parliamentary representative and the rest of the community is operative only within that community and is not transferable: "Now can this *identity* of interest subsist between the legislature of one community and the people of another? If it cannot, every act of power exercised by that legislature over the people of another community, is a *usurpation of the fourth natural right of mankind*" (i.e. that of self-defence).[70] Ireland is seen as "forming a *different* state in the *same* empire. For in a *free* empire, composed of different states, one *community* is to another, exactly what in the same community, one individual is to another".[71] The constituent states of the empire are entitled to self-determination in all matters of internal government and should surrender this individuality only with regard to foreign policy, which should be common to all the states.[72] His clumsy justification of Britain's right to "lead" the empire stems from its "being better inhabited and more wealthy than the others". Under a superior system of government such as that of the British constitution, "it is only necessary that they [other states of the empire] should be intimately *connected with*, not *dependent upon* the superior state".[73]

Sheridan accepts Montesquieu's interpretation of the empire as a set of "confederated communities", the unity of which "is maintained by the common relation of these states to *one executive power*".[74] Curiously, his rejection of the republic as a form of government rests not upon the obvious point of "levelling principles" but rather on its tendency to break up the empire by the necessary removal of that "bond of union" the king. But it is clear that this is less an argument in itself than a means to facilitate Sheridan's arrival at the *point d'appui*, namely that the current power of the British parliament encroaches unjustly on that of the king. This clumsy exercise seems designed purely to emphasise the fact that it is the British parliament and *not* the king that is the target of the Patriots' attack.[75] The pamphlet's concluding postscript to Lord North affords a brief insight to the Patriots' view of British politicians' motivation: "Certain it is that the casual circumstance of our king's residing among you ... gives to you, groundless, and strange ideas of a superiority over us, to which you have no pretensions or ideas, [and] which we conceive owe their existence only to the insolence of pride".[76]

Sheridan's second pamphlet[77] did not confine itself to discussing the Declaratory Act but ventured also to repudiate the concurrent Patriot argument for modifying Poynings' Law and for an Irish mutiny act. Clearly the long recess had not altered fundamentally the original format of the assault on the Declaratory Act — the Declaration of Rights attempted by Grattan on 19 April 1780 as a counter-claim to the "Declaration" of 1720. Sheridan's rejection of this move as unnecessary on the grounds that the British parliament had already been seen to surrender the exercise of their supposed authority (i.e. through its inability to enforce British law in Ireland) reveals the Patriots' awareness that the victory they were seeking was theoretical rather than practical.[78] But more interesting is his point that the Declaratory Act itself conferred no legislative authority but "is only a specification of rights presumed to be antecedently existing".[79] The awareness of this fact would later be reflected in the debates on the proposed repeal of the Declaratory Act, but it helps to explain why the Patriots in April 1780 did not press for an immediate repeal of the act. It was obviously felt that the repeal of an act of declaration would not in itself repeal the legislative authority to which it gave expression, but that an inverse expression in a similar declaratory format would cancel the earlier declaration. This would restore the pre-1720 situation and facilitate the related plan to modify Poynings' Law.

Sheridan's treatment of Poynings' Law contains an explicit revelation of the roots of Patriot discontent. The origin of the "executive's" (Sheridan's own word) power to alter Irish measures is seen as lying in their inferior format as "heads of bills" rather than as actual bills. Secondly, the administrative procedure peculiar to Irish heads "necessarily prevents their being supported by that joint weight and influence which the cooperation of both Houses of Parliament would otherwise procure for them with the crown".[80] Significantly, Sheridan finds it convenient to substitute the term "crown" when he means "British privy council". Still refusing to cite the British privy council specifically he claims in response to the Patriots' second argument that the lack of interference afforded British bills stems not from different procedure but rather from the "special care" which is taken that "no bills should pass those Houses, but such as are pre-assured of receiving the royal assent".[81]

Sheridan is, however, prepared to admit to the existence of the Irish privy council, a body, he claims, to which the king has delegated the power of the royal negative. Since the use of this power is popularly seen as "ungracious", the crown "will naturally endeavour to shift the ostensible part of it from itself, and, if possible, to render some intervening body instrumental in preventing the necessity of having recourse to it".[82]

Much of the historical importance of Henry Flood lies in the fact that, in his advocacy of an alternative "Patriot" plan, he forced the Yelverton-Grattan group into an expository defence of their own proposals' superiority. One of the crucial exchanges between Flood and Yelverton, when the issue was resumed late in 1781, concerned the failure of Yelverton's draft bill on the modification of Poynings's

Law to affect the alteration and suppression powers of the British privy council. This tactic was not intended by Flood to advance an argument personally favoured by him at the time (at this point Flood wanted merely a committee of enquiry into the history of Poynings' Law) but was designed to expose the weakness of the proposed settlement. Yelverton retreated from the challenge: "I think it unnecessary to declare my opinion; I think it impolitic and I will not do it".[83]

Yelverton's obvious discomfort on this occasion and the strange reluctance of the Patriots throughout the campaign to attack the illegality of the British privy council's power to alter and suppress Irish heads of bills stemmed in all probability from the equally strange dichotomy which existed as regards the theory and practice of the eighteenth-century constitution. Official conceptions of the British constitution still did not afford recognition to the privy council as other than a body of *advisers* to the king who was still seen as the seat of executive power.[84] Therefore for Yelverton to suggest that the British privy council had the power to alter or suppress Irish measures would have been to accredit it with a power which it was not in theory recognised to possess. Thus it was that the authors of Baratariana, and Sheridan in his second pamphlet, found it necessary to use the term "king" when referring to the privy council, and why Yelverton felt unable to press home his attack on the British attorney-general on 11 October 1781.[85] Since the only recognised "power" possessed by the British privy council was its ability to give expression to *the king's* assent or veto, any attempt by Yelverton to reduce the power of the privy council would have been seen in contemporary terms as an attack on the royal prerogative.[86]

It can therefore be said that the constitutional settlement proposed and carried into legislation in 1782 was based not upon the realities of practical politics but rather upon a deliberately-maintained illusion which left the settlement incomplete and vulnerable to encroachment. The reasons for this failure could only stem from the Patriots' unwillingness to further separate the two kingdoms by seeming to reduce the bond of union between them — the king. It is clear from the attack on the Irish privy council and from the fact that the abolition of those powers was made the part-basis of the 1782 settlement that the Patriots did not view that council as a mere counterpart of the British body. In theory the council's position as such a counterpart is supported by its role as advisory to the lord lieutenant in the same manner as the British council was seen to advise the king.

However, all Patriot writings and speeches are characterised by a tendency to ignore the existence of the lord lieutenant and to treat of the Irish privy council as a body which interferes unconstitutionally to obstruct the transmission of parliament's wishes to the king. The Patriot silence on the lord lieutenant seemed designed to emphasise his status as a mere *representative* of the king and to strip him of even the mildest pretensions to personal authority. Although contemporary theory recognised that the words of the lord lieutenant represented the wishes of the king, the Patriots found it politically expedient to ignore this and persisted in their attitude that the lord lieutenant was a royal clerk in receipt of bad advice from unconstitutional advisers.[87]

The motion for the introduction of Yelverton's bill on Poynings' Law was carried unanimously on 18 December 1781, but no further moves were made in the matter until the following March.[88] In the intervening period the sound defeat of two motions declaratory of the legislative equality of the Irish parliament and implying the illegality of the 1720 act revealed to the Patriots the effectiveness of the government's argument regarding estate titles and land settlements.[89] Before the proposed constitutional settlement could be proceeded with, these fears had to be quelled. Thus came into being the heads of a bill "for extending certain of the provisions contained in an act of his late Majesty, Henry VII confirming all the statutes made in England, concerning property and commerce" which related to Ireland.[90]

Without the latter bill it would not have been possible to proceed with the denial of the 1720 act, although the proposed modification of Poynings' Law would not have been affected. This would seem the ultimate testimony that the two parts of the settlement were intended to complement each other. The Patriots' awareness (as revealed in Sheridan's second pamphlet) that the removal of an act declaratory of legislative supremacy would not affect the exercise of that supremacy was borne out by Grattan on 22 February 1782. In a speech heavily reliant on historical precedents he asserted that such supremacy had never had legal existence.[91]

It is likely that Grattan's famous declaratory resolution of 16 April 1782 would have been carried by virtue of the bill to confirm British statutes even had there not been a change of government in England during the Irish parliament's recess in March. However, the almost two-faced behaviour of "solid" government supporters (and employees) on that day testifies to the importance of this latter factor, and I would suggest that it was of crucial significance in procuring the unanimous vote on which Grattan's fame chiefly rests.[92] Indeed the effect of the crisis in England was revealed with startling clarity on the eve of the recess with the seemingly-miraculous convertion to Patriot views of Thomas Conolly, in recent times a supporter of government.[93]

44

(3) *The Government*

This seems a not inappropriate point to examine the roles of the British and Irish governments in the emergent situation. A crucial point regarding the 1782 settlement was that it was concluded with the second Rockingham administration, and there is some reason to believe that had the North administration survived, the settlement would have taken a somewhat different form. Due to the vicissitudes of the American war North's position on Ireland was necessarily subject to alteration, but his relationship with the king prevented him from making those necessary changes. Apart from the king, North's previous perseverence with regard to America made it all the more difficult for him politically to adopt a radically different posture towards Ireland. In the aftermath of the free trade crisis North's Irish policy was clearly one of "thus far and no further". In early December 1779 he had expressed to Buckinghamshire his hope that constitutional issues would be kept "out of sight".[94] Despite the warning sent to North in January 1780 containing details of the Yelverton programme, the first explicit communication of the cabinet's policy was apparently not made until late March and only then by virtue of the Irish Speaker's presence in London.

Following a two-hour meeting with North, the Speaker Edmund Pery reported that "the cabinet had resolved not to admit of any innovation in the constitution of Ireland, and this is the public language of all persons connected with the administration". Between the lines of this report it may be clearly seen that the cabinet's standpoint was not reached through any consideration of the issues. When Pery pointed out to North the difficulties of adhering to such a position on questions such as that of the judges' tenure and the habeas corpus bill, "some of them appeared to have weight with him", as though he were hearing them for the first time. He even appeared "not unwilling to relax in some points, yet he said he could not take upon himself alone to do it". The meeting was obviously followed by a hurried conference between North and the attorney-general, the latter of whom then called upon Pery to assure him that the judges and habeas corpus bills would be returned.[95]

The chief reason for the cabinet's inertia on a point on which it had resolved to take such a determined stand probably lay in the false security into which Buckinghamshire had unwittingly lulled the ministers regarding any serious threat to amend the constitution. Painfully aware that the free trade crisis had lost him the confidence of the ministers in London, Buckinghamshire was anxious to impress upon them that he had regained control of the situation, but also to emphasise the difficulties under which he laboured. Hence it was that on 17 February 1780 he airily predicted the defeat of Carysfort's mutiny bill in the House of Lords. Hillsborough, the secretary of state, took his word for it.[96] Hence also did he complain to Germain that "no opportunity has been omitted of misrepresenting my conduct by a few gentlemen who have found means to persuade Lord North's interior cabinet of their having found a degree of weight in this kingdom which by no means belongs to them"; that "some weeks ago I evidently traced a concerted plan to frighten me from hence at the same moment that insinuations were propagated in England of its being impossible for me to carry on the business".[97] Although Buckinghamshire's protestations of being surrounded by intrigue did have some foundation in fact, the two sets of letters when coupled with his occasional hints that his days in office were numbered give an overall impression of a viceroy under severe mental stress.

Hillsborough also seemed unaware of the nature of Patriot objections to Poynings' Law. On the day of Pery's meeting with North he ordered Buckinghamshire to use the Irish privy council to suppress bills containing "any latent design of making attacks on the constitution".[98] Although Buckinghamshire pledged himself to this in his reply it was clear from later events that he was prepared to do nothing of the kind.[99] The cabinet's attitude having been laid down so firmly the Irish government did not seek to supplant it even partially with one of its own. The tactics of government members in the spring of 1780 displayed no originality but rather a determination to rely upon their patronage-built majority. "You have no means of preserving the country except by a majority in parliament", wrote one government member in March.[100] As long as the British government's position in London did not deteriorate that majority seemed secure. Buckinghamshire had pointed out how "every inconvenience must necessarily be increased from the disastrous state of the mother country; the doubts of the stability of the English administration cannot but lessen the authority of those who act under them".[101] It is notable that the Irish government's success in carrying the altered money bill in August 1780 came in the wake of British victories at Camden and Charleston.

In February, March and April of that year two of the most influential members, the Duke of Leinster and Thomas Conolly, supported the government's contention that constitutional issues should be postponed until the end of the American war; neither had anything to gain from violent disagreement with a cabinet so soundly placed at Westminster.[102] Buckinghamshire claimed to have the support of Shannon also.[103] A point made by John Scott on 19 April regarding the doubtful validity of estate titles in the event of any modification of the constitution was the Irish government's only significant contribution to the debate, and its impact proved the value of the effort.[104] The British cabinet's refusal to consider Irish demands on constitutional issues was almost certainly grounded on their refusal to concede to American demands. The Irish demands, like those of the Americans, were seen not as representative of a general imperial malaise, but as yet another manifestation of colonial perversity. Informal opinions on Ireland by cabinet members during these months are rare, but Burke's description of Grattan as a madman who should be stopped could be taken as a (admittedly extreme) reflection of contemporary English views.[105]

Certainly the Patriot programme did not meet with obvious support in any area of official opinion. More disturbing however was the fact that the cabinet's policy was characterised by its double-refusal to make any public statement of its position on Irish affairs and also to justify that position as privately expressed. By this behaviour the ministers left their Castle spokesmen in Dublin unable to respond with logic and reason to Patrior arguments. This in turn undermined the support normally offered to government by the more influential politicians. While Conolly and Leinster were indeed vocal in their support of the government their arguments tended to reflect the rather unsubstantial expressions of the Castle members that the time was unpropitious for constitutional issues and postponement the most desirable way to travel. Shannon and Ponsonby, controllers of many votes, remained virtually silent throughout. The consequences of the government's ideological poverty was starkly revealed on 19 April 1780 in the disturbingly high number who divided with the Patriots.[106]

When the cabinet did act it acted in haste and ignorance. When the Patriots voiced their objections to the powers of the Irish privy council the cabinet responded with an order to Buckinghamshire to quash the objections. When the Irish mutiny bill, a representation of the Irish legislature's equality with that of Westminster, was transmitted to London it was dealt with in a manner which tended to confer legitimacy on Patriot arguments.[107] We have seen how narrowly were avoided similar *faux pas* on the judges' and habeas corpus bills. However, it is highly probable that the British ministers' failure to construct a coherent Irish policy during 1780 stemmed in some degree from their lack of confidence in Buckinghamshire to successfully implement any more complicated strategy. His refusal in the summer of that year to comply with the cabinet's wish to prosecute seditious newspapers could only have seemed symptomatic of his general weakness.[108] More than a week before Hillsborough had congratulated Buckinghamshire on his successful handling of the altered mutiny bill North had informed the king of his intention to replace both the lord lieutenant and the chief secretary.[109]

The new viceroy Lord Carlisle and his chief secretary William Eden had few illusions regarding the situation which faced them in Ireland. Eden regarded the appointment as a potential danger to his career.[110] On the eve of his departure he bluntly told Hillsborough that he felt the state of Irish affairs to be "very disjointed, critical, and alarming", and insisted that policy be clearly and timely expounded in London.[111] The secret of Carlisle's well-being for most of 1781 lay, in his own view, in the fact that he did not have to face parliament:[112]

Our political stupor continues, owing to the general dispersion of those who, when collected together either with or without design, are seldom long together without doing some mischief. The great people declare themselves satisfied with what England has done for this country; the English of which is, that they do not know what new demand to make in regard to their commerce, and in their cool moments look with more alarm at constitutional innovation than his Majesty's representatives do. But the conviction that nothing can be so dangerous for themselves as extending the jurisdiction of the House of Lords, destroying Poynings' Law, or in short, weakening the connection between the two countries, gives me no sort of confidence but that when the parliamentary fever is at its height, every one of these destructive measures may be proposed and with difficulty defeated.

To all appearances the support of important figures such as the Speaker, Leinster and Conolly had been successfully purchased. Daly, John FitzGibbon, Lords Shannon and Ely all seemed inclined to support the government. The main threat came from Charlemont and Grattan who were "in determined opposition", and from Yelverton who "will not risk his popularity by any connection with us". Ponsonby "rather keeps at a distance".[113] By the opening of the session in October Carlisle still fully expected "the most mortifying disgraces ... in spite of all the caution that prudence can suggest".[114]

Despite Eden's early insistence that his role be simply that of implementing policies made in London it soon became clear that the British cabinet was determined to be even less involved with the decision-making process on Irish affairs than it had been in Buckinghamshire's time. By July 1781 Eden had received only one private letter from North. Hillsborough "is really attentive and punctual; but he wants either power or energy, and too often leaves us to fight our own battles at a great disadvantage when a slight exertion on the spot would do the business".[115] Lack of explicit directions less than a month before the resumption of parliament led the Castle to formulate its own proposals.[116]

The proposals show the Castle's determination to continue the policy adopted in Buckinghamshire's time of flat opposition to all issues affecting the constitution. Motions on Poynings' Law, the mutiny act and the Declaratory Act were forecast. A lack of certainty regarding the likely format of the assault on the Declaratory Act led the Castle to reserve to itself the right to resist it in a manner of its own choosing. On the continuing difficulties relating to the desired separation of the post offices, the judges, the habeas corpus bill and the sugar duties, the Castle was prepared to make recommendations but emphasised the need for "the most early and explicit instructions upon them; as they will otherwise come upon me in such a manner as to oblige me to act from my own judgment".[117]

The replies from both Hillsborough and North were negative, unhelpful, and displayed a failure to appreciate the parliamentary difficulties faced by the Irish administration. Attempts to advance constitutional matters were to be stonewalled "totis viribus". The Castle's concessionary proposals on the more minor issues — which had clearly been designed to facilitate the intended resistence to constitutional motions — were blasted almost without exception. Those proposals which did not draw an immediate negative response were postponed for later consideration or irritatingly left to Eden's own discretion.[118]

Carlisle's government won all but two of the divisions on constitutional or constitution-related issues which took place between 1 November 1781 and 2 March 1782. In analysis this meant that the Castle defeated two successive motions by Grattan and Flood to repeal the mutiny act; defeated a proposed amendment on a loyal address which was then carried; two successive motions by Grattan and Flood on the Declaratory Act; two motions on Portuguese trade, sugar duties and public accounts designed to embarrass the government; and Flood's motion for a committee on the history of Poynings' Law. The two Patriot victories both belonged to Yelverton who obtained *unanimously* leave to introduce his bills to modify Poynings' Law and to confirm the validity of previous statutes.[119] Except for these two divisions, which occurred months apart, the government wavered without obvious pattern from 51 to 81. It soared only on 4 December 1781 (to 128 and 130) in the divisions on the loyal address which followed the British defeat at Yorktown, Virginia. This latter event, together with the consequent collapse of the North government in March 1782, did not by themselves bring about the shifts in alignment by which the Irish settlement of 1782 was reached, but they did help to create the climate in which such shifts became inevitable.

That the military significance of the Yorktown disaster was fully appreciated in Dublin is clear from the debate of 4 December which turned on the issue of continuing the American war. Interestingly this issue split the Patriot ranks. The conflict was probably more a reflection of a difference of opinion as to tactics than of any fundamental lack of unity regarding Ireland's position in the empire. It would have been felt by many that Grattan's opportunism in opposing the loyal address was in bad taste at such a moment.[120] The division figures (167 to 39 and 167 to 37) indicated that most Patriots sided with Yelverton in support of the address. But as the real impact of Yorktown on the British cabinet's position was not immediate, nor was it so in the Irish context. Buoyed up by the support of Daly, Bushe, FitzGibbon, the Ponsonbys and the Donegals, all of whom had been charmed into the government camp by mid-November, the Castle managed to defeat Grattan on 7 December and Flood four days later.[121]

The significance of the debate on 4 December was that it marked the beginning of an association between Yelverton and the chief secretary, of which Grattan certainly certainly knew nothing, and which was designed to facilitate the introduction of Yelverton's bill to modify Poynings' Law. On the day before this debate of 4 December (and therefore too late for London to stop him) Eden had reported to the cabinet that Yelverton had agreed to personally bring forward the loyal address in exchange for government neutrality when he would move for leave to introduce his bill on Poynings' Law. Following the debate Eden emphasised to the cabinet that the loyal address had been thought impossible to carry, "and if I had not contrived to have the business brought forward by Mr. Yelverton it would have succeeded with less effect. He is a well-meaning man; of strong understanding and generous feeling; personally kind towards me; but decidedly opposed in his general system to every possible administration".[122]

Despite Eden's claim to have reserved the right to oppose Yelverton's bill itself, and his offer to renage on the deal if the cabinet so desired, the fait accompli had been perfectly executed. The cabinet could scarcely order Eden to dishonour his word in a matter connected with a loyal address.[123] The unanimity of the vote of 18 December (the day on which Yelverton collected his dues) signified that the principle of the 1782 settlement had been conceded by the Irish government and, by implication, the cabinet in London also.

The question remains as to why Carlisle and Eden brought about such a drastic reversal in policy. The move could scarcely have been brought about by the loyal address of 4 December which, however desirable, was not a necessity. There are some indications that Eden's view of Irish policy had never really coincided with that of the cabinet, and his reluctance to accept the post of chief secretary may have had roots deeper than fears for his career. By December 1781 the cabinet had moved in the direction opposite to that of legislative independence and was instead inclined towards an union with Ireland. On the day on which Eden reported his agreement with Yelverton, Hillsborough wrote to Carlisle of his hopes of such an union, "and I very sincerely hope the glory of your Excellency's administration may be crowned with the completion of that important and salutary measure".[124] As early as January 1780, months before his appointment to Ireland, Eden had shown "some degree of reprobation" on this subject and had been in touch with one who (although differing from him as regards an union) thought the Patriot effort on free trade "a virtuous one" and wished them well.[125] Eden's stated opinion of Yelverton demonstrates that he was far from seeing the Patriots as shatterers of empire. But until Yorktown there is no evidence that Carlisle and Eden intended to deviate from the cabinet's general view on constitutional issues, even if lack of instructions forced them to initiate their own tactics.[126] After Yorktown the opinions of government supporters at Westminster moved into three camps as regards the American situation. The view that the war must continue was set against the view that negotiation was necessary to stave off inevitable defeat and the more extreme third standpoint that America should be immediately abandoned.[127] It is unclear whether Eden would have adhered to the second or the third view, but his Irish policy indicates his belief that the moment had come to preserve the empire by readjusting, either by negotiation or concession, the territorial relationships within it.

But he was not without misgivings. "I do not know whether to regret or rejoice", he wrote following an attempt by Flood on 2nd March 1782 to pre-empt Yelverton's motion to introduce a bill confirming British statutes.

It is a difficult situation in which I stand: I do not know what will or indeed ought to be the result of the proposed experiment but I know that I would infinitely rather see it in the hands of so respectable a man as Mr. Yelverton than taken as a piece of popularity by Mr. F[lood].

While it is clear that Eden had been given no details of the bill prior to Yelverton's move to introduce it in parliament, he accepted it as a necessary and desirable corollary of the bill to modify Poynings' Law — "nothing can be less exceptionable". Thus it was that leave to introduce the bill to confirm British statutes was given unanimously (except for Flood) on 2 March. On the matter of the bill itself Eden could not take "any ostensible part" but relied on his supporters to ensure that the provisions of the bill were sufficiently broad to "show a fair disposition towards Great Britain". A significant element of this letter was the revelation that Grattan's standpoint on the bill was not a foregone conclusion.[128]

Although Grattan was to staunchly support Yelverton against Flood in March and was one of the framers of the bill to confirm statutes,

Yelverton's voice had not been heard in support of Grattan on 22 February when the latter's motion on the Declaratory Act was massively defeated. The alliance between the two men was clearly less well-defined than has been believed. It is possible that Yelverton was among the many who were affected by the attorney-general's argument regarding the validity of estate titles, and that his support for a resolution nullifying the Declaratory Act was dependent (like the support of many others) on the passing of a bill assuring the validity of those titles. Thus, in supporting Yelverton's stand against Flood on this issue and in helping to frame the bill itself, Grattan was merely facilitating the passage of his own favoured resolution on the Declaratory Act on 16 April.[129]

In official correspondence the concession to Yelverton's second bill was represented by Carlisle and Eden not as the result of a policy shift on their part but rather as a manifestation of the people's will and as a convenient way of silencing the Volunteers.[130] The cabinet disapproved of the bill in principle: "This bill ... would amount to a virtual disclaimer of all legislative authority in England over Ireland and take away the sole support which now remains to that claim, namely the interest which the Irish have in the maintenance of the laws intended to be thus confirmed". It was viewed in London as a matter worthy to be discussed by the Westminster parliament, and on this pretext the cabinet was willing to allow the passage of the bill through the Irish parliament at Eden's discretion. But far from representing a change in policy this move by the cabinet was merely an unavoidable exercise in expediency. Loughborough confided that North's government had now reached the state where even an Irish embarrassment could topple it.[131]

The time had gone when the attitude of North's cabinet to Irish affairs had any significance. Yelverton's bill on Poynings' Law, the scope of which necessitated a debate in the Westminster parliament, was perused in mid-March by ministers who knew themselves to be incapable of successfully carrying this bill or any other.[132] Whatever Eden's motive may have been for the petulent outburst which he made in the British Commons early in April, this speech (at the climax of which he moved the repeal of the Declaratory Act) was his last manoeuvre in the policy which he had pursued since 28 November 1781. A few days before the outburst Carlisle, in one of his last official letters to Hillsborough, had opined that such a repeal would be "a measure equally becoming and wise", and recommended it to the serious consideration of the incoming government.[133]

The men through whose hands the 1782 settlement was to become a reality lacked background knowledge of the situation, experience of Irish parliamentary patriotism, and above all the time necessary to restore these deficiencies. The settlement agreed to by the

Rockingham government represented a surrender to Patriot demands, not in consequence of any defeat but rather in fear of such. Rockingham's own involvement in Irish politics since he had spearheaded the efforts to block a proposed tax on absentee Irish landlords (like himself) in 1773 had not been impressive.[134] A brief note from the eccentric Lord Bristol, Bishop of Derry, c.1778 is all that remains of his and Rockingham's discussions on "our favourite topic of a relaxation of the popery laws in Ireland".[135] The first public assault by the British opposition on North's conduct of Irish affairs was not intended (unlike all those which followed) to use the growing Irish unrest as a means of embarrassing the government. Rockingham's motion in May 1779 was not a bold demand for free trade but merely called for "particulars relative to the trade and manufactures of Great Britain and Ireland".[136] There was no concerted or pre-arranged plan of opposition. Rockingham owned land in Ireland. Several letters exchanged with his Irish agent Denham about the time of the motion show his acute awareness of the poverty on his estate and on others. The motion, the earlier part of which made reference to "the distressed and impovrished state of Ireland", seems to have been personally inspired. Making no references to his Whig colleagues, Rockingham on the failure of the motion promised Denham that he would "probably strive again".[137]

Despite Rockingham's admission in November that he did not know the opinions and attitudes of his colleagues in regard to Ireland and his stated hope that they would not be in a hurry to get involved in the free trade dispute, opposition tactics during the winter debates of 1779 were better organised.[138] However, the lengthy speeches of Fox and the motions of censure on the government advanced by Shelburne and the Earl of Upper Ossory that winter were intended purely to exploit the Irish situation; they betokened no development of an "Irish party" on the part of the Whigs.[139] Shelburne's motion of censure was obviously the result of pressure from Rockingham: "I will endeavour to think of some resolutions about Ireland", Shelbourne wrote three days before the motion, "for besides having summoned the House, we must not ... be overrun".[140]

When the free trade concessions were finally announced by North on 13 December Fox was without any response other than to declare that his approval of them would wait upon that of the Irish parliament.[141] But behind this lame bravado lay a genuine attempt by the Whigs to form an alliance with the embryonic Patriot group in Dublin. Individual Irish members had been written to by Burke, Fox and Thomas Townsend in support of a proposed alliance which had apparently originated in contacts between Fox, James Adair and Forbes. But the effectiveness of any such alliance would of course have depended upon its expansion in Ireland beyond the confines of the small group of Patriots:[142]

When I had a communication with you on the state of Ireland, or when I had the honour of a conversation on the same subject with Mr. Fox I did not perceive so clearly as at present the impracticability of any cooperation between the oppositions in the two groups: I see now that this circumstance cannot obtain unless matters in your country proceed to such *extremities*, as I trust will not be the case: your opposition and ours must always stand on different grounds; in Ireland where no genuine spirit of Whiggism prevails, nor the least idea of a systematic opposition; an operative or effectual opposition can only originate from a jealousy conceived against Great Britain *at large*, this being the only subject on which the sensibility of our people can be awakened, and without compulsion on their part the majority of our parliament will never resist any measure whatever, which is proposed by English administration: thus you must perceive that the only means, which can quicken an opposition of ours into life, must under the cooperation of yours, [be] if not impossible, at least very difficult and precarious.

In this same invaluble missive the Whigs were informed that constitutional grievances remained to be settled:

I have some reason to believe that Ireland would be content with obtaining the five following laws; vizt: repeal of the Test Act, and 4th cap. of 20th Hen. 7th commonly called *Poynings' Law*, Habeas Corpus bill, act to secure independency of judges, and an act to establish our exchequer on constitutional grounds.

This campaign, Forbes confided, was due to begin after the Easter recess of 1780.[143]

At this point the proposed alliance appears to have been frozen. The Whigs remained silent on Irish affairs while the mutiny bill was being debated in Dublin during May and August. By November 1780 the Duke of Richmond's private opinions on Ireland had developed no further than a conviction that the present connection was "founded upon absurdity and injustice". The question of possible alternative forms of connection Richmond preferred to leave to "those who have a head assiduity [sic] sufficient for undertaking such a work".[144] By early 1781 the Whigs' neglect of Irish affairs was being revealed in the form of parliamentary confusion. Fox, in demanding the rcommittal of the British mutiny bill (the word "Ireland" had been omitted to avoid upsetting the Patriots), claimed that the omission "directly overturned the constitution of this country, and gave up all right to supremacy over Ireland".[145] Three days later when Fox spoke again on the issue he was better prepared. All references to British legislative supremacy were dropped and the perpetuity of the

Irish mutiny act was attacked on the traditional ground of the threat it posed to the constitution. Fox denied that he desired the re-insertion of the word "Ireland" in the British act and arranged for his objections to reflect those of the Patriots — the perpetuity of the Irish act, the omission of the preamble, and the non-limitation of the number of troops.[146]

The Whigs' failure to formulate a definite attitude to Ireland continued even into early March 1782 by which time the fall of North was inevitable. But when they kissed hands on 27 March the new ministers were fully aware that the impending settlement of Irish constitutional grievances required immediate attention. Of all the politicians to have held the post of lord lieutenant of Ireland in the second half of the eighteenth century The Duke of Portland was perhaps the most senior in political status. His appointment to a post normally given to aspiring politicians indicates that the seriousness of the situation was indeed appreciated by the ministers.[147]

The immediate problem lay not with either of Yelverton's bills but rather with the need to plan a response to a forthcoming motion by Grattan on the Declaratory Act scheduled for 16 April. The Whig Richard Brinsley Sheridan had been warned by his brother Charles in Dublin that the government "dare not, cannot oppose" legislative independence.[148] The consequences of an attempt by the new lord lieutenant to oppose the motion were nebulous and the attempt itself uncertain of success. Despite the willingness of Flood, Daly, Yelverton and Burgh to concede an adjournment, Grattan — supported by Charlemont — insisted that the motion go forward on the 16.[149] This was not an indication that Grattan had taken over the leadership of the Patriots. It rather reflects his awareness that with the passing of Yelverton's bill to confirm statutes, and the change of government, he no longer needed the support of the other Patriots to ensure a respectable parliamentary following.

Worse than the lack of time was the dearth of information. Picqued by the necessarily sudden dismissal of Carlisle, Eden in London in early April refused to discuss Irish affairs with Shelburne the new secretary of state.[150] Portland's attempts to reason with Grattan were hampered by the latter's anxiety to avoid accusations of compromise and his consequent refusal to communicate with the Castle except through the somewhat public medium of Charles Francis Sheridan.[151] In the event, the Irish government's need to commit itself and the cabinet in London to any *particular* settlement was removed by the simple expedient of a king's message asking the Irish Commons to consider some "final adjustment, as may give mutual satisfaction to ... Britain and Ireland". The new chief secretary Richard Fitzpatrick was therefore not bound to answer Grattan in the latter's own terms. The only accurate account of Grattan's speech on this day shows that he relied for his theoretical justification upon Lockean principles. However, rhetoric and emotive appeals left little room for logical argument. He concluded with commendable clarity by setting forth his demands in terms of inadmissibility:

6th of Geo. I inadmissible — foreign judicature inadmissible — legislative power of the council inadmissible — perpetual mutiny bill inadmissible. Limit and mould the new mutiny bill — extinguish the legislative power of the council — restore the power of the Lords — establish the independency of parliament.

It was within these terms that the 1782 settlement was to be framed.[152]

Two less well-remembered facts about Grattan's performance were that his address to the king (in which the above demands were more politely set out) was carried not by a division but by virtue of the fact that it was not vocally opposed; and secondly, that those who supported it from the government benches were cautious rather than effusive.[153] Portland certainly was not convinced:

For by what I have been able to collect from between thirty and forty gentlemen of the first rank, property and ability, to every one of whom ... I put the question distinctly upon the final judicature, independent legislation, and modification of Poynings' Law I should have considered myself warranted in saying that there were not four opinions in favour of any alteration of the apellant jurisdiction, either by writ of error, or by appeal to the House of Lords in England; that they were nearly divided respecting the law of Poynings and that among those who wished an alteration of it there were considerable differences as to the extent of the modification, and that the only point contended for, in which perfect unanimity prevails is the independence of their legislature.

But even Portland was bewildered by the general failure of these divisions to manifest themselves in response to Grattan's speech. Totally oblivious to the probability that the absence of any sign of leadership from the government front bench was at the root of the phenomenon, Portland recommended to the cabinet concession in accordance with the terms of Grattan's demands.[154]

But the other factor which undoubtedly influenced the members' behaviour, Portland's recommendations, and probably the cabinet's decision, was that of the Volunteers. Having played a crucial role in the free trade dispute the Volunteers had continued to shadow the development of the constitutional campaign, ignoring even a parliamentary repudiation of their expressed interest. They became a source of unease even to those politicians who were nominally their leaders. The politicians' leadership was indeed nominal; that the Volunteer units had lives of their own had been demonstrated by the attempt in 1780 to dismiss the Duke of Leinster for supporting the government on the altered mutiny bill, and by their efforts to dictate the behaviour of other members on the same issue.[155]

The Volunteers represented the threat of armed rebellion in Ireland. When under the influence of politicians their existence was sufficiently disturbing; without that influence they presented a terrifying prospect. As Dr Smyth has pointed out, there were "no clear guidelines" to the Volunteers' relationship with parliament.[156] Despite the fact that his Patriot colleagues had joined Conolly and Leinster in repudiating the Volunteers' offer in January 1780 to support the campaign, Grattan had decided to involve them insofar as was practicable.[157] "You seem to be less afraid of the Volunteers than people are here", wrote Lord Lucan shortly before 16th April 1782, "but I am of your opinion, since I see that the whole country are [sic] become of one opinion. The danger was that the parliament and the people at large might have differed in their sentiments".[158]

The demand for a political settlement was being supported by the unspoken threat of a military coup. How many of the Patriots might have acted as leaders is not known; only Grattan privately expressed his determination to *"proceed as if refused"* if no satisfactory response was forthcoming by the end of May 1782.[159] Portland was not in favour of a government attempt to seize the initiative in the political dispute by militarily crushing the Volunteers.[160]

They know and feel their strength, and are equally sensible of your situation and resources. They are not so ignorant of the effects of a peace [i.e. with America] as not to be convinced that if you had the good fortune to conclude one tomorrow it would not be in your power to send over such a force as would compel them to relinquish their claims; and having so recent an example of the fatal consequences of coercive measures before you they are in no fears that Great Britain will attempt a second experiment of the same sort.

It only remained for the cabinet in London to ascertain the precise nature of the settlement demanded and to decide upon the extent to which this demand could or should be acceded to. Portland's recommendations were too general in purport to be of any real assistance to the ministers.[161]

It would have been very lucky if he had explained whether he thought it adviseable to enter into any treaty with Ireland, and if he did what mode of treating would be most pleasing. If nothing of this sort is to take place I wish he had suggested what steps he could wish to be taken here, whether a mere repeal of the 6th of Geo. I would do. I own I still adhere to my opinion that giving way in everything without any treaty or agreement which shall be binding on both countries, can answer to no end but that of obtaining quiet for a few months.

An unsolicited letter from Grattan stating his belief that all the demands were inseparable clarified nothing and served only to irritate Fox with its "strange and affected" style.[162] However, Grattan displayed to Portland a surprising flexibility regarding the actual terms in which his demands were to be met. In regard to the proposed repeal of the Declaratory Act he said, "I would not despair of some middle term being thought of, which would answer the purpose, if I was instructed to assure them that the independence of their legislature would certainly be conceded".[163]

Though it was never stated explicitly, the importance of the settlement for the British cabinet was not linked with imperial prestige but rather with domestic security. The terms in which the ministers expressed their concern indicate that the potential loss of face was far less important than the possible reduction of Britain's power to defend its western approaches. This is probably the anxiety which lay behind the separate suggestions of Fox and Portland for a parliamentary commission to fix the limits of legislative independence.[164]

My opinion [wrote Fox] is clear for giving them all that they ask, but for giving it them so as to secure us from further demands, and at the same time to have some clear understanding with respect to what we are to expect from Ireland in return for the protection and assistance which she receives from those fleets which cost us such enormous sums, and her nothing.

Despite an obvious lack of any developments in early May, Fox by the 11th of that month was looking towards the settlement with greater optimism.[165]

But Portland's absence, Burke's evident lack of interest, Rockingham's deteriorating health, together with the fact that responsibility for the conduct of Irish affairs was vested not in Fox but in Shelburne all coalesced greatly to reduce Fox's influence over the cabinet's decision. Shelburne indeed had taken advantage of all of the above circumstances to ensure that the cabinet's decision would reflect his own. A speech of Shelburne's several days after Grattan's motion "was received here", reported Portland acidly,[166]

with the utmost exultation and joy. For it was considered here as an unequivocal proof not only of the inclinations of the king's ministers, but of the parliament on your side, and particularly of the House of Lords, and the conclusions drawn from it, amounted almost to a conviction in the minds of the people there that you coincide in all their wishes, that you allow them to be founded in justice, and that they must be granted of necessity.

Lobbied by one of Grattan's friends, Robert Day, Shelburne displayed the "warm feelings of an Irishman, and the anxiety of a sincere patriot".[167]

But even Shelburne was anxious about the possible consequences of the readjustment:[168]

If those ties by which the two kingdoms have been hitherto so closely united, are to be loosened and cut asunder, is your Grace yet prepared to advise whether any and what substitutions, are thought of for the preservation of the remaining connection between us? If by the proposed modification of Poynings' Law so much power is taken from the two privy councils ... are we to look for agreement in any new institution of council, which may answer the purposes of keeping up the appendency and connection of Ireland to the crown of Great Britain, and of preventing the confusion which must arise in all cases of common concern from two parliaments acting with distinct and equal powers, and without any operating centre? In addressing these queries to your Grace I make it evidently appear that I seek for information, and do not yet hold myself competent to offer any digested plan, or propose any definite resolution upon them.

Portland was able to reassure Shelburne that the British privy council would still possess powers to enable it to act as an adequate "operating centre".[169] It is, however, likely that Shelburne drew more reassurance from Pery who felt that the repeal of the Declaratory Act "will, in fact, be giving up nothing but a mere nominal power". It was to Pery that Shelburne was to gratefully write: "It will be satisfactory to you to know the weight your letter had, at least in forming my opinion".[171] The lord lieutenant's further suggestion that commissioners be appointed was useful but a poor substitute for the "middle term" which Grattan was prepared to consider.[171]

When no further developments had appeared by 11 May[172] Shelburne, probably under pressure from Robert Day, pointed out to Rockingham and Fox the impropriety of any further procrastination and requested a cabinet meeting for 13 May or the evening of 14 May. By this time Rockingham's illness was becoming a source of concern to his colleagues.[173] No satisfactorily detailed account of this cabinet meeting has survived[174] but the ministers' justifications were spelt out in parliament on 17 May. Verbatim resolutions were passed in both Houses signifying agreement with the Irish addresses of 16 April, and in the Commons leave was obtained to introduce a bill to repeal the Declaratory Act. In the Commons Fox defended his decision regarding the Declaratory Act on the grounds that the British parliament could not in justice legislate for the internal affairs of persons "who were not represented among those by whom such laws were made".[175]

Curiously, Fox did not try to justify the proposed discontinuation of appellant jurisdiction on grounds that it was inseparable from the repeal of the Declaratory Act, but rather because it had proved impossible to enforce British decrees in Ireland.[176] His indictment of Poynings' Law was founded on the supposition that it undermined the integrity of the Irish parliament, "that men who did not wish to oppose popular opinions, which they did not approve, should nevertheless unanimously give way to those opinions, merely because they knew they would be rejected in the privy council". The perpetuity of the mutiny act was of course repugnant to the constitution of both countries and was damned accordingly.[177]

Thus was the Irish case presented at Westminster as one founded in justice. The implication that England had therefore been guilty of acts of injustice was side-stepped by asserting at key points that such things were the natural by-products of North's administration.[178] It was explicitly denied that the concessions represented "a day of humiliation" or a capitulation through fear.[179] But the most interesting element of the speech was the statement that the final settlement of the relationship between the two kingdoms did not rest with the concessions. Negotiations towards the final settlement would be entered upon by the Irish administration, supported at a later stage by British commissioners, to establish "a treaty which should be sanctified by the most solemn forms of the constitutions of both countries".[180]

In the House of Lords Shelburne defended the concessions against loud accusations that they represented a surrender to imaginary grievances.[181] But Shelburne did not attack the power of the British privy council: He[182]

disclaimed the idea of treating England and Ireland as distinct dominions, united under one sovereign. A doctrine so dangerous and unconstitutional had never entered his mind; nor was it to be found in the addresses of the Lords and Commons of Ireland, which expressly declare, that they desire all acts may pass under the great seal of Great Britain. The king, therefore, as the executive power of this country, will still hold the sovereignty of that, and all acts of state flow, as before, from his Majesty in his privy council of Great Britain.

Taken altogether, the Whig performances of 17 May reflect the decision of a cabinet with its back to the wall and without a viable alternative plan. For this latter deficiency Portland naturally got the blame. Sheridan reported to Fitzpatrick that Shelburne's despatches had[183]

a reserve and disingenuous management in them that cannot be very pleasing to you who must act under them. There is a caution of fixing the Duke of Portland's representations of the state of Ireland as the sole responsible ground for the concessions which have been made. He is to be the person answerable for the consequences, and every acquiescence which he has thought necessary to the carrying on the government is dwelt on as a particular grace and grant of power to him.

60

Despite their obvious failure to agree in the matter of the privy councils, Shelburne no less than Fox was anxious for "the immediate attainment" of some assurance "in the most precise and unambiguous terms" that no further demands would be made. Portland's proposed commission would only risk "keeping that ferment alive".[184]

The carrying of Grattan's address of gratitude to the king on 27 May was the last occasion for more than a year on which the two parliaments could be said to have been in harmony. The Rockingham government spent the remaining weeks of its short life engaged in a vain attempt to formulate an agreement which would not infringe the concessions but yet ensure that the essence of British influence over Ireland would remain unaltered. Rockingham, breathing his last, hoped for an "union of power and strength, and mutual and reciprocal advantage", and for "the adjustment of any matters which might hereafter cause any disputes or misunderstandings".[185] But the plan suggested by Portland and which proved agreeable to Shelburne was[186]

an act of parliament . . . by which the superintending power and supremacy of Great Britain, in all matters of state and general commerce, will be virtually and effectually acknowledged; that a share in the expense, in carrying on a defensive or offensive war, either in support of our own dominions, or those of our allies, shall be borne by Ireland in proportion to the actual state of her abilities; and that she will adopt every such regulation as may be judged necessary by Great Britain for the better ordering and securing her trade and commerce with foreign nations, or her own colonies and dependencies, consideration being duly had to the circumstances of the country.

Shelburne, clearly impressed by Portland's promises of Irish support for the plan, "lived in the most anxious expectation of some such measure offering itself":[187]

No matter who has the merit, let the two kingdoms be one; which can only be by Ireland now acknowledging the superintending power and supremacy to be where Nature has placed it, in precise and unambiguous terms.

Within weeks adverse reaction from the Volunteers (who had evidently got wind of the plan), and probably also the situation in the Irish parliament, caused Portland to advise the abandonment of his proposal.[188]

For during these weeks the Irish members were locked in an ever-loudening dispute as to whether the concessions formed an adequate protection against incursions of British influence. The Renunciation dispute of 1782-83 had its origins in the weaknesses of the May concessions. It was now pointed out that the repeal of the Declaratory Act would not affect the objectionable power of which that act was declaratory. It was now observed that Yelverton's bill on Poynings'

Law "only transferred the power of altering from the Irish to the British privy council, and the British attorney-general". It was now remarked upon that the concessions carried no safeguard against the repeal of any or all of them at the whim of a future British government.[189]

The Renunciation Act of 1783 put not an end but rather a period to the great readjustment of Anglo-Irish constitutional relations which had begun in 1779 and was to continue for the rest of the century. The events of 1779-83 had caused a shift of legislative power in favour of the Irish parliament. The significance of this transfer was demonstrated by Shelbourne's efforts in June 1782 to obtain a clarification of the new relationship favourable to Britain. It was further demonstrated by the attempt of William Pitt in 1785 to reinterpret that relationship within the terms of the settlement but again on lines favourable to Britain. Most of all it was demonstrated by the primarily defensive and (sometimes irrationally) suspicious posture adopted by the Patriot members of the Irish parliament who in the years after 1783 jealously guarded the settlement and viewed all attempts to build upon or add to it as sacrilegious and sinister.

The Government (1): The Commercial Propositions Affair, 1784-5

The Renunciation Act of 1783 merely set a seal upon the concessions of the previous year. No commissioners had been appointed nor any legislation passed to define the new relationship between the two kingdoms. The spirit of the agreement appeared to suggest that a form of "dominion status" had been conferred on Ireland; that the Irish would have control of their own internal affairs while deferring to London in matters of foreign policy. However, this was nowhere stated in the letter of the agreement. Certainly the king's Irish subjects were bound to support him in the event of war, but nothing bound them to support the British parliament or privy council. Certainly also the Irish taxpayers contributed to the imperial exchequer, but only by virtue of their contribution to the king's exchequer. The kingdom of Ireland was indeed related to the British Empire, but only by virtue of the fact that the king of Ireland happened also to be head of that empire. It seems significant that in the late eighteenth century the British government considered the person of the king to be an unsatisfactory "operating centre" of such a relationship.[1]

In any case the incomplete state of the settlement at the time of his taking office meant that Pitt had to have an Irish policy, as distinct from just an extension of his domestic or imperial policy. The settlement had left Britain at a potential disadvantage as regards the defence of her western perimeters. This was due to the fact that the mechanisms by which those defences would be mobilised were in the hands of a parliamentary body whose relationship with Britain was ill-defined and whose obligation to mobilise had been left unspecified. The very incompleteness of the settlement was of such a nature that Pitt had few alternative lines of action in his efforts to redress the imbalance. He could have simply accepted the position as created in 1782-83 and relied upon the spirit of the agreement. This would have exposed both the king and the imperial parliament to major embarrassment should the two parliaments take up opposite standpoints on a matter which concerned both kingdoms. Secondly, he could have attempted to repeal all the relevant legislation of 1782-83 and reinstitute the Declaratory Act, thus re-creating the former constitutional position. Thirdly, he could have brought about an union of the two kingdoms and thus institute an entirely new constitutional position. But both of these latter alternatives would have required military force to succeed and would also have initiated a period of intense civil disorder. This would have conflicted with Pitt's other Irish policy of restoring order and public calm. And it was not Pitt's way to obtain one important goal at the expense of another.

The final alternative was the commercial plan of 1784-85 which was designed to reduce Britain's disadvantage under the 1782-83 settlement while not appearing to actually do so.

The 1784-85 plan may have assumed a commercial format because Pitt "was always excited by problems of trade and finance", and because he could scarcely proceed with his planned revision of Britain's other commercial relationships without an assurance that he could speak on behalf of the Irish parliament. In their original detail the propositions may have owed something to Pitt's admiration for Adam Smith.[2] It is even possible that Pitt had come upon some such plan among the office papers of the preceding coalitions.[3] In any case the lord lieutenant in 1784, the Duke of Rutland, was anxious for "a fixed and systematic plan ... for the future government of Ireland" and hoped to be "delivered from the wretched and disgraceful task of governing from day to day by temporising and expedients".[4] There is evidence that the Irish popular and parliamentary mind was ripe by the autumn of 1784 to receive a commercial settlement. The government's refusal to accede to a parliamentary demand for protective duties on coarse woollen goods in April of that year had serious repercussions outside parliament where mob violence acted in concert with local corporation resistance and press abuse.[5]

At the closing of the session in May Richard Griffith, "one of the more moderate leaders of the protectionist party", tried to include in the Commons address of thanks to the lord lieutenant a request "to take the distressed state of the manufacturers into consideration and to co-operate with his Majesty's ministers in England in forming a reciprocal arrangement of commercial intercourse between Great Britain and Ireland". That Pitt had not yet assembled his ideas on the matter was demonstrated by the quashing of Griffith's proposed amendment. However, the seriousness of the proposal was shown by the appearance of Conolly and some of Leinster's supporters in the minority, and by the petulent attempt on the following day to oppose the address *in toto* and to remove the expression of approval normally attached to the measures of the session.[6] The chief secretary Thomas Orde, wishing to avoid trouble in days of such sparse attendance and perhaps mollified by the relative vagueness of the amendment, allowed its insertion in the address when the ever-persistent Griffith produced it again as the session ended.[7] Rutland explained that the concession "was of a conciliatory nature" and was harmless in that "it pledges nothing but discussion and decision and makes no particular stipulation whatsoever".[8] In view of the fact that the first evidence of Pitt's interest in such a scheme surfaced at the end of May 1784 it is an open question as to whether Pitt's propositions originated in the Griffith amendment.[9]

Pitt outlined his plan to Orde when the latter visited him in June and July and forecast the persuasion "of those of the Irish nation who will admit of any persuasion".[10] The first and most easily persuaded was Rutland himself who believed that the conclusion of some definite arrangement was "indispensable".[11] But Rutland by his own admission was not sufficiently familiar with treasury matters to design such an arrangement. The architect was the Irish chancellor of the exchequer John Foster. His proposals, which were transmitted to Pitt in September, reflected Orde's view that the "great and material objects to be settled" were "those of the navigation act, of the trade between the two countries, or protecting duties, and the footing upon which Ireland is to be considered in foreign treaties".[12] In detail Foster's plan provided for[13]

a reinterpretation of the Navigation Act ... so that Ireland would be permitted to re-export British colonial goods to Great Britain itself; articles of home growth and manufacture should, generally speaking, pass between Great Britain and Ireland at the lower rate of duty currently chargeable, if there was a difference in the rate ...; and though bounties on exports were generally to be eliminated, the bounty system ... was not only to be preserved, but was to be rounded off by a reciprocal preference for taking corns, etc. from each other before either apply to foreign states for a supply.

But already Pitt's mind was operating on a more grandiose level. Purely commercial readjustments were all very well, he wrote to Orde on 19 September, but[14]

We must, in order to make a permanent and tranquil system, find some line according to which the parliaments of the two countries may exercise the rights of legislation, without clashing with each other on the one hand, or, on the other, being encumbered by the necessity of actual and positive concert on every point of common concern.

Acceptance of Irish legislative independence, recognition of the problems created by it, and willingness to work within the existing framework rather than a desire to radically alter it are all implicit in this statement. The attempt to link this broad policy to a commerce-based solution makes it clear that Pitt had learned from the free trade dispute that economic inequalities were the real basis of mistrust between the two kingdoms.

Foster's attempt to reduce the inequality of advantage which was at the root of the mistrust was admirable but must have seemed a little partial. As his colleague Beresford was later to say (jokingly) to Pitt, "our view is to get every advantage, and not to partake of any of the disadvantages of England".[15] Pitt declared that his proposed system should "extend the aggregate wealth of Great Britain and Ireland to its utmost limit", but "without partiality or preference to one part of the empire or the other". In order both to balance the relationship and to strengthen the connection between the two kingdoms. a new tax was hinted at, perhaps one involving the navy.[16]

But Pitt still had not decided on the details. A letter to Orde of 25 September showed him yet "endeavouring to prepare myself with materials as well as I can" and enlisting the aid of Scott and Beresford.[17] By early October however, he was ready *"to give Ireland an almost unlimited communication of commercial advantages,* if we can receive in return some security that *her strength and riches will be our benefit, and that she will contribute from time to time in their increasing proportions to the common exigencies of the empire"*. Two other considerations may have influenced the "totality" of the offer: Pitt, appalled by a summer of riots in Dublin and nebulous plots to separate the two kingdoms entirely, hoped that the offer would remove "every temptation to Ireland to consider her interest as separate from England". He also hoped to cement the coating of goodwill by "a prudent and temperate reform of parliament".[18] But the prospect of Pitt-inspired parliamentary reform for Ireland was to perish along with its counterpart in England. However, the former hope that an economic settlement would remove "all temptation" from would-be revolutionaries reflects yet again Pitt's belief in the essential simplicity of the Anglo-Irish grievance. The issue now was, in Pitt's words, one of "some security" in return for the proposed concessions.

Much of October was spent in efforts to remove or clarify sources of possible misunderstanding. "The principle must of course be at once understood and ascertained", wrote Orde, "that, the bond of connection being indissoluble, there can be no other object to each more prevailing than the best possible contribution to the aggregate wealth and strength of the whole.[19] While no obvious effort seems to have been made to come to terms with the question of "some security", Orde felt it necessary to point out that Ireland did not want a navy, could not afford one, and indeed would scarcely know how to employ one at present. Foster offered proofs ("not well founded", said Orde) that the propositions should be seen as a boon and not as a right.[20] However, fragments of doubt such as Pitt's erroneous belief that England might become an "overflow" market for superfluous Irish goods (which since the duties were to be equal could only occur in the unlikely event of redundant products) testified to the inadequacy of the pen as a pacifier of misguided fears.[21] On 17 October Lord Sydney dispatched a slightly irritated note to Rutland requesting the immediate presence of "leading people" to discuss the matter as "nothing of this kind can be settled by the king's English servants alone".[22]

It is clear that Pitt had reached his decision on the best kind of "security" before the arrival of Foster and Beresford in London. To Beresford he

talked of a general plan between the two countries, and stated that such a plan must go upon one of two ideas, either upon the system of our former connection viz. looking up to G. Britain as the superior, and allowing her certain advantages, (which he thought the worse plan) or upon a system of perfect equality in trade, to all the dependencies of Britain, Ireland contributing so far as her abilities would allow, to the general support of the empire, that to be varied as her circumstances increased, and at the same time Ireland regulating her trade with all foreign countries, so as to meet England upon equal terms in their markets.

Nor was Pitt unsupported by his ministers. Beresford found Henry Dundas "very liberal" on the plan "only wishing to know what will give content, and how that shall be given in such a way as to shew that what is given is voluntary concession, not extorted, and is to be looked on as final". Grenville and Thurlow also seemed agreeable.[23]

To Rutland the prime minister explained "that there is no difficulty that may not be surmounted, if Ireland can be brought to repay, as she ought, the concession of full *equality in commerce* by a very *moderate* contribution to our burdens, particularly to our sinking fund".[24] So Pitt's object was to strengthen the Anglo-Irish nexus by linking the Irish and British national debts. That he had already heard the opinions of Foster and Beresford on this proposal is clear from his assurance that the proposed contribution was "very moderate". For Foster and Beresford had failed to see the point, the former feeling that "it were better for Britain to leave the affair to the liberality and ability of the moment when our aid might be necessary", and the latter believing that "it was the best policy to keep the commercial subject by itself, and to leave the imperial concerns to the general unexplained but well-understood situation in which they are".[25] It seems not to have occurred to either Foster or Beresford that Pitt was endeavouring to render specific, explicable and clear that which was "general", "unexplained" and "well-understood".

Rutland who was at pains yet again to point out his inability "to speak with precision on the commercial points in question", agreed with Foster and Beresford. In his opinion the proposed new revenue was "impracticable, inconsistent with the principles of true policy, and, I fear, would completely defeat the main object of your munificence, that of quieting faction and of constituting the foundations of a permanent good understanding between the two kingdoms".[26] He further reminded Pitt that the maintenance by Ireland of 15,000 troops within the country represented no mean contribution to the imperial well-being, and that the "notion of a paltry revenue lost America to Great Britain".[27]

Even as Pitt, Foster and Beresford adopted their separate stances, Rutland proceeded to take up a third standpoint. Enmeshed in an attempt to replace the now-declining Volunteers with a Castle-controlled militia, Rutland hoped to be allowed to use the commercial concessions as a bargaining counter to push a militia bill through the Irish legislature.[28] Orde, followed by the now strangely-reluctant Foster and Beresford, was dispatched to put these thoughts to Pitt in person.[29] But while several days of discussion and more than one heated communication from Rutland impressed upon Pitt the unwisdom of his proposed contribution, they did nothing to remove his serene conviction that "these objections may be removed". Against Rutland's assertion that the Irish contribution to the empire was already sufficient, Pitt interpreted the proposed contribution as payment for "all that has been given since the first concessions from the year 1778 downwards". This disastrous explanation ignored the fact that the "concessions" to which he referred were regarded as rights by those on whom they had been bestowed".[30]

This self-revelation of the limit to which Pitt understood the Anglo-Irish mind was preceded by Orde's stated belief that the prime minister's position in cabinet on the matter (despite the avowed support of Thurlow and Dundas) was not entirely secure.[31] To this we may add the fact that Rutland's opposition, had it been carried to its extremity, might have had serious consequences. The previous month one of Rutland's London informants had assured him that he was the "principal supporter" of the ministry. Even Orde believed that the lord lieutenant's good record in Ireland would lead the cabinet to endorse any measure supported by him.[32] Both Orde and Pitt testified to the favourable reception afforded Rutland's militia proposal but it was clear from the outset that the prime minister regarded it as a side-issue and one which he was not prepared to link with the commercial propositions.[33] Orde's letter of 6th December contained no new information and its tone seemed to suggest that negotiations were deadlocked; Pitt, against all advice, would insist on the contribution.[34]

Serious illness intervened to prevent Rutland from engaging in further written recriminations and he learned from Pitt a week later that "we have scarcely any longer any difficulty, if *some mode* and *time* of contribution (accomodated in any manner to the temper of

Ireland) can be fixed". It was no longer "if" but "when" and "how". That his cabinet colleagues had not been amenable to a one-way agreement was hinted at by Pitt's remark that without a contribution "difficulty is infinite". Personally he would refuse absolutely "to bring forward a lame and imperfect system, adding to concessions on the one hand, without affording a reasonable secure expectation of return on the other".[35] On 6 January Rutland, still not fully recovered, was officially directed to urge "the indispenable necessity" of the contribution as part of the commercial package deal to be laid before the Irish parliament at the re-opening of the session. The cabinet had decided that the contribution should take the form of "the appropriation of any surplus that may hereafter arise from an increase of the hereditary revenue, beyond its produce, as estimated at present from the medium of the last five years, or any other term that is thought a fair one". Rutland was to secure the passage of an act "appropriating the future surplus of the hereditary revenue to be applied in aid of British parliamentary grants to the navy". It was to be made quite clear that this was an additional revenue and not to be considered as a substitute for any existing tax, and that it was a peace-time tax which was liable to be increased in time of war or similar emergency.[36]

As they emerged from the post-Christmas cabinet sessions the propositions appeared as a set of resolutions: The navigation act was to be made reciprocal, which meant that Ireland would henceforth have the right to export colonial products (but only, it seems, American material) to Britain. Import tariffs in the two kingdoms were to be made equal — "the same duties to which they are subject if imported directly from the place of growth". The third resolution provided for the lifting of import bans such as that which existed in England on Irish silks, lace works, copper and brass. But the main articles on which the Irish duties were lower than their British counterparts were beer, old drapery, loaf sugar, spirits, silk, tallow, starch and soap. The fourth proposition provided that "in all cases where the duties on articles of the growth and manufacture of either country are different on the importation into the other, it is expedient that they shall be reduced in the kingdom where they are highest to the amount payable in the other".[37]

This missive was accompanied by a private letter from Pitt, sweetly optimistic that the combination of Irish gratitude and Rutland's persuasive abilities would yield the desired result. Pitt indeed thought it[38]

impossible to believe that your friends and supporters should really have any hesitation, if they once understand . . . that the settlement between the two kingdoms, and of course the giving tranquillity to Ireland, and security to any interest they have at stake, must turn on this fundamental and essential point, of *reciprocity in the final compact to be now formed.*

69

Having thus dealt with possible objections Pitt went on to explain his view of Ireland's position as one within the empire and subordinate to Britain, not in terms of legislative power but rather in its recognition of Britain's position as the mother-country of the empire to which Ireland belonged as a self-governing internal "associate". That this was Pitt's view of the Anglo-Irish connection is borne out by his insistence that the commercial resolutions represented a concession and *not* a right. The colonies, he maintained,[39]

belong (unless by favour or compact we make it otherwise) *exclusively to this country*. The suffering Ireland to send anything to those colonies, to bring anything from thence, is itself a favour, and is a deviation, too, for the sake of a favour to Ireland from the general and almost uniform policy of all nations with regard to the trade of their colonies.

The concessions, according to Pitt, amounted to nothing less than permission to Ireland to supply Britain with the produce of its own colonies. "Can it be said that Ireland has any right to have the liberty of thus *carrying for us*, because we have the liberty of *carrying for them*, unless the colonies with whom the trade subsists are as much their colonies as they are ours?" Pitt would not recognise the required contribution as manifesting Ireland's repayment for the proposed concessions. The commercial resolutions, he reiterated, represented *"a mere and absolute favour"*, and one on which Ireland "appears to set a high value".[40]

But as Pitt entered more deeply into his reasoning it became increasingly clear that the "mere and absolute favour" had been worked out with careful attention to the possible effects, however long-term, upon its bestower. The hereditary revenue had been specially chosen not just as a means of repayment for past favours, but as a barometer of the effect of the other resolutions on Ireland's prosperity, since the amount of the surplus would rise or fall in accordance with the fortunes of Irish commerce: "If Ireland does not grow richer and more populous, she will by this scheme contribute nothing. If she does grow richer by the partcipation of our trade, surely she ought to contribute ...".[41] We may assume that the proposed Irish contribution was among the "various circumstances" in which Pitt placed his trust "in believing that no branch of trade and manufacture will shift so suddenly as not to allow time, in every instance as it arises, for the industry of this country gradually to take another direction". His faith in the elasticity of markets eliminated any fear "in this liberal view to encourage a competition which will ultimately prove for the common benefit of the empire".[42]

Pitt's ethical interpretation of the proposed agreement was that it served to eliminate "local prejudices and partial advantages, in order to consult uniformly and without distinction the general benefit of the empire". This agreement would make "England and Ireland *one country* in effect, though for local concerns under distinct legislatures; one in the communication of advantages, and of course in the participation of burdens".[43] Yet Pitt eschewed the idea of "a bargain" as analagous in its odiousness to "a treaty between two separate crowns".[44] In this may be seen the prime minister's struggle to reconcile the stated reality of a concession to an implicitly subordinate kingdom with the rather obvious appearance of an inter-regnal trade agreement. The pivot of the contradiction was of course the existence of a distinct and separate legislature in Dublin. Pitt's acute awareness of the reality of the situation is signified in this letter by his substitution for the term "union" (which was common currency in connection with Irish affairs even at this time) the more vague word "unity".[45]

In the relation of Great Britain [with Ireland] there can subsist but two possible principles of connection. The one, that which is exploded, of total subordination in Ireland, and of restrictions on her commerce for the benefit of this country, which was by this means able to bear the burden of the empire; the other is, what is now proposed to be confirmed and completed, that of an equal participation of all commercial advantages, and some proportion of the charge of protecting the general interest. If Ireland is to be at all connected with this country, and to remain a member of the empire, she must make her options between the two principles. . . .

To conceal the extent to which Ireland had succeeded in distancing herself from the empire she was being given an opportunity to help run it.[46]

That Foster, Beresford and Orde had been active in suggesting alternative arrangements is indicated by Pitt's condemnation of proposals that the contribution be left to depend on "the strongest general pledge" on the part of Ireland, or that the surplus hereditary revenue "should be left to Ireland as a means of gradually diminishing her other taxes".[47] The latter proposal — that Ireland should be allowed to apply crown revenues to the reduction of its own national debt — would of course have served only to emphasise the separation of the two kingdoms and so defeat the underlying intention of the measure. But it was in the rejection of the former proposal that were sown the seeds of mistrust which were eventually to precipitate parliamentary opposition in Ireland and ultimately bring about the cancellation of the entire plan.

But as Rutland testified repeatedly, Irish mistrust of the British government already ran so deep that the resolutions were likely to be subjected to every conceivable misinterpretation from their first appearance. He warned Sydney that the equalisation of the duties would be represented simply as the removal of all obstructions to the full exploitation in Irish markets of Britain's "great capital and extensive establishment in manufacture". The altered navigation act would be regarded as operating "only accidentally in the instance of foreign goods, and hardly ever on goods from the plantations, the proprietors of which are resident in Great Britain and will draw the produce chiefly thither".[48] Worse still, it would be said that if the freedom to set or alter bounties was removed, "all hope of encouraging any trade to Great Britain in manufacture" would be "cut off for ever". The proposed contribution would arouse opposition both within and without parliament, and would be viewed as a malicious mechanism designed to counteract any possible improvements from the other propositions.[49] Rutland foresaw the rejection of the contribution initially on grounds of existing taxation (military establishment etc.) and secondly due to mistrust of the commercial resolutions and an unwillingness to believe that their benefits would outweigh the compensation to be exacted.[50]

There were in Ireland, wrote Rutland, three descriptions of men:[51]

The Dissenters who seek for such an alteration of the constitution as will throw more power into their hands by bringing the government nearer to that of a republic. The Roman Catholics whose superior numbers would speedily give them the upper hand if they were admitted to a participation in the legislature. And those men who oppose government upon personal considerations. The first two classes are naturally jealous of each other from principle, and the third class is not upon any principle a friend to either.

Nor by any means was the "third class" a friend to Rutland. In a personal memorandum the following day he referred to its members "with a *few exceptions*" as "an interested, selfish, savage race of harpies and plunderers".[52] The issue of the contribution, he warned Sydney, might well prove to be a disastrous unifying factor.[53] To the exhausted Orde ("I am literally obliged to see and converse with every man who comes up to attend parliament")[54] fell the task of canvassing the opinions of leading government supporters in Ireland.[55] Three days after the opening of the renewed session on 20 January 1785 Rutland reported that "all the confidential friends of government" were "distinctly against" the contribution. The lord lieutenant felt justified in damning it as "an impolitic and ill-timed measure".[56] To Pitt he emphasised the danger that the contribution might re-kindle the suspicion of British influence and so provide a fresh *raison d'etre* for the Volunteers.[57] His afterthought that the investment of the surplus's appropriation in the British parliament would prove "obnoxious" was fully borne out by the sensitive "friends of government".[58] To Pitt, however, this was a point of some importance in his efforts to define clearly Ireland's position in the empire. He[59] conceived it impossible that anything more than a general account of the money paid on the proposed contribution should be laid before the Irish parliament. I am confirmed in thinking that anything more would let them into a control on the executive government of the empire, which must *completely* reside here.

Any hope which might have existed that Grattan would support the measure and so split the opposition vanished when he informed Foster that he regarded the contribution as a "subsidy", a "compensation for rights restored, for favours conferred, or for equality", and as a generally impolitic proposal.[60] As January drew to a close Sydney impressed upon Rutland the importance of his role. The cabinet would be unwilling to introduce the propositions at Westminster unless the Irish would agree to accept the contribution clause. British Whig Opposition murmuring was now to be heard and Sydney also feared protests from British manufacturers.[61]

Orde having taken to his bed in a not uncharacteristic moment of weakness the presentation of the resolutions to the Irish parliament was re-scheduled for 7 February.[62] In the interval Rutland tried desperately to reconcile Pitt's insistence on Britain's right to the disposal of the Irish surplus with the Irish members' disapproval of any such assertion. In view of Pitt's stated attitude Rutland knew that any reconciliation would be little better than an illusion. However, Sydney was not impressed by Rutland's suggestion that the Irish parliament transfer the surplus directly to the upkeep of the imperial navy in Ireland.[63] "The idea of her contributing *only* to the support of the services, for her own *immediate and separate benefit*, is the direct reverse of the principle", responded Sydney. The contribution, he emphasised, was for the good of the empire and could not therefore be "under separate control".[64] In an effort to mitigate what was rapidly developing into a naked power struggle, Sydney offered the lord lieutenant permission to sign the warrants to issue the appropriation, to make its English recipients legally accountable in Ireland, and to ensure that the surplus would be used to supply the imperial navy with Irish products.[65] The cabinet was also prepared to consider an alternative plan: "The growing surplus of the hereditary revenue ... might, at once, by the authority of an Irish Act, be appropriated to make a part of a sinking fund, for reducing the national debt of this country".[66] This clever device had the double advantage of giving the appropriation the appearance of an Irish parliamentary decision while retaining the principle of its employment for the imperial benefit generally. So impressed was the cabinet with this idea that Sydney urged it on Rutland as an expedient even more desirable than the original proposal. But above all he was not to accede to the appropriation by the Irish parliament of the Irish surplus for purely Irish purposes, unless his difficulties proved "insurmountable" and the very concept of contribution appeared in jeopardy. The cabinet had bent to this latter extent, said Sydney, "from the absolute necessity we feel of securing the contribution in some shape or other, before an idea can be entertained here of bringing forward the commercial arrangements".[67]

The most startling aspect of Sydney's letter is the revelation that the cabinet was prepared to sacrifice the reality of an Irish contribution to the empire in exchange for the appearance of that fact. That an illusion was indeed aimed at is suggested by the determination to secure the contribution "in some shape or other". That the main object of the illusion was to hoodwink the British Whig Opposition is indicated by the linking of this proposal with the introduction of the commercial arrangements in London. Pitt felt the alternative proposal to be "just better than nothing, because with it we may venture to bring forward here the commercial arrangement, and with less than this we certainly could not stir a step".[68] If this was indeed the cabinet's motive in thus allowing Rutland the freedom to concede under duress, then the sincerity of the offer is in considerable doubt. The facts that the option was presented to Rutland only as a last resort and that the cabinet hoped it would never be used do not mitigate the risk taken by the ministers in advancing a proposal to which they seem to have had no real intention of giving their sanction.

The relative silence with which the Irish Commons received the propositions on 7 February was indicative less of a favourable response than of the understandable hesitation in the face of complex economic detail. The significance of the last proposition — the contribution linked with an Irish Act as per cabinet suggestion — was commented on only by William Brownlow who "could hardly repress his indignation" at the notion that Ireland should be made "a tributary nation to Great Britain". Under the combined counter-attack of Orde, Gardiner, Burton Conyngham and Foster, and the temporising gestures of Conolly, Forbes and Sir John Parnell, Brownlow withdrew his remarks. But Rutland knew the Irish Commons too well to be optimistic; he was already prepared to jettison the new expedient in favour of the original proposal.[69] Moreover, a new problem had arisen. Sydney had urged Rutland to ensure that the appropriation of the surplus was acknowledged ro be perpetual. Rutland now painfully pointed out to him that the Irish parliament would probably insist on having control of the appropriation.[70]

On the evening of 7 February Rutland, despite obvious misgivings, had "rather favourable hopes of the success of the whole measure as it is now stated; but I cannot yet speak with any positiveness".[71] He could not have lived long in such hopes. In a matter of days Grattan, speaking as he claimed, for "many", responded to solicitations from Orde and Foster with promises of "the most decided and powerful opposition" to any further removal of revenue from a country already overburdened with debt. The opinion of "every intelligent and knowing man" leaned towards the securing of the country from further financial calamity before any consent would be given to the contribution.[72] In fact Grattan's responses reveal that the Castle, in paying him such close court, had made a serious tactical error. The real consequence of this error was the shifting of the normally reliable government supporters into the Grattanite camp. Orde was insolently warned by Grattan "not to deceive himself" but that "the gentlemen highest in office and confidence . . . were cordially indisposed" to the propositions as they stood.[73]

Grattan now foretold the doom of the measure "unless the expenses of the government should be made equal to its revenues". But some at least of Grattan's supporters realised that they were in strange company. At a noon meeting in Orde's apartments on 11 February the law officers and government servants did not demand but rather "burst out with entreaties" for the revision of the resolutions:[74]

They offered to raise the revenues by additional taxes to equalise the charges of government, and they solemnly engaged to do that upon so full and liberal a plan as should satisfy every idea of the most ample provision. They did all of them avow, that however in their individual capacities they allowed the propriety of giving the assistance required by Great Britain, yet if it were not done in some such mode as they recommended, they could not combat Mr. Grattan's arguments in the face of their country; and although the measure should be carried by the influence of government, a foundation would be laid for such a strength of opposition in parliament, and for such universal dissatisfaction throughout the country, as might end in the subversion of all peace and harmony.

The propositions were to be debated in the Commons within an hour of the meeting's conclusion and even those who owed their livelihoods to government were unwilling to support Orde on the issue. The opposition demand was not conformable to any contingency plan espoused by the cabinet. But no time remained in which to consult London and it was too late to postpone the sitting. The only alternative being defeat in the Commons and the consequent abandonment of the propositions *in toto*, Rutland on his own responsibility directed Orde to alter the contribution clause and to insert a further clause embodying the opposition demand.[75] The essence of the alteration to the contribution clause was that the surplus, instead of consisting of the *entire* sum over and above a fixed amount of the hereditary revenue for each year, would consist of *the same sum less whatever amount was required to defray the outstanding expenditure of the kingdom for each year*. In brief, the size of the annual contribution would be made to depend on the balancing of the Irish budget.[76]

The alterations did not mollify the non-Grattanite opposition before which Orde re-presented his wares that afternoon. The commercial proposals were attacked at length by a variety of members "as particular objects struck their minds". These "particular objects" differed little from those forecast by Rutland in his warnings to Sydney.[77] The opposition evidently regarded the entire plan as a stratagem to emasculate the growth of Irish commerce and felt that the apparently generous provisions were devoid of any real advantage. The contribution was vilified as "a tribute marking the abject situation of this country and her subjection to Great Britain". The vocal element in the non-Grattanite camp included Flood, Corry, Gardiner, Hartley, A. Montgomery, Griffith, the Recorder, Molyneux, Parsons, Doyle, Dunn, Wolfe, Forbes, O'Neill and Brownlow. However, the support of Grattan, who had of course won his point (as well as the support of the unpredictable Ponsonby), led to the renewal of spirited support from the regular government men and to the carrying of the propositions. The solidarity of government supporters and "country gentlemen" was particularly pleasing to Orde.[78]

But both Pitt and the king were enraged at the alterations. To his confidant, George Rose, Orde complained bitterly that he was "shocked at heart by the manifest displeasure which seems to be taken at my conduct in this business". He considered resignation.[79] Sydney responded to Rutland's explanations with the charge that his interference had rendered "the application of the surplus entirely precarious". Ominously, the cabinet's objection was based on the fact that the hitherto sound economic proposition had been reduced to a matter of trust. One author has suggested that the cabinet's underlying fear was that a colonially-minded Irish chancellor would evade the contribution by "a series of small and profitable deficits".[80] However, a more plausible fear may have been the possibility that the contribution, depending as it did upon the amount required to defray existing overheads, would decline into insignificance or even vanish under the increasing weight of Irish expenditure. The cabinet wondered aloud whether "the stipulation" had been agreed to by the Irish parliament "in order to defeat the main object".[81] Rutland was sharply told that he should have risked defeat rather "than to have given for a moment the *apparent* sanction of government to this alteration"; that he had neglected to ensure the perpetuity of the appropriation and that he had left unspecified the objects to which the appropriation was to be applied.[82]

However, the cabinet in the last analysis was not prepared to abandon the project. Sydney had begun his vitriolic epistle with the news that the British Commons had smiled on the propositions *provided* that the perpetuity of the appropriation was acknowledged.[53] Fox and his followers had fallen into the trap of roundly denouncing the propositions as a collective danger to British economic well-being, thus causing the Irish opposition to wonder if the plan wasn't so bad after all.[84] Pitt in a surprisingly kinder tone assured Rutland that he fully understood the pressures which had forced him to make the alterations.[85]

But the extra-parliamentary opposition to the plan, so long feared by the cabinet, had begun to manifest itself.[86] The previous January the cabinet had prepared the way for the propositions in England by seeking the views of British manufacturers on Anglo-Irish trade. The Committee of Trade and Plantations which conducted the examinations strategically refrained from revealing the imminence of the propositions. The manufacturers "tended to reflect a calm confidence in the ability of British goods and workmanship to hold their own in competition with Ireland". The obvious feeling, after the advancement of the propositions, that they had been duped, fused with the manufacturers' irritation over government behaviour during the discussions on fiscal policy.[87] More than sixty British towns, some of them encouraged by the Whig Opposition, petitioned against the plan. From Lancashire alone 80,000 manufacturers petitioned the Commons against the admission of Irish cotton. A General Chamber of Manufacturers of England and Scotland was formed under the guidance of Josiah Wedgwood. Its proposed solution was "a real union with Ireland under one legislature".[88]

In the meantime Rutland, in an effort to repair the strained relations caused by his alterations, dispatched Edward Cooke to London to further clarify the Castle's position. Cooke seems to have exceeded his instructions, for Sydney's despatch of 3 March contained drafts of freshly altered propositions. The contribution clause was altered by removing from it the stipulation that the budget should be balanced from the revenue surplus. An additional clause inserted at an earlier point provided instead for the prevention of future budget overheads by damning as "inexpedient that any new services or expenses should be incurred unless a specific provision shall be made at the time of allowing the same for defraying the charge thereof". This clause was inserted immediately following the provision that Ireland's annual revenue should equal its annual expenses.[89]

Now thoroughly alarmed, Rutland sent Orde to London as well.[90] The chief secretary arrived on 13 March to find Pitt determined to render the propositions more palatable by further diluting the contribution clause.[91] Pitt, according to one biographer, had made a tactical error. Encouraged by the favourable reports of industrial opinion which had preceded the petitions, and doubtless further invigorated by the February victory in Ireland, Pitt allowed himself to be stampeded towards an announcement on 3 March of a motion to adopt the resolutions within one week. The opposition's accusations of suspicious and indecent haste had now caught the ears of the independents and waverers. Pitt had not publicised the advantages of the plan as effectively as the opposition had aired its objections to it.[92] The opposition paraded an endless series of "petitions, papers and evidence" before the Commons in the full awareness that "the delay and timidity of government" were improving their case.[93] Orde, realising that delay at this point in London would mean corresponding and suspicion-inducing delays in Ireland, could only look on "distressed and mortified" and "under an agitation of mind not to be described".[94]

However, he did succeed "in bringing the cabinet to reason", as he reported a week after his arrival: "They are sensible of the advantages and satisfied of the security".[95] But Orde's attempt to pass on the sensibility and satisfaction to the British Commons created such anxiety amongst the City merchants "as if they were going to lose the River Thames", and it was rumoured that Pitt was going to disown some of Orde's statements.[96] In a note of 27 March telling of his imminent return Orde reported that "we have maintained our ground".[97] But the cabinet, having inspected Rutland's draft bill, inserted a further provision designed to ensure the perpetuity of the appropriation. The mode to be adopted was to tighten the regulations surrounding the actual collection of the revenue itself. Since the hereditary revenue was perpetual, it was argued, the manner of its collection should be correspondingly so, if only for the sake of ensuring its safe receipt. Moreover, wrote Sydney getting to the point, "without such permanency it might be practicable at a future day to diminish the hereditary revenue by withholding or changing the operation of those laws which from time to time have been found necessary for its collection".[98] The cabinet, which had now added to its tactics vilification of the Whig Opposition on the grounds of the latter's concessions to Ireland in 1782-83, hoped that its newest alteration would not prove unpalatable.[99]

Rutland, clearly alarmed lest such a bald admission of inter-regnal mistrust become thus public, disinterred numerous precedents militating against interference with collection regulations and pointed out the possibility of withholding the royal assent in any future Irish attempt to reduce the surplus.[100] An irritated reply from Sydney offered only to allow the re-insertion of the perpetuity provision in a subsequent revenue act rather than in the commercial plan if this would facilitate matters. The cabinet was agreeable to a suggestion from Orde that this subsequent revenue act should originate in Britain.[101] By this time Rutland would have been in full agreement with his London informant, Daniel Pulteney, who opined that "Pitt has not managed [the Irish business] with his usual foresight or spirit".[102]

Pitt seemed to be waiting for the various elements of opposition to exhaust themselves, but this tactic (if such it was) was interpreted as fear.[103] The arguments against the propositions in England, as spelt out by more than twenty pamphlets, "were based for the most part on reports of the low price of Irish labour and the supposedly favourable geographical position of Ireland for the colonial trade".[104] By 23 April the petitions were "languishing", and Fox had followed his disapproval of the propositions on the grounds of their "irrevocability and conclusiveness" by claiming that "they seemed not so final and conclusive as they ought to be".[105] When no petitioners appeared on 2 May Pitt prepared to bring on the measure.[106] Rutland expressed himself to Sydney as "very glad" that he would not have to present the bill in Dublin before the resolutions on which it was based were passed in London.[107] He might well have been so. Three days later Orde was telling Grattan of his "real concern on finding your opinion to be unfavourable, as I conceived the explanation thus introduced into the bill to be neither new nor inconsistent with the spirit of the 11th resolution, as originally intended".[108]

The bill was indeed creating difficulties. Rutland and Orde objected to the manner in which part of it was worded and it is probable that Pitt was informed by Orde of Grattan's new attitude.[109] The bill reproduced the original eleven propositions in the form of twenty clauses. Although they did not justify the later assertion by Henry Grattan the younger that they were "new propositions, wholly different to those he [Pitt] had agreed to", the wording of the bill differed so substantially from that of the resolutions as to give rise to pardonable misunderstandings.[110]

Pitt, despite dire warnings from Orde, had tried to please everybody.[111] The expansion of the resolutions represented to a large extent Pitt's efforts to assuage or remove the fears of nervous manufacturers in Britain. The prevailing tone of the altered resolutions was, as Orde hinted, one of profound mistrust of Irish intentions.[112] Fox damned the resolutions as representative of a new set of propositions, "and the reverse of the former". There followed a debate in which a confused Fox, having stated that the prospects of a political union of the two kingdoms had been retarded, went on to claim that the fourth clause "demanded from Ireland a surrender of her liberty and independence".[113] In fact it was not until "it became clear that nothing could prevent the passage of Pitt's twenty resolutions" that "the opposition assumed the role of Irish patriots and decried the propositions on the ground that they were prejudicial to the independence of Ireland".[114] The fourth clause provided that such alterations of the navigation laws as would be made in Britain should also apply in Ireland "by laws to be passed by the parliament of that kingdom for the same time, and in the same manner as in Great Britain". Pitt's assertion to Orde that the clause represented merely a "voluntary compact" was apparently not clear enough in the clause itself.[115]

But for Pitt the initial success in carrying the first resolution was overshadowed by Fox's promise that he would "fight the whole of it inch by inch; he would debate every resolution, every amendment, and divide the House upon each".[116] But the Whig backbenchers were already losing interest. As Pitt dragged individual resolutions through the Commons in May the opposition melted away.[117] The Lords examined witnesses and debated the measures in June and July. From Dublin Rutland continued to rave at Pitt against the required perpetuity of the revenue collection. The Irish Commons in general "would as soon vote the repeal of Magna Charta", and Grattan in particular "terms it a covenant which for the extension of commerce sacrifices and destroys the constitution".[118] Pitt responded less dramatically but with similar sentiments regarding the British Commons.[119] Both Orde and Rutland pointed out to the cabinet the probable reluctance of the Irish parliament to pass the fourth resolution in its bill format.[120] Grattan indeed bore out Orde's foreboding that he was likely to prove "very impracticable" by declaiming against the resolutions in the Commons in mid-June. The Whigs, wrote Lord Mornington to him in reproof, had expressed "the greatest triumph" at this.[121]

The substitution for Orde, who was battling against a painful eye infection, of Beresford as promulgator of Rutland's views in London proved unwise. Pulteney reported him to have alarmed the cabinet into a fresh state of indecision.[122] Meanwhile, efforts in Dublin to bring Grattan around were unsuccessful. In early July Orde described him to Beresford as "wholly lost".[123] Rutland told Pitt that Grattan was "impracticable in a degree scarcely credible". Evidently, Grattan's

ideas of objection were such as to render them impossible to be obviated. He said that he could admit nothing which intrenched on old settlements; that it seemed an attempt to resume in peace concessions granted in war; that rendering the fourth proposition conditional was of little avail; that everything should be left to national faith, and nothing covenanted. He objected to the American and East Indian clauses, and that which relates to the permanent collection of the revenue. He seemed not to think it possible, by any explanations, to remove the difficulties, but held firm in his opinion that anything, except the eleven specific propositions, as they went from Ireland, was perfectly inadmissible.

Grattan threatened "a very unpleasant scene of discontent", followed, if the issue was carried, by "a perpetual struggle". "In short", wrote Rutland, "he appears to have adopted a decided line of opposition, and has returned to his vomit, and to the support of the desperate views of an English abandoned faction in Ireland".[124]

On 19 July, following a violent debate, the resolutions (with one amendment by the Lords) were accepted by the British Commons. The contentious fourth and twentieth resolutions were not, however, altered to any material degree, and Rutland soon reported Grattan to be "wild on the business", that his "general notions" were "wild and extravagant" and wide from "any mark or possible compromise".[125] The last days of July saw Orde engaged in efforts to mitigate the expected impact of the fourth resolution by inserting a sentence incorporating recognition of Irish legislative independence.[126] Though this was done it was clear to Orde that it was unlikely to prove effective.[127] Orde then tried to persuade the still-divided cabinet not to transmit the resolutions.[128] When this failed he conceived of a scheme to introduce an altered bill and then to have it referred to a committee in order to work into conformity with the resolutions as approved in Britain.[129] Implicitly in this plan is revealed Orde's dismay at the prospect of having to face two divisions on the dreaded propositions; one to obtain leave to introduce them in the form of a bill, and secondly the bill itself. A delay to facilitate discussion in committee might have been valuble; but delay merely for the purpose of moulding a *fait accompli* into a legislative instrument would only encourage festering resentments. Orde felt able for one division but not at all for a second. Still suffering greatly with his eyes he confided to Rose in the early hours of 28 July that he was "stupid with talking and arguing".[130]

When he moved to introduce the bill on 12 August Orde was opposed first by Conolly "whose arguments turned almost entirely upon the wording of the fourth British proposition ... as that resolution appeared to him to strike essentially at the independence of the Irish constitution". In a debate which lasted until nine the following morning similar points were made by Grattan, Flood, Sir Henry Cavendish, Corry, Burgh, Wolfe, O'Neill, Curran and others. The government carried the division on the introduction of the bill by only nineteen votes (127 to 108).[131] The extent to which county members had responded to constituency pressure is suggested by the fact that only ten such members supported the motion, a further forty-nine opposing it.[132] A majority of the ten supporters were reportedly placemen or sons of placemen.[133]

At some unspecifiable point during the next few hours Rutland and Orde decided not to introduce the bill and to temporarily abandon it as a parliamentary measure. In grave tones Rutland relayed the information to a "disappointed and hurt" Pitt that he would advance "an effort of our united strength to get the bill printed, that at least it may remain as a monument of the liberality of Great Britain, and of my desire to promote a system which promises such essential advantages to the empire".[134]

A major post-mortem on the failure of the propositions would yield little that has not already been revealed. However, the fact that the settlement's doom was sealed largely by the fourth proposition inspires a certain curiosity as to the origin of the clause.

In the matter of elucidating for his own benefit the complex economic data which was the stuff of the settlement, Pitt was as dependent on Charles Jenkinson as Rutland was on Beresford and Foster. Jenkinson's views on colonial matters, while not diametrically opposed to those held by Pitt, were sufficiently at odds with them to make him a dangerous fifth columnist. He had not been prominent enough in the circle of North's advisers to share in the prime minister's downfall in March 1782. He survived the period of coalitions and his expertise in matters of national finance secured him a place in the inner circle of Pitt's "confidential" servants.

Perhaps had Pitt been a little older and wiser he would have been more sensitive to the possibility that skilful manipulation of administrative detail could frustrate even the most unambiguous ministerial intentions. Certainly Pitt could not have been unaware of Jenkinson's views. During the debate on regulating the government of Massachusetts Bay Jenkinson stated that "it was a great mistake that the establishment of a parliament precluded Great Britain from taxing that kingdom. He looked upon all inferior assemblies as being like the corporate towns of England, and as having a power like theirs of making bye-laws and nothing more".[135] Privately Jenkinson had disapproved of the 1782 settlement and especially of the idea that Castle personnel in Ireland should be appointed and dismissed on a party basis: ". . . I shall think them mad if they endevour [sic] to make a general change in the administration of the Government of that Kingdom as they have done here".[136] More generally,[137]

He had also expressed certain views about the colonies: the increase of the colonies, he had stated, was certainly what was wished for, but they should so increase as to be useful to the mother country. Whatever regulations were essential to that object and to the maintenance of the principles of the Act of Navigation, though they might to a small degree prevent the increase of the colonies, were an which in his opinion ought to be submitted to "for the good of the whole".

No mention of the navigation act had been included in the propositions of February 1785.[138] At least one contemporary observer believed that "Pitt relied principally and almost exclusively upon Jenkinson in his efforts to bring about commercial union".[139]

Years later, on the eve of the union Jenkinson admitted privately that "With respect to the commercial regulations ... I had the principal share in a committee of Privy Council which took the subject into consideration ...; and in the report made on that occasion, which was drawn by myself, I fully delivered my opinion on the subject".[140] In the draft of this report which survives among his papers, Jenkinson believed it[141]

impossible, that Great Britain and Ireland can carry on their trade with equal advantage, unless the laws that grant exclusive privileges to ships and mariners, and that regulate and restrain the trade to and from the British Colonies and Settlements in America, the West Indies and on the coast of Africa are the same in both kingdoms. This truth is self evident to any one who has the least knowledge of commerce. ...

His recommendation as to the navigation act itself was couched in terms unfortunately similar to those which passed into the final version of the fourth proposition: "Great Britain proposes therefore, that the parliament of Ireland shall enact and thereby subject the trade of Ireland in these respects to the same regulations and restrictions to which the trade of Great Britain is now or may at any time hereafter be liable".[142]

Unlike Pitt who (as has been pointed out above) refused to view the proposed agreement as a "bargain" and tried to design it so that it would operate within the framework of the 1782 settlement, Jenkinson held no such attitudes. When defending the fourth proposition in the British Commons he described it as "no more than a condition which one independent nation thought it necessary to stipulate for from another, in a bargain which was to be mutually beneficial. Such conditions were frequently required in negotiations between rival nations, in defensive or offensive as well as in commercial treaties".[143] In his private report to the cabinet Jenkinson even regarded the "reasonable request" of the fourth proposition as a fair exchange for the other advantages to be obtained by Ireland from the overall settlement.[144]

But it was while putting forward in private the reasons for his recommendation that Jenkinson's mask of impartiality began to slip. "Does the parliament of Ireland", he began, "wish to be more independant [sic] or greater than the parliament of Great Britain?"[145]

Which of these kingdoms first formed and brought to perfection these laws of trade and navigation? Which of them first planted and raised these colonies and settlements to their present flourishing condition at a great expense? Which of them now confers on the other the great benefits arising from them - Which of them is most interested in the preservation of them? Which of them is best acquainted with the principles on which the laws of navigation are founded and on which the colonies and settlements ought in future to be continued and supported. Every candid and reasonable man will answer to all these questions, *Great Britain*; It is absurd to suppose that at the same time that G. Britain confers on the people of Ireland such great benefits, she will relinquish to another power, an equal share in the management of her interests in all these respects.

As will be seen in a later chapter, Pitt tended to see the failure of 12 August 1785 purely in terms of political mismanagement. He was apparently blind to Jenkinson's active role in undermining the proposed settlement. In fairness it should be pointed out that no conclusive evidence dating from the most relevant period 1784-85 exists which would confirm that Jenkinson designed the fourth proposition with deliberate sabotage in mind. But his general views on colonies, and on Ireland in particular, suggest that he would have been averse to any agreement which would strengthen the 1782 settlement. Moreover, the supportive documentation of the fourth proposition does not give the impression that an over-strenuous effort was made by its designer to soothe the fears of Irish parliamentarians.

In conclusion it is perhaps worth noting the opinion of a specialist that Jenkinson "undoubtedly had . . . something to do with turning Pitt away from the soundness of the political economy of Adam Smith, and with luring him into all the mazes of the old system".[146]

The Politics of Parliamentary Opposition, 1782-1800

(1) *March 1782 - December 1783*

Aside from the 1782-83 settlement and the conditions it imposed upon Irish politics of the late eighteenth century, the campaign from which the settlement emerged had the effect of establishing a pattern of opposition politics not only with regard to the Irish government but also to the Whig Opposition in London. Like the settlement itself this effect resulted from the interaction of Irish and British political ambitions and achievements. The refusal of the Patriot members in 1780 to form a close political alliance with the Whigs had consequences unforeseen by either side. The strong anti-government stance adopted and practised by the patriots and the absence of any formal understanding between them and the Whigs meant that when the Whigs came to power in March 1782 their relationship with their Irish counterparts was already circumscribed. However "well-disposed"[1] they had been toward Irish grievances in the past, the Rockinghams in March 1782 became not allies in power but merely the old enemy with a new face.

The failure of the Rockingham government to place the relationship on a more co-operative (if not more amiable) footing was nowhere more evident than in Fitzpatrick's complaint that the patriots were offering them "no more confidence than they would have done the last Government".[2] Portland's attempts to court the approval of the patriots through the dismissal of some of the principal office-holders under Buckinghamshire and Carlisle were less than successful. The patriots seemed not to respond to the aroma of office with the same sensual enthusiasm that characterised the British Whigs. Grattan was prepared to recommend the dismissal of "notorious consciences"[3] but not to be the replacement of any one of them. In the dark hours before the dawn of 16 April 1782 Grattan had refused to accept office in exchange for an adjournment.[4] After that date his acceptance of the £50,000 "reward" made him unwilling to take office lest he should seem to have been "bought".[5] Forbes, once projected as solicitor-general, also failed to take office.[6] Indeed, of the patriots who had taken part in the campaign of 1779-82, only Yelverton and Sheridan accepted office from Portland, and both were suspiciously short of money.[7] Moreover, Portland's dismissals did not all go smoothly. His attempt to remove John Lees altogether from office backfired when the charges of criminal maladministration levelled against him were proven to be unfounded. Portland recanted and Lees was reinstated.[8] The abrupt dismissal of Maurice Coppinger after 22 years service to make room for George Ponsonby, of one the "great interests", merely tarnished Portland's reputation as a humane man.[9]

John Beresford, who survived the transition, found that "there is no confidence between his Grace and his Secretary nor between the Castle and any of the new ministers; Mr. Ponsonby is the only real confidant; he advises everything, and I know certainly that his Grace's inclinations are communicated to Yelverton, Burgh, &c., through George Ponsonby; Mr. O'Beirne is the confidential Secretary.[10] That arrangements were being made to effect a reconcilation was hinted at by Sheridan who noticed in late June that Grattan had "grown into great favour with the Duke".[11] But Portland's Irish days were numbered. A week later Rockingham died, Shelburne was given the Treasury, and a number of cabinet ministers, along with Portland, resigned as a consequence.[12]

Despite the obvious shortcomings of the 1782 settlement it is difficult to interpret the behaviour of Grattan and Flood over the Renunciation issue as other than a struggle for personal power and influence in the Commons. Portland's failure to absorb the patriots and so re-assert the authority of the Castle over parliament meant that when the new lord lieutenant, Earl Temple, took over, Grattan still had nominal command of the Commons. Government, having been seen to lend its support to "simple Repeal" in April, was unable to prevent itself from being dragged in Grattan's wake when the latter began to defend that "simple Repeal" (and his own leadership) against Flood and Renunciation.[13] In the circumstances Temple's private attempt between July and September to woo Leinster, Charlemont, Conolly and Ponsonby away from Grattan was a mistake; all of them smelt blood and tried to exploit the situation for their own benefit.[14]

The Mansfield Writ of Error made it increasingly difficult to pour scorn on Flood's case for Renunciation.[15] Clearly fearing the loss of country independent support and that government would be dragged by Grattan into defeat, Temple recommended to London that the Writ be used as an excuse to pass a bill of Renunciation at Westminster — "a solution which will save the credit of both Parliaments".[16] The passing of Renunciation had to wait upon the conclusion of the Treaty of Paris in January 1783, but strategic prorogation of the Irish parliament saved Temple from further embarrassment.[17] In the interval Temple busied himself with the new Order of St Patrick, the last but perhaps most promising attempt on his part to woo the great names back to the support of government.[18] But by the first week of April the Shelburne administration had fallen and the viceroyalty of Ireland had again changed hands.

Temple's successor, Lord Northington, began his term of office with neither a Declaratory Act nor a Renunciation dispute to contend with, and so was in a somewhat better position to negotiate with unco-operative patriots. Charlemont and Grattan certainly saw no reason why they should not now accept the invitations to attend the privy council meetings.[19] Grattan, however, was not without terms:[20]

He wished much to engage me in some plan of retrenchment, not of a sort to affect the patronage of administration so much as you might apprehend: I think I rather contrived to beat him out of this idea and he neared at last to a plan of reform, to affect only the creation of additional salaries in future to places of no responsibility.

The patriot urge to economise may have been quite genuine, but an alternative effect of restraining further sinecures was to prevent government from using the executive power to create a phalanx of obedient members. "Yelverton and Forbes of course acceded", as more reluctantly did Foster.[21] However, the unlucky choice of John FitzGibbon to replace Yelverton as attorney-general ultimately led Forbes to refuse the post which had been ear-marked for him (solicitor-general) since Portland's time.[22] For the first and last time the Irish opposition held sway at the Irish privy council.

The history of Northington's six-month term of office was less than happy. It was quickly sensed by his privy councillors that Northington's chief secretary, William Windham, was the stronger half of the viceroyalty and pressure was brought to bear upon him accordingly. A draft copy of his resignation which survives among his papers indicates that Windham was ready to quit after only six weeks in office.[23] In the end a simmering quarrel with the Ponsonbys over patronage drove him from Ireland.[24] In his own words the strength of his aversion to office was equalled only by his belief that Northington lacked confidence in him.[25] Certainly Northington's angry letter accepting Windham's resignation leaves little doubt that the lord lieutenant had a weakness for Castle gossip: "your strong disinclination to the confinement and business of your situation had not escaped the attention of the *Eagle-eyed* observers of the Castle". Northington made it plain to Windham that a man who was the butt of office jokes could not be a useful chief secretary.[26]

Nor was Northington a successful policy-maker. On behalf of his privy council he advocated annual sessions of parliament "to accelerate the decisions upon appeals, which are now confined to the House of Lords in Ireland" and "to prevent a delay in adopting any new

commercial regulations that may be made in the British Parliament".
Northington now privately believed that annual sessions "will knit
more firmly together the supports of Government, marshal the
phalanx more readily".[27] An absentee tax, if proposed, should be
resisted as "a measure so prejudicial to the landed interest of this
Kingdom". Any extra-parliamentary attempt to advance parliamentary
reform would also be resisted. In the area of commerce the ghost
of the 1781 sugar dispute was resurrected, and Northington was
prevailed upon to suggest that the Irish refiner be given a monopoly
(by prohibiting the importation of British sugar). In regard to Irish
silk and woollen manufactures he proposed that the current duties
on English goods be increased or else that the duties on Irish goods
in England be lowered. The Irish Post Office was to be remodelled
"as a foreign one".[28] North's immediate reaction was to forbid the
introduction of annual sessions as "very undesireable" (*sic*).[29]

But it was on the more trivial matter of the sugar duties that the
Irish privy council successfully rebelled, forcing the new chief
secretary, Thomas Pelham, against the express wishes of the cabinet,
to accept a duty of twelve shillings instead of the nine shillings on
imports of refined sugars from England: ". . . part of our friends,
which is usually called in this country, the Duke of Portland's friends,
persisted in their opinions, that the duty of 12/- which they had
formerly asked for, they must continue to support". This incident
also provided a clue as to the balance of power amongst "the Duke
of Portland's friends". Grattan, supported by La Touche, had
originally held out for a duty of sixteen shillings. The Ponsonbys,
while declining to accept the government's nine shilling duty, also
refused to support Grattan. Apparently without committing
themselves to either extreme, Forbes (probably consulted
independently), Metge,[30] Ogle,[31] and finally Yelverton refused to
accept the nine shilling duty.[32]

Finding then that the probability was, that I should be in a minority of
which, it would be difficult to form a just calculation, when the Attorney-
General voted against me, I thought it most prudent to consent to the 12/-,
to which Mr. Grattan and all our friends assented.

The significance of these occurrences was not lost on Pelham. The
attempt to absorb the patriot and non-patriot opposition had failed.
Instead the government was being used as a counter in a power-
struggle not altogether dissimilar from those of the old Undertaker
days. In September it had been necessary to hold a cabinet dinner[33]
in order to obtain Grattan's agreement not to propose embarrassing
amendments to a forthcoming address in the Commons. To eliminate
all possible misunderstandings, Yelverton, Forbes and Sheridan had
also to be invited to hear Grattan thus give his agreement.[34] It was

88

becoming clear that the government was saving itself from parliamentary embarrassment at the price of a different kind of humiliation.

Moreover, the policies advanced by the councillors were not finding favour in London. Part of the problem may well have lain in the attitude of Lord North, now home secretary, but it could scarcely be overlooked that the Irish council's policies were national rather than imperial in concept; collectively they gave the impression of a council seeking the aggrandisement of Ireland through a high degree of political independence and commercial advantage, even at the expense of Britain.[35] Portland refused to accept that Grattan was sincere in his demands for reform and retrenchment in public expenditure, that he merely advocated them "to satisfy certain engagements which he conceives himself to have entered into".[36] North urged Northington to resist "those fresh demands and fresh projects of trade which the Irish are continually forming to the prejudice of this country".[37] One fresh project was the concept of a separate Irish foreign policy. North countered this with a blunt refusal to lay imperial peace treaties before the Irish parliament: "If the King is to take the advice of the Irish Parliament in matters relating to war and peace, and foreign states, the utmost confusion must be the consequence".[38] Fox echoed this sentiment.[39] Northington's "proposals of prohibitory and protecting duties, are both objectionable", as was his suggested interference with silk and wool duties.[40]

Both Northington and Pelham were deeply concerned at the struggle between Grattan and the Ponsonbys for influence over the country independent element in the Commons. The Ponsonbys had taken advantage of their traditional close links with the British Whigs to influence Portland[41] who was not quick on the uptake. "Will you believe it?", shrilled Northington[42]

He [Portland] has the vanity to think that his own friends consist of a sixth part of the House of Commons of Ireland, and that they are chiefly under the management of G. Ponsonby. The only way he can possibly support it, is by a supposition most perfectly ill-founded, that the great interests are united under such a leader. For interest [instance?] that Lord Shannon with 20 votes, is to take his cue from G. Ponsonby and to lose his vice-treasurership if he so pleases, and that Tottenham Loftus with 8 votes, himself with a pension of £1,000 for [illegible] than but one pensioned or placed is to be equally at the disposal of such a jackanapes.

By the time the sugar dispute arose Portland had seemingly been informed of the true position, but, as Pelham pointed out, this did not represent a solution to the overall problem:[43]

I mean the separation of our friends, and the dependence upon those, whom your Grace does not thoroughly approve of for support: If I had carried the question [i.e. on the sugar duties], they would immediately have claimed a larger share of confidence than I have hitherto given, and if I had failed, they would have justly claimed a merit in supporting us at a time, when I was deserted by those, from whom I had the best claims to assistance; In short . . . this division of our friends drove me to the alternative of yielding the wishes of your Grace's friends or risking the being in a minority, with the certainty of all your friends being against me.

Pelham was prepared to dismiss the sugar duties affair as

an instance of the instability in the Irish, which justifys a coalition of parties in this country, in order that you may force one party, by shewing them, that you have other friends, whom you may trust to for support, when they begin to waver.

But the money bill dispute of 1753 had long since demonstrated that for government to play one parliamentary group against the other was not invariably successful and certainly was a poor substitute for a solid and steady Castle phalanx. The privy council as assembled by Northington was unmanageable. Even before it had been formed Grattan had identified his enemies as "the dregs of the old opposition" (i.e. the former Undertaker families) and "the outcasts of the old court".[44] Both categories were represented in Northington's council.[45] To the departed Windham Northington admitted that the council was proving "difficult to manage from the cursed jealousy each man entertains of the other".[46] Years later Charlemont was to claim that for reasons of personal aggrandisement Grattan had deliberately excluded fellow-patriots Yelverton and Forbes from positions of effective influence on the council and that this had been the reason for Charlemont's breach with Grattan.[47]
Pelham was also fully aware of the shortcomings of the situation. Perhaps the worst shortcoming was the council's potential ineffectiveness, despite its formidably broad bottom, should "the outcasts of the old court" join forces with the other discontented elements in the parliament. Even as things stood, "the success of affairs in the House of Commons has as yet been more owing to the weakness and ignorance of opposition, than to the strength of administration".[48] Furthermore, Pelham had little confidence in Yelverton who, he felt, "cannot be very zealous in suggesting measures, the fate of which, he is indifferent to". Likewise FitzGibbon who, Pelham believed, would give no constructive support "until his office calls upon him".[49] Scott and Carleton, both dismissed by Portland, had been re-employed for the sole reason that, joined to Flood, they would have made a dangerous opposition.[50]
In fact Northington and Pelham had learned what Portland and Temple had been too ill-circumstanced and short of time to discover;

that "there are two parties in this country, as well as in England, but their principle very different, their objects are different, and their institution dissimilar";[51] that the "unity" of 16 April 1782 had been an illusion; that the patriots were a frugal collection of individual politicians, jealous of each other and waning in their influence (the re-employment of Scott and Carleton indicated that government could no longer have been kept afloat by the patriot aura alone); that the great interests who had supported the patriots on 16 April in fact had little in common with Grattan and that their deepest desire was to obtain enough personal patronage to turn the clock back to 1770.[52] Of Grattan's own aims at this stage little evidence remains. In a council of such heterogeneous proportions it would have been difficult to make headway, especially in the absence of traditional supporters like Yelverton and Forbes. Although Grattan's influence was clearly visible in the policy proposals of September 1783 even these could not be carried against the disapproval of the British cabinet.[53] The revolt over the sugar duties was, as Pelham believed, an island of "instability" in an ocean of futility.

For the moment the fissures in the council were concealed (publicly at least) by the pressing need to maintain the rule of law against calls within and without parliament for parliamentary reform. "Opposition" in Northington's Ireland, "consist of men unfriendly to England, county members under the influence of their electors, and a few disapointed [sic] individuals, who are hostile to the reigning Lord Lieut".[54] Opposition behaviour as reflected in the Commons tended to be haphazard but generally in line with this conclusion. Of the twenty-six significant[55] divisions which occurred during the session (14 October 1783 to 3 March 1784 - i.e. until Northington left Ireland) the government won all but three. The outstanding three divisions were on opposition proposals to raise the salaries of the lord lieutenant and chief secretary. Northington was unwilling to accept the proposed increase because he feared that it would be used as "a weapon" and that thenceforth he might be the "dupe" of opposition.[56] Despite the facts that opposition members did not uniformly support the motions and that the motions were opposed by leading government spokesmen, government supporters seemed too confused to rally in the half-empty house. Separate addresses to the king requesting rises in the salaries of Northington and Pelham were carried by 77 to 54 and 71 to 28. The line-up of supporters of the motions indeed included "a few disappointed individuals", notably Daniel Toler, Thomas Burgh and John Blaquiere. Confusion in the opposition ranks was manifested by the fact that other "disappointed" men such as Sir Henry Cavendish and "men unfriendly to England" such as Sir Edward Newenham opposed the addresses. Grattan was absent.[57] Division figures throughout the session were relatively low and suggest that attendance was poor. Only on five occasions did the figures exceed 200. The highest figure (229) was obtained not on the day of the debate on parliamentary reform but over a "procedure" dispute on the acceptance of a petition from the Dublin Chamber of Commerce (which individual members of the Chamber had neglected to sign).[58] The line-up of speakers on the issue indicates a straight collision between the government and the opposition. On this issue at least it proved possible for the opposition to maintain an apparently-high degree of unity.[59] It was something of a tribute to Grattan that, after he had joined the government, none of the patriots who stayed on in opposition were able to bring forth a majority for their motions. Curran, asserting the traditional patriotic point that the Irish Commons had "the sole and undoubted privilege ... to originate all bills of supply and grants of public money" was opposed even by Brownlow and Langrishe and was unable to raise even a dozen votes.[60] (Admittedly there were only eighty members in the House).

Brownlow's behaviour was inconsistent throughout the session. He supported Flood's amendment on 10 November regarding the need for retrenchment in the army establishment,[61] but opposed Corry's proposal to congratulate the Prince of Wales on the latter's twenty-first birthday. (Corry could only raise ten votes on this issue.)[62] Less than a week later he opposed the government over the Chamber of Commerce petition but, as noted above, refused to support Curran's motion on the House's right to originate bills. Corry was one of the more consistent patriots. On only two of the ten occasions on which he spoke during the session did he support the government viewpoint. One of these deviations was Corry's support for a proposed committee to consider the vexed matter of Irish-Portuguese trade relations; the other (less easily-explained) shift of position on his part was his support of the proposed bonding of tobacco duties.[63]

The most spectacular debate of the session—on Flood's parliamentary reform proposal — was spoiled to some extent by the fact that the debate turned not on the bill itself but rather on the question of leave to introduce it. Parliamentary ethics allowed Flood and his followers to attract support by using the "secondary" nature of the question as a mitigating circumstance. Opposers of the measure could claim that those who voted for the bill's introduction thereby committed themselves, as men of honour and consistency, to support the measure itself. Nevertheless, in a House of 218 members, an unusually high number (50) spoke. A brief comparison of the list of speakers with the membership list of the Monks of the Screw reveals that the movement of Grattan and others to the government benches had shattered the ephemeral unity of the patriots. Newenham, Ogle, Kingsborough, Arthur Browne, Forbes, Hardy, Curran, Hartstonge, and John Doyle,[64] all Monks of the Screw, supported Flood against fellow-monks George Ponsonby, Peter Metge, Yelverton (all office-holders), Arthur Wolfe and Denis Daly.

But it was also the end of the privy council as it had been constituted, for this was the moment chosen by Grattan, its leading "oracle", to desert it. Near the end of the debate he arose and briefly supported Flood's motion.[65] The evidence of collusion between Grattan and his former comrades is too sparse to be considered conclusive, but enough Monks supported Flood in the division to raise the suspicion of pre-arrangement.[66] Northington had certainly been warned by Grattan in advance:[67]

Grattan, having pledged himself to the idea of a reform of parliament, could not see the distinction between the refusal of leave on the ground of its having come from an exceptionable body, and the absolute denial of receiving any plan of reform. He voted against us, and spoke; but his speech evidently showed that he meant us no harm, and on the question of the resolution to support Parliament he voted with us.

Northington evidently hoped to get him back.[68]

Grattan's motives for the defection are a matter of speculation. Half a century later his son was to claim that "His wish was to keep the Volunteers of Ireland and the country well affected to the Irish Parliament, no less than to the British connection".[69] At the time Grattan "declared himself decidedly a friend to the parliamentary reform"; that he "love[d] to blend the idea of parliament and volunteers; they have hitherto concurred in establishing our constitution in the last parliament, and I hope they will do it in the present".[70] These words were all the more extraordinary in view of the fact that Grattan had spoken against both of Flood's attempts earlier in November to reduce public expenditure on the army as a gesture of confidence in the Volunteers.[71]

The truth probably lay in Grattan's discovery that in Ireland, unlike England, entry into office was not accompanied by the acquisition of power. The decision-making process was not vested in the Castle but between the Irish parliament and the British cabinet; whoever held sway in the former would, by the spirit of the 1782-83 settlement, possess an effective veto over the British cabinet. The Castle was, in Northington's time, merely an agency of executive power. Between April and June 1782 Grattan had learned the effectualness of the Irish parliament as an instrument of legislative power. Since July 1783 he had had first-hand knowledge of the powerlessness of the Castle and the British cabinet without conclusive control of the Irish legislature. He had made the error of moving from a position of supreme power (or so it must have seemed to him) to the ranks of the powerless. It could not have escaped his notice that Flood was gradually replacing him on the opposition benches. (It is notable that Flood's proposals, although heavily defeated, drew the largest minorities.)[72] In vocal terms Grattan's desertion was tentative but revealing. He had recognised that the British government's concessions of the previous year were not the result of purely constitutional agitation but arose rather from a combination of parliamentary and extra-parliamentary pressure; thus it was that Grattan "love[d] to blend the idea of parliament and Volunteers". However potentially dangerous was the Volunteer card he was determined to play it in order to regain his pinnacle of April 1782.

(2) December 1783 - November 1788

The coalition government in London began to totter on 11th December, and by January 1784 the Treasury had been given over to William Pitt.[73] Despite an apparently-sincere letter from the new home secretary, Lord Sydney, stating that the new government would be pleased to retain him as viceroy, and a warning from Fox that he should not resign until all doubts surrounding Pitt's ability to command a majority at Westminster had been resolved, Northington was determined to go.[74] He persisted in his refusal to meet the Irish parliament on its resumption date of 26 January and two further adjournments were necessary to allow Northington's successor time to arrive.[75] This in turn led to a short but rancorous debate on 9 February, when it was argued that Northington, having resigned as lord lieutenant, had no right to ask the House to adjourn.[76] Grattan did not speak but enough patriots joined in opposing the requested adjournment (Brownlow, Arthur Browne, Major Doyle and Curran) to make Northington shrink from a head-on collision. Government eventually supported an amendment by Brownlow for a shorter adjournment. This tactic successfully split the opposition, but significantly, did not completely absorb it. Against the 108 members who supported Brownlow's amendment was an unusually high number — 42 — who clearly wanted no adjournment at all.[77] By the eve of Rutland's arrival the anti-adjournment lobby had swelled to 48.[78]

The eighteen months which followed the settlement of 1782 had imposed a pattern on future relations between the main opposition groups in Dublin and London. Similarly the brief part-session of 26 February to 14 May 1784 laid the foundations of a relationship between government and opposition in Dublin which was to be invariably stormy and almost invariably defined in terms of confrontation. For opposition members the Rutland administration began in division and confusion but ended in a hardening of battle-lines unknown since the days before 1779.

94

The basic division amongst the great interests was between those who were prepared to gamble on Pitt's survival at Westminster and those who were not. Despite his role of sullen obstructiveness after the fall of the British coalition, Northington co-operated with the incoming Rutland.[79] Rutland for his part seemed particularly anxious to ensure against mass desertions from the government's ranks by disappointed individuals. A surviving account of the strange arrangements proposed by Northington before the government's collapse in London indicates that he had intended to bind the Ponsonbys and Shannons firmly to him.[80] It is virtually certain that these were the arrangements the most important of which (with some adjustments to detail) were passed to Rutland on his arrival.[81] Only the Leinsters adopted the incongruous parallel suggested by James Adair in 1780 (and speculated upon by George Ponsonby in 1783) by following the British Whigs into opposition.[82] Leinster refused to give any reason other than *"that he must oppose the administration"*. Rutland had no doubt that this statement "seems to announce an attempt in him to raise a Party here, and make the present state of English politics the ground of opposition to the measures of Government in this Kingdom".[83]

In response to a feeler from Richard Brinsley Sheridan on the possibilities of such a "system", Charles (who had lost touch with his brother) pointed out that the campaign of 1780-83 had been "the only instance . . .in the history of Irish politics, where a party ever appeared to act upon public principle", and that "it is not probable that we shall in future furnish any other example that will do honour to our public spirit".[84] Charles Sheridan, unlike Grattan, was forced to remain with the Castle through necessity. But like Grattan, he also had discovered it to be a situation devoid of real power. It was the ultimate irony that Sheridan, whose avid pursuit of power was eventually to ruin him, had been instrumental in the transformation of the Irish privy council into a powerless body, only to find himself trapped by his circumstances within its ranks:

. . . we have in fact no *Irish government*; all power here being lodged in a branch of the *English* government, we have no cabinet, no administration of our own; no great offices of state, every office we have here is merely ministerial, it confers no power but that of giving advice, which may or may not be followed by the Chief Governor. As all power, therefore, is lodged solely in the English government, of which the Irish is only a branch, it necessarily follows that no exertion of any party here could ever lead to power, unless they overturned the English government in this country, or unless the efforts of such a party in the Irish House of Commons could overturn the British administration in England, and the leaders of it get into their places; — the first, you will allow, would not be a very wise object, and the latter you must acknowledge to be impossible.

Interesting echoes of Forbes's reply to Adair in 1780 are present in Sheridan's assertion that "The great leading interests in this kingdom are ... strongly averse to forming any such connection on your side of the water, as it would tend to create a fluctuation in the affairs of this country, that would destroy all their consequence". The Irish adherents of the British Whigs were "few in number", would be unable to be of direct assistance to the Whig cause, and moreover would have nothing to gain.[85]

Nevertheless, Sheridan was correct in stating that Rutland and his chief secretary Thomas Orde had come "with the olive branch in their hand".[86] Even the importunate had expressed certain reservations about supporting government unless their offices and sinecures could be guaranteed even in the event of Pitt's failure at Westminster.[87] The limits of the administration's self-confidence were made embarrassingly public at the beginning of April. Foster, having stated the government's opposition to a Ponsonby-proposed address on charter schools, was forced to give way when Ponsonby was supported by Sir Lucius O'Brien and the Provost.[88]

The main obstacles of the session, as Rutland saw them, were Flood's parliamentary reform bill and the increasingly loud clamour for protecting duties as a trade recession gripped the country.[89] In the event, the old division between Flood and other opposition members did surface, but it did not decide the issue of reform. Despite the fact that Flood proceeded on this occasion with the legitimate support of county petitions and not by Volunteer pressure, his motion for the committal of the reform bill was lost by 159 to 85. Government arguments against the bill were singularly uninspiring ("innovation", "anti-constitutional", "violating chartered rights"),[90] but support for the bill, which came from a number of patriots, was backhanded. Grattan himself echoed the wish that the bill be committed in order that its many defects could be put right.[91] No member of the Shannon, Ponsonby or Leinster connections in the Commons spoke in support of Flood.[92] Orde believed that the majority might have been even greater had not some members' yielded to their constituents' advice or felt bound by election promises.[93]

But before the matter of protecting duties could be dealt with, Grattan laid (however unsuccessfully) the foundations of an opposition policy which was one day to become a central plank in the patriot platform. Having been engaged for some time in chairing a parliamentary enquiry into the management of the public revenue, Grattan at the end of March brought forth a detailed case for reform and retrenchment in the Castle's revenue department. Despite the fact that he had uncovered no evidence of extravagance he concluded by moving a resolution "to prevent the grant of any future additional salary to custom(s) officers".[94] At this stage Grattan's assault on the well-established practice of distributing rewards and pensions to obedient members under the guise of customs officers' salaries was no more than an administrative reform.[95] But his refusal to dilute the provocative wording of the resolution forced the government to adopt an argument to oppose it which was also to become an established part of the pattern of confrontation between successive administrations and the opposition - that the proposed resolution would imply the right of parliament to restrain the king's prerogative.[96] The bulk of Grattan's proposed reforms, being merely administrative in content, were carried. His resolution, however, was lost without a division, and Grattan was supported vocally only by Sir Lucius O'Brien (who was probably reminding the Castle of his aspirations to office).[97] Unity had not returned to the patriots. Their refusal to support Grattan on this occasion paralleled the debate a fortnight earlier when Grattan (who *was* present) remained silent as Molyneux, Hartstonge, Hartley, Corry, Dunn and Forbes laboured in vain to halve the proposed increase in postage.[98]

The patriots' voices were occasionally to be heard amongst those of the concerned members who attempted on 2 April to carry resolutions declaratory of the poverty of unprotected Irish manufacturers and of the need to assist them. Despite the support of Hartley, Warren, Boyle, Roche, Cavendish and Blaquiere, Gardiner (normally a supporter of government)[99] was unable to prevent Foster from carrying a division bypassing and dismissive of the resolutions by 110 to 36.[100] Gardiner lost a second division on that same day by 123 to 37 when he tried to introduce an additional duty on imported old drapery.[101] Rutland, who had feared that the House would be "much divided on the issue", had pleasantly found those divisions to have operated in his favour.[102]

By the end of the session lines of co-operation between the various strands of the opposition were still uncertain, but an undercurrent of anti-government feeling had a startling clarity. The address to the lord lieutenant, with which sessions were normally closed, was not an ideal issue on which to take a stand, since opposition to the address could be interpreted as a personal reflection on Rutland. However, William Todd Jones was determined to make the most of the opportunity:

For what bounties received from the Duke of Rutland were the people of Ireland to offer up this thanksgiving? Was it for the rejection of their favourite bill to reform the representation in that House; and to renovate the constitution? Was it for the precipitate dismissal of the equalisation bill, without deigning it any offer of redress, any slight promise from the minister, to sooth the disappointed? Was it for that lenient and equitable act, the post-office bill; the adoption of which from a former administration only aggravated the injury? Was it for the contemptuous rejection of every resolution proposed there, to enforce the residence of certain absentee great officers of the state, who draw immense salaries from this kingdom, and squander them in another; inattentive to, and negligent of the duties annexed to these offices; if there are any duties annexed to them? Was it for filling the streets of the capital with an armed host, not amenable to the controul, and derogatory to the privileges of its peaceful citizens? Or was it for transforming the House of Commons into a court of star-chamber, and converting the Castle from an Irish court to a French Bastille, or a Granada inquisition?

This catalogue of supposed grievances was in fact a gross misrepresentation of the session. The "equalisation bill", the affair of the customs officers' salaries, and the liberty of the press bill had attracted only desultory debate and an uneven, disjointed opposition. But the important fact was that a speech of such sweeping condemnation had not been made since the late 1770s. Jones, supported unreservedly by Molyneux, was clearly advocating systematic opposition.[103] Forbes ("absent in the country" for most of the session),[104] Brownlow and Corry belatedly rose to condemn the address but were handicapped by the widespread feeling that such condemnation would seem to slight the viceroy. Even Richard Griffith ("warm for reform of Parliament and protecting duties")[105] and Gardiner felt the condemnation to be badly timed.[106]

Grattan, morally unable to condemn the behaviour of a government which had so readily accepted his administrative reforms, "supported the address and pointed out many beneficial acts by which this session had been distinguished".[107] Rutland had the satisfaction of defeating a Corry-proposed amendment to the address by 97 to 36, but noted ominously that the minority had included the Duke of Leinster's three brothers and other of his supporters, together with the Conolly connection "and most of the County members who were in town".[108] The withdrawal of Leinster's support was not unexpected: he was "so fickle and unsteady in his opinions, and so weak in all his public conduct, that I hardly knew how I shall be able to dispose of him. There seems to be a perpetual conflict and struggle in his mind between avarice, pride, and ambition".[109] Clearly the office of President of the Council, the offer of which had secured Leinster's support in March (it was ultimately never created), was no longer sufficient.[110]

Rutland was learning that successful negotiation with the great interests as well as with unconnected but ambitious members depended upon the successful shuffling of offices. To meet all demands for offices and pensions at any one time would have been financially ruinous and ultimately counterproductive. The lower rungs of the patronage ladder could be controlled by judicious use of carrot and stick. Members aspiring to office could be kept at bay for a limited period by promises, while members in office were vulnerable to threats of dismissal for parliamentary misbehaviour. This latter course probably operated in the case of Charles Sheridan, whose sole parliamentary duty for most of the 1780s was to propose, on behalf of government, the annual mutiny bill.[111] Deaths, retirements, promotions and horizontal movements were relied upon to ensure that applicants were not kept waiting beyond their patience. But it was in the upper echelons of the patronage ladder that difficulties frequently arose. Great interests were not only wealthy enough (in appearance at least) to disdain threats of dismissal, but were likely to be short of patience and capable of taking many members with them into opposition.

Conolly had begun the Rutland period in avowed opposition in sympathy with his Whig friends at Westminster, but was so violently opposed to Flood's reform bill that he felt it his duty to support government at least until the bill should be rejected.[112] The focal point of the sense of grievance surrounding the address was clearly the local matter of the distressed and unprotected manufacturers. Griffith failed to get an amendment declaratory of the situation inserted in the address on 11th May.[113] Two days later — the day after Leinster and Conolly deserted government in the division on Corry's amendment — Griffith proposed a separate address inclusive of the same sentiment but also requesting "some well-digested plan" to regulate commercial relations between Britain and Ireland.[114] Despite the fact that this proposal seemed to coincide with the government's still-undefined thoughts on a commercial settlement, there is no evidence that Griffith colluded with the Castle.[115] Orde had responded to Griffith by revealing that plans for some commercial settlement were afoot, but he also opposed the proposed address as unnecessary.[116] By the time Foster came to make his successful conciliatory gesture to Griffith[117] a short debate had taken place in which Hartley, Corry and Brownlow had joined forces with malcontents such as Molyneux, anti-government figures such as Newenham, and an habitual government supporter Joseph Hewitt, in support of Griffith's address.[118] The great interests apparently gave no sign during the debate but their behaviour on the previous day made the government reluctant to risk a division. Foster's gesture was made with the full approval of his superiors.[119]

In May 1784 the government estimated its strength as 184 in the Commons.[120] The most ominous comment of the session was perhaps that of Griffith who deplored the (allegedly "light and trifling") treatment of the address "by any gentleman who sits on that side of the House".[121]

One of the manifestations of Rutland's control over the Irish parliament was the shortening and regularising of its sessions. As

99

governments rose and fell in the early 1780s the parliament in Dublin, although it retained its opening date in October of each year, had had its proceedings interupted by a series of haphazard adjournments and prorogations. The most likely explanation for the movement of the opening of parliament from October 1784 to January 1785 is the difficulty experienced in formulating the commercial settlement. The official "permissions" to prorogue hold no clues and no evidence exists that Rutland at this point took advantage of his position to avoid meeting a troublesome parliament until the last possible moment.[122] Nevertheless, the pattern established in 1785 was the one which was to survive. The Irish parliament never again (until 1796) met before January. The peculiar business of 1785 caused the session to last well until September of that year, but in succeeding years sessions tended to peter out in mid-April.

As Orde, and later the Castle servants, wrestled with the embryo commercial settlement throughout the second half of 1784 Rutland continued his efforts to win the support of "respectable characters".[123] The testing-ground of parliament having been removed, Leinster, Conolly, Clifden and Ponsonby needed little coaxing to ensure their attendance at privy council meetings.[124] Shannon also identified himself with the ranks of the "well-disposed".[125] There is no evidence that Rutland and Orde extended their discussion of the commercial settlement beyond the "inner cabinet" of Foster and Beresford. Indeed the terms in which Rutland stated his objection to Pitt's proposed "contribution" on 13th January 1785 are anticipatory and suggest that the "respectable characters" of the privy council were even yet being kept in ignorance of the details.[126] It was not until the following day that he resolved "To be very accurate about the state of Parliament",[127] and on the eve of the opening of the session Orde was still interviewing individual members.[128]

The parliamentary proceedings in the period up to the initial debates on the propositions in mid-February demonstrated that the viceregal efforts had been worthwhile. The "leading interests", with the exception of the volatile Duke of Leinster, firmly supported the government.[129] Opposition, as the session opened, was composed of the patriots Brownlow, Forbes, Corry, Arthur Browne, Michael Smith, Hartstonge, William Todd Jones, and Edward Newenham, together with Lord Edward Fitzgerald and Sir Edward Crofton who opposed the government on principle.[130] Grattan was conspicuously absent from the above list of those who attempted to oppose the address itself or the clause of the address expressing routine disapproval of Rutland's measures.[131] Orde, who had striven to remain on good terms with Grattan during the autumn of 1784, now seized upon the apparent opportunity either to capture the patriot

100

vote or (if Grattan's hegemony was less than complete) at least to split it.[132] The fawning letter imploring Grattan's "opinion and approbation" of the proposed commercial settlement included an offer to carry the details to him in Wicklow.[133] That this gesture failed to secure Grattan's co-operation may not have been unconnected with the anxiety with which it had been sought.[134]

However, Grattan's reluctance to commit himself entirely to the government may have stemmed from the continuing (though now less frequent) presence of his rival Flood on the opposition benches. Flood seemed to have been handicapped by his not-infrequent absences in London during the session, but when present his behaviour suggested a fresh attempt on his part to seize control of events. At the start of the session he introduced the emotion-charged issues of protecting duties and parliamentary reform. He failed to attract the support either of patriots or great interests, but the discomfiture of the patriots was so obvious that Flood felt encouraged to pursue the issue by bill early in March.[135] In fact, of the eleven occasions on which Flood participated in the debates, he played a secondary or supportive role in only four of them. On the other seven occasions he either introduced the issue himself, or proposed a motion on an existing patriot policy or attempted to amend a patriot motion and thus transfer the attention of the House to himself.

Not too surprisingly, Flood found himself best supported on the issue of parliamentary reform. Brownlow, Newenham, Corry, Forbes and Michael Smith agreed to assist him in drawing up the bill.[136] When the bill was debated on 12 May, O'Neill, Hartstonge and Major Doyle supported it also, despite Grattan's stated opinion that the measure was unnecessary.[137]

Despite Grattan's relative silence for much of the sesion, the patriots pressed forward with policies which, though as yet tentatively expressed, were to become the main planks of the patriot platform. Patriot concern regarding public money and its misuse for political purposes underlay Forbes's seemingly innocent request at the start of the session for an account "of all additional salaries, pensions and annual payments, of what nature soever" on the civil list since 1778.[138] O'Hara's promise on 11 February "to put a stop to the practice of bartering places for pensions" was followed in early March by Forbes's promise to exclude from the House by bill those members "who shall accept, for themselves, or any of their family, any pension for years or lives".[139]

A further focal point of patriot concern was the absence of an Irish foreign policy as distinct from the mere participation of Ireland in an imperial foreign policy. Corry, supported by Newenham and Forbes, demanded a committee of enquiry in order to discover which of the foreign treaties entered into by Britain in the previous several years could be said to involve "the common interest" of Britain and Ireland. The government's reaction was to adopt a variation of of their response to Grattan's resolution of the previous year on customs officers' salaries — that Corry seemed to "doubt his majesty's royal word" and to "call in question the king's veracity". Orde was more explicit, but he also took cover behind the "king" fiction in his assertion that "It is not the province of parliament to form treaties, but to take advantage of them when formed, and to improve their consequences to the benefit of the nation".[140] When the issue was brought forward again a few days later the "king" fiction had become an established part of the government's political vocabulary: "The prerogative of the crown, of making peace and war, ought not to be infringed; it is a power which was vested in the crown because of its superior intelligence".[141]

A source of unity amongst the patriots and of additional support for their "side" was their demand for an enquiry into the King's Bench decision of 1784 to proceed in certain cases by attachment instead of trial by jury, and their subsequent condemnation of that decision when the government refused to concede an enquiry.[142] The patriots had the full[143] support of the Leinster group on this issue, and Brownlow's motion of 24 February that a recent attachment case "was contrary to the principles of the constitution" brought them their highest division figure of the session (i.e. before 12 August), even though they were defeated.[144]

The commercial settlement did not become a party issue until August 1785. Rather than adopt a distinct attitude to the propositions, the opposition tended to suspend operations when presented with them. As pointed out in the previous chapter, opposition members displayed an inability to grasp the financial details of the settlement when it was laid before them in February.[145] The Commons was generally in favour of a commercial agreement. A loyal address thanking the king for the propositions drew almost unanimous support in February.[146] In the same month the patriots split over Corry's resolution on foreign policy, as Todd Jones was "unwilling to give any embarrassment to government" until the propositions were debated. In April Corry was forced to withdraw a motion demanding equal construction of the navigation act in the face of his colleagues' accusations of bad timing.[147] A curious factor in regard to the pre-August debates on the settlement was that although vocal attacks had clearly been suspended after 11 February, division figures (with the exception of the loyal address) remained stable. The opposition numbers never fell below 33 or rose above 42 in any of the four divisions between February and June.

The impression that opposition had attained some level of cohesiveness at least on this issue is strengthened by the fact that

102

three of the four divisions were on matters connected with the settlement but not actually focussed on it. The Commons divided along party lines vocally as well as in the division lobbies over Hartley's demand on 9 February for more time to consider the settlement. The motion was rejected by 156 to 37.[148] The only debate to come to a division on a technical aspect of the settlement commanded 33 votes against the government's 178.[149] Flood did somewhat better on 14 February when he wisely buried a possible division on the eleventh proposition in the more "general" motion "that an immediate and effectual retrenchment in public expenses is necessary". He lost by 121 to 42.[150]

Grattan remained silent for most of the session and opposed the patriots when he did speak.[151] But despite this fact and despite the division figures, the government remained solidly under the impression that his support was essential to ensure the success of the settlement. It is a point of considerable interest that Grattan's influence over the country gentlemen was believed (by the government, if by nobody else) to stem from his personality and parliamentary track record rather than from his traditionally-supposed position as leader of the patriot group. Yet throughout the first half of 1785 Grattan sat securely on the fence , publicly supporting the government on the February propositions and on the militia clothing arrangements, but privately making it clear that his support could not be taken for granted.[152] It was the measure of Grattan's showmanship that he not only helped to stampede the Castle into opposing Pitt's arrangements on 11 February (above, pp. 75-6), but that when he ultimately returned to opposition in June he slid with little difficulty into a prominent position. On 13 June the revised propositions became a subject of debate in the Irish Commons. But while Forbes and Corry wrestled with the less-than-central problem of getting circular letters sent out to ensure a full attendance for a major debate on the issue, it was Grattan who arose to declare the "new" propositions "subversive of the rights of Ireland".[153] A fortnight later (30 June) Grattan tested the strength of his influence over the patriot group with favourable results. In opposition to a government request for a fortnight's adjournment Hercules Rowley moved that further debate on the propositions be postponed until the following session. Corry, Forbes and Curran failed to adopt identical positions on the question. Despite the support of Conolly, Rowley instantly concurred with a request from Grattan, who supported the spirit of the motion, that it be withdrawn.

A further significant feature of this debate was that with it began the flow of desertions from the government ranks which was to bring about the near-defeat of the administration in August. "Solid" government men such as Cavendish and General Luttrell[154] had duly opposed Forbes's move for circular letters on 13 June.[155] But by the end of the month Cavendish felt the propositions to be "a vital stab to the legislative independence of Ireland". He and other government supporters such as Godfrey Greene and Denis Browne wanted the propositions postponed until the following year.[156] There is a strong temptation to suggest that the government's view of Grattan's influence over the House was justified and that it was in response to his declaration on 13 June that the desertions to the opposition benches began a fortnight later. But Grattan had spoken *before* Cavendish and Luttrell on 13 June and neither member seemed to have been influenced by his statement at that point. Moreover, Grattan was one of the last to speak on Rowley's motion of 30 June. The "alternative" patriot leaders — Forbes, Corry and Curran — had reacted in a confused manner to Rowley's motion; Grattan could therefore have seized the escape route from the propositions offered by Rowley and still have retained his prominent position in the patriot group. The balance of probability is that Grattan, in reaching his decision to cancel Rowley's motion, was influenced by the desertion of the government members and of the formidable Conolly, all of whom had spoken *before* him on 30 June. Therefore, while it was the deserters from government who were to decide the outcome of the fateful decision of 12 August, it was Grattan who decided that the confrontation would actually take place.

When 12 August came, Grattan spoke at length. This was important in regard to his role as the patriots' leader[157] but scarcely necessary for the issue itself. It was, as he had previously said, "the old question and the old cause", and it did indeed "produce the same spirit".[158] Grattan might have influenced the course of events but the events themselves were still very much in the hands of government supporters and the country gentlemen. The true extent of Grattan's influence with these latter gentlemen was perhaps revealed in September when he foolishly attempted to oppose the end-of-session address to Rutland and found himself in a minority of thirteen.[159]

Rutland's response to the events of 12 August was conciliatory rather than reactionary. The near-defeat of the government had been brought about less through desertion by Castle employees than by a lack of commitment on their part. There had been , he informed Pitt, "many truants".[160] Rutland's failure to dismiss the deserters from their offices almost certainly arose from the need to withhold this threat against the outcome of a further crisis. Within days of the last debate on the propositions Edmund Pery signified his wish to retire from the Speakership of the Commons. Ponsonby, allegedly supported by Leinster, Loftus, Conolly and Shannon ("with all his strength") planned to recapture the position which had been occupied by his father until the Townshend period.[161] But Ponsonby himself could not have been blind to the balance of forces on 12 August. Moreover, the defeat of a government candidate in a contest for the Speakership and the consequent demise of Rutland's administration would have been of little benefit to Ponsonby if Rutland's last act was to be the dismissal of every office-holder who had opposed his candidate. Rutland had left him in no doubt that this would indeed be the response to any such contest.[162] This threat, together with the lack of certainty that he could carry the day, eventually drew Ponsonby to the Castle to wait on the lord lieutenant and "explain his conduct".[163] Had he but known it, Ponsonby had contributed immeasurably to the recovery of Rutland's political strength. Many of those who supported the uncontested John Foster for the Speakership on 5 September were aware in their unanimity that they retained their offices not through the government's weakness but by its mercy, and were suitably grateful.[164]

Paradoxically it was Pitt who presented the greatest danger to Rutland's political recovery. The prime minister's immediate desire was for revenge, and he sought "with great impatience for a more particular account" of "the deserters who reduced our force so low".[165] Moreover, although Pitt had acquiesced in the temporary abandonment of the propositions he was not prepared to postpone the re-match any longer than was necessary. To Orde who visited him in September he suggested that a policy of systematic resistance be adopted to all opposition measures no matter how reasonable or negotiable, until the Irish law sense on the propositions. However, Orde did manage to persuade him against mass dismissals and to be satisfied with the token removals of the Ponsonbyite William Burton[166] and Edward Hunt (of the minor O'Neill connection)[167] and the curtailment of Lord Bellamont's pension.[168] Pitt seethed for months. It was late October before he came upon the treacherous letter from a leading Castle administrator accusing Orde of incompetence and of mismanaging the Commons on 12 August.[169] Pitt reacted so precipitately that only Rutland's spirited defence of his chief secretary kept Orde in office.[170]

The 1786 session was relatively short and as quiet as Rutland had anticipated,[171] and has consequently been ignored by virtually every historian who has dealt with this period.[172] In fact the session saw significant progress in the development of the patriot group as an appropriate party possessing a distinct set of policies and representing a serious alternative to the Castle government

Pitt took a direct personal interest in the Irish government's plans for the session. However, the transcript of the conversation between him and Orde on 15 November 1785 suggests an unwillingness on Pitt's part to interfere with Rutland's plans.[173] All further moves on the commercial scheme were "to depend on its being called for".

Orde also managed to dissuade Pitt from his earlier plan of resisting the introduction of all measures, necessary and otherwise, until the propositions should be accepted. Such necessary measures included the proposed establishment of a militia and an anti-Volunteer bill. It was in this context that the police bill (the only measure for which the Irish session of 1786 is remembered) came into being.

The Dublin police bill, as introduced by the government to the Irish commons in March 1786,[174] was based on the London and Westminster police bill. This latter measure had been sponsored by Pitt's cabinet the previous year but had been withdrawn due to strong local opposition.[175] The manner of its introduction into the November conversation between Orde and Pitt suggests not that the prime minister was trying to smuggle the bill into Westminster through the Irish "back door", but rather that Orde saw the measure as a means of undermining the Volunteers. A considerable part of the Volunteers' *raison d'etre* after 1783 related to the absence of adequate policing. The successful establishment of a hierarchically-structured, centrally-controlled police force with relatively-sweeping powers of law-enforcement would eliminate yet another reason for the Volunteers' continued existence while avoiding the potentially-explosive proposal of an anti-Volunteer bill. In exchange for Pitt's proposed militia Orde suggested that the rotation of cavalry units stationed in the two kingdoms would provide a sufficiently stable (and less contentious) military presence. Pitt showed no signs of disagreeing with these proposals. Nor did he demur when Orde laid before him Rutland's brainchild of an Irish system of public education on the lines of Eton and Westminster. But it seems to have been Orde himself who added the suggestion that an institution be established in Ireland for the training of Catholic priests.[176]

Rutland's government was well prepared for the new session. Despite the desertions and truancies Rutland had noted with satisfaction that considerable connections such as that of Lord Shannon (12 members), Lord Tyrone (6 members), Lord Clifden (7 members) and Lord Hillsborough (8 members) had been "steady and decided in their support" on 12 August.[177] The latter names featured among those listed by Lodges Morres in December 1785 when he pointed out to Rutland that "if three great interests were to unite in representing a matter of the Crown ... surely it would be an unhappy circumstance. On past occasions Shannon, Loftus and Ponsonby[178]

were beat by a division and know that they could effect great matters by a union, and they are highly well-disposed to each other. They would no act together upon slight occasions, but I know certain points upon which they would sacrifice [*sic*] every consideration to unite.

106

But by the opening of the session Orde had "seen and conversed with almost every member of either House of Parliament of whose conduct we could have any doubt". He had (with apparent success) laid down

the general principle of commencing from this moment a special warning to all the persons connected by office or emolument with His Majesty's Government that they would in peril of their particular interest be expected not only to support us when they should be present, but also to attend to summons upon any occasion of business.

The Ponsonbys were reinstated in Rutland's good graces on the condition that Lord Shannon would be responsible for them. It was clear also that Orde knew in advance of the patriot programme for the session.[179]

Although doomed to fail, the patriot programme was carefully planned[180], skilfully executed, and conducted with an impressive degree of unity. Grattan was present for much of the session but, as usual, it was Corry who was allowed to lead the patriots in defeat. The beginning of the session was taken up with Corry's requests for details of government expenditure over a considerable number of years.[181] Government was agreeable to most of these requests but baulked at Corry's demand on 7 February for details of its investments in the National Bank. On this occasion patriot strength was starkly revealed as 9 against the government's 144.[182] But the financial details were important. The patriot plan was, firstly to gain the support of as many country independent members as possible by attacking the high level of taxation. Secondly, the patriots hoped that by blaming taxation levels on the pension list the fury of the country gentlemen could be directed against that list. The third part of the plan was to cite the pension list as an artificial means of keeping the Castle in power and therefore as representing an indirect attack upon the 1782 settlement.

Government's failure to rescind the extra £140,000 in taxes which had been voted the previous year in expectation of the commercial settlement left them open to attack since the settlement had never materialised. On 9 February Conolly, supported by Hardy, Newenham, Brownlow, Forbes, Corry and Grattan, moved that, in view of the greatly increased taxation, the government should now have no difficulty in keeping the national expenditure within the national income.[183] Two days after Corry's disaster over the bank investments issue the patriots brought forth an impressive 73 votes while the government party merely held its ground with 149 votes.[184] Before proceeding with the second part of the plan Corry tested the water by objecting to a proposed newspaper tax. Absences reduced the figures on both sides this time but the division of 118 to 51 showed clearly that the patriots still held an appreciable part of the "country" vote.[185]

The size and composition of the pension list was a personal headache to Orde and he wished that he could "give way upon a liberal compromise" to the expected opposition proposal.[186]

Yet in the state of the country it seems hardly possible to venture upon such a measure, which would from the peculiar circumstance of the Hereditary Revenue previous to any settlement appear to be so strong an encroachment on the Royal Prerogative; and (what is perhaps of more real consequence) would deprive Government of a means (how prudently soever to be used) of defeating the combinations of party or popular violence, as any formidable symptoms of them should from time to time be manifested.

Forbes's request on 20 February for leave to introduce his bill "to prevent persons holding places or pensions under the crown from sitting or voting in the House of Commons" was deftly turned aside. Blaquiere for government "declared his approbation of the principle of any bill which tended to restrain the undue influence of the crown in that House, if any such existed", and suggested that the pursuit of the issue would merely delay the more urgent supply bills. Conscious that he had been out-manoeuvred, and that he would appear unreasonable if he pressed on, Forbes postponed the issue.[187]

A fortnight later, the supply bills having been passed, Forbes merged the two remaining parts of the patriot programme.[188] The attack on the pension list was carefully structured to appeal to the country independents:[189]

The pensions of Ireland ... exceeded the pensions of England: Upon what ground could this be justified? Were the revenue, the commerce, the resources of Ireland greater than those of England? Was the number of persons who deserved reward in Ireland greater than those who deserved reward in England? If not, could any man say that pensions were granted with any other intention than to overturn the independence of the parliament of Ireland. It was idle ... to talk of an independent parliament, whose members received wages from the crown; it was not in human nature, for so long as the hope of reward, and the fear of receiving injury, would operate upon the mind of man, so long would pensions given to members of parliament be able to sway them from their duty. A pensioner is but a man, and until the minister could exempt him from the common condition of humanity, he must be influenced by his pension.

This appeal to sweet reason was preceded by a reference to an attack on the pension list in 1757. The citation of such a precedent was designed partly to appeal to the gentlemen's sense of history but mainly to counteract in some degree the government's argument that the patriots were attacking the crown's prerogative.[190] It was pointed

108

out moreover that "the House of Commons could not control the power of the crown while its members were dependent on the crown during pleasure"; that in Britain this imbalance in the constitution had been redressed by legislation similar to that now advocated by Forbes.[191] The proposed legislation was allotted an historical position as Forbes appealed to the gentlemen to continue their sterling service of August 1785 and "secure the constitution from future attack".[192]

Reason, history and justice having been exhausted, Forbes finally asked the gentlemen to use their votes to improve the position of the Irish parliament as a power-sharing entity within the framework of the 1782 settlement: "By adopting a measure of self-denial on the subject of pensions ... we establish a character in the nation which will procure us a greater degree of influence than we ever possessed".[193] Forbes's last tactic in the assault was to preserve the structure of his intended bill by temporarily withholding it. Had he brought forward the bill and lost, Forbes would have been unable to introduce it in the following session without some material alteration. The motion merely stated that "the present application and amount of pensions" were "a grievance to the nation" but did commit the House to redressing it.[194]

The careful timing and handling of the assault helped the patriots to retain the bulk of the support they had attracted earlier in the session. But the loss of the motion by 128 to 70 represented in real terms the zenith of the patriot achievement and the end of their hopes for that session. But Forbes, to whom leadership of the patriots had been temporarily given,[195] was encouraged rather than dismayed, and insisted on introducing the bill. Although the approach of the quarter sessions had begun to reduce the number of its members, the government felt confident enough to allow the introduction of Forbes's bill. When the confrontation came on the motion to allow the bill a second reading the Castle felt no compunction to further expand its argument that the royal prerogative was being molested. Perhaps the most significant development of the patriots' policy for several years was the refusal to evade this argument or to adopt a variation of it as had been done in the past. The patriots' answer in 1786 was that the whole concept of the crown's prerogative as defined by the Castle was invalid:[196]

The power of parliament over the prerogative was too firmly established to admit of a question; not a power of limiting it only, but also a power of superintending its exercise within the limits and bounds already set to it. This superintendence forming the characteristic, distinguishing ours from an absolute monarchy, and the notoriety of those limits and bounds forming, as a great writer observes, one chief boast of our constitution; to deny that

109

superintendence and control, what would it be but again to set up unlimited power and passive obedience.

The significance of this counterargument lay not in its essence but rather in the fact that it had been stated in terms which suggested that the Castle held an opposite or different view. In fact the Castle could not, in keeping with Whig orthodoxy, explicitly disagree with the statement. But the Castle's refusal to concede the practical application of the principle in repeated instances allowed to patriots to suggest (with potential credibility) that the government was abusing the royal prerogative and upsetting the balance of the constitution. The political stance of the Whig party at Westminster was being increasingly adopted by the patriots in Dublin. The bill was lost by 134 to 78.[197]

Patriot unity and discipline had held fast throughout the campaign, Corry and Grattan by obvious pre-arrangement adopting supportive roles. That it had not been enough was due in part to the government's success in the securing the support of the great interests. However, the patriot attack on the pension list did not (by any evidence known to us) originate in any formal agreement with the Westminster Whigs, and the dolorous career of those Whigs even after Burke's Act could scarcely have made the latter measure worthy of imitation merely for its own sake. Yet the patriots were to revive the "Forbes" programme of pension and place bills annually in the years ahead. It is therefore suggested here that the voting power of the government in the Irish Commons depended not exclusively on the support of the great interests but to a significant extent upon the support of members who had not the resources to be truly country independents but who remained outside parliamentary groups. The support of country independents could be attracted (though not always reliably) by particular sets of circumstances — uncontrolled taxation or "the constitution in danger" — but the persistence of patriot opposition to pensioners and placemen makes it clear that the balance of power in the Irish Commons lay with those who could be *bought*. It will from this be obvious that the patriots' motivation is now being called into question and that it is being suggested that their primary *raison d'etre* was the pursuit of parliamentary and executive power. This suggestion will be explored further when dealing with the Regency Crisis. But for the present it is worth noting that even before the 1780s the pension list had almost invariably increased from year to year. There was a grim truth in FitzGibbon's statement that "It is somewhat odd that the honourable gentleman [Forbes] could not perceive any extravagance in Lord Northington's government, while that worthy gentleman remained here, though now his indignation breaks forth so violently".[198]

110

The government's failure to bring forward the police bill until the middle of March stemmed not from their determination to take advantage of the quarter sessions but from Pitt's sudden loss of interest in Irish affairs. In a letter of 15 March Orde revealed that Pitt had failed to reply to the chief secretary's long missive of late January.[199] The successful resistence to the patriots on the pension issue had been conducted entirely on Orde's initiative. The police bill was introduced on 20 March, as Orde felt it inadvisable to wait any longer for the revised draft from London "from which however we very much wished to have derived new lights".[200] The main thrust of the patriots' opposition to the bill centred on an attempt to delay its committal until the return of the country gentlemen who were absent at the quarter sessions. To achieve this it was necessary to harness the support of the remaining country independents by transferring to the police bill the odious mantle of an attack on the constitution. The clauses providing for the appointment of police officials by the Castle facilitated the patriots' efforts to emphasise the continuity in spirit between the government's pension and place policy. The police measure, it was claimed, was "a bill of armed patronage".[201] But the very absence of the members in the hope of whose support the patriots tried to delay the committal of the bill rendered even the most vociferous opposition futile. The patriots could muster only 37 votes against the government's 139 on the question of deferring the bill's committal to the beginning of May.[202] The patriots' alternative argument that the bill represented "an invasion of the chartered rights of the city of Dublin" proved more effective. A further attempt to delay the bill's committal, supported by the arrival of a petition from the freemen and freeholders of Dublin, raised the opposition's division figure to 46 and lowered the government's to 125.[203] These figures hardly wavered (130 to 44) when on the same day the patriots moved to adjourn before the committee could get under way.[204]

Despite the government's protestations that no hurry was intended there is no doubt that the police bill was rushed through parliament.[205] Introduced on 20 March, the bill was given its second reading and was committed on 22; it was discussed in committee on 25 and 27 and passed its third reading on 28.[206] The lack of positive support from London, the fact that the measure on which the bill was based had been defeated at Westminster the previous year, the peculiar success of the patriots in retaining the support of normally volatile country gentlemen (however numerically insufficient), the unavoidable loss of a proportion of Castle support due to the quarter sessions, together with disturbing resemblence between the anti-police campaign in the Dublin press and the successful similar campaign in London in 1785, were undoubtedly the factors at the root of the government's desire to hurry the bill

111

into law.[207] The extent of the government's nervousness on the issue is suggested by the fact that concessions were granted and the bill altered in committee in the obvious hope of luring away some of the patriots' country support.[208]

The debate on the police bill brought to light one further development in the growing polarisation between the patriots and the government — the explicit abandonment by the patriots of the "king" fiction which since 1780 had bound them to the Castle in an illusory but almost-inescapable unity. During the campaign for the 1782 settlement Yelverton and those members who had then formed the patriot nucleus had refused to carry their assault on the Irish privy council to its nominal counterpart in London. Even during the pension bill debate of 1786 they had failed to rally at the Castle suggestion that their position represented an attack upon the crown. The tactical usefulness of Corry's assertion that parliament had power over the prerogative (above, p. 109) could not disguise the patriots' failure to come to terms with the prerogative itself. The manner in which the Castle had exploited this chink in the patriot armour made such a confrontation inevitable. Thus it was that when the solicitor-general played the "prerogative" card during the committee stage of the police bill, Grattan responded: "The control of the crown is another word for the control of the minister".[209] The stigma of imaginary treason which had for several years prevented the patriots from making use of all possible tactics against the Castle had at a stroke been removed. The king had in one sense been expelled from Irish parliamentary politics.

Important as the developments in the patriots' political evolution seem in retrospect, the failure of these policies to bring forth victory in 1786 gave rise to an understandable but counterproductive impatience on the part of the members concerned. The sessions of 1787 and 1788 saw the addition of further items to the patriots' list of "national" grievances and the further development of their identity as a possible alternative government. But their unity crumbled and with it all their hopes of attracting independent support. Natural impatience may have been supplemented by the realisation that due to the size of the government's pension list (and the Castle's new determination on discipline after August 1785), no amount of country support would be sufficient. The patriots were effectively doomed to permanent opposition.

The patriots began the 1787 session united but without any apparent plan of action. Half-hearted efforts to blame the Castle firstly for provoking by its inertia the social unrest which was then sweeping the country, and secondly for failing to quell the outbreak, were followed by disjointed criticisms of government expenditure.[210] Forbes hinted darkly that he would again raise the pension issue.[211]

112

The lord lieutenant's opening speech had in fact been doctored to allow the opposition as few grounds as possible on which to attack the government.[212] The patriots took advantage of the government's vague promise of legislation to quell the agrarian violence and claimed that such interference with local magistrates was unnecessary. At this point the patriots' brittle unity failed them. When amendments were proposed embodying the opposition's objections a number of patriots left the chamber, leaving Curran and Richard Longfield[213] without vocal support.[214] "Opposition", chortled Orde with good reason, "is certainly very weak both in numbers and in concert . . .".[215]

On 3 February Corry, supported by Stewart (of Killymoon), John Wolfe and Burgh (of Old Town), attacked the government's disbursement procedures and lost a division by 127 to 35.[216] It was the end of Corry's leadership, of patriot unity, and of systematic opposition. A few days later Conolly, supported by Grattan, proposed a motion agreeing "chearfully" [sic] to the renewed grant of the contentious £140,000 first voted in 1785, and hoped that Rutland's "frugal and just management" would prevent "the further accumulation of debt, or increase of taxes". Orde grasped the olive branch and the motion was carried unanimously. A somewhat soured Corry warned that the current money bill merely represented "a vote of credit" and that without retrenchment new taxes would inexorably follow. Before the day ended Grattan made clear who was in charge: "Satisfied with having carried a principle, I applaud the ministers' assenting to the motion, and withhold animadversion on the articles of expense".[217]

But there yawned a considerable gap between those patriots who had lost confidence in Corry and those who were prepared to follow Grattan unreservedly into the Castle yard. In a straight competition with Corry it was Grattan who came off the worse. Even had there been no split in the patriot ranks the government's bill "to prevent tumultuous uprisings", designed to restore the rule of law in Whiteboy-ravaged areas, was not a propitious object for parliamentary opposition. Grattan took the opportunity to test the extent of the Castle's desire to reclaim him. John Wolfe, Stewart (of Killymoon) and Curran — all followers of Corry — attacked the bill as "hostile to the liberties of the people" and likened it to the British Riot Act.[218] Grattan wished to know

Whether it was meant to press the bill with all its clauses? Whether it was intended to submit it to alteration? — If the former he would oppose it in the first instance; if the latter, if his alterations were acceded to, he would vote for the commital.

In the event, the government merely made use of Grattan's new stance to emphasise the rift in the patriot group. The attorney-general rejected all of Grattan's proposed alterations except one.

As the debate continued it became clear that Grattan was almost without a personal following amongst the patriots. Stewart, Wolfe, Dunn, Kearney, Michael Smith and Curran violently opposed the bill. Only Brownlow, Arthur Browne, Hardy and Forbes agreed to support the measure, and each of them stated that they did so only on the understanding that objectionable clauses would be altered in committee. Both sides of the patriot group were embarrassed. Forbes regretted that "on this occasion he must differ from some right honourable and honourable friends, with whom he was used to co-operate". Stewart "was sorry he was under the necessity of differing with some gentlemen, with whom he gloried in co-operating". It was Stewart who eventually forced the division which the government by 192 to 30. If the earlier division of 3 February had been a true indication of patriot strength at this point, then the five members who reluctantly supported Grattan on the committal of the bill represented the full extent of Grattan's influence in the Irish Commons in 1787. Under these circumstances Corry's silence throughout the debate must have added considerably to his personal standing.[219]

Thus it was that Grattan's attempt to capture the helm of the patriot group had the ironic effect of papering over the cracks. He did not try to interfere when, a few days later, Corry, supported by Forbes and Curran, demanded (in vain) time to consider in detail the newly-signed Anglo-French commercial treaty.[220] He remained silent when, in mid-March, Forbes (supported by Hardy, Todd Jones and Curran) again wheeled in his ill-fated bill to exclude pensioners and placemen from the Commons. The unusually-impressive division figure of 65 (against the government's 129) on this occasion can be attributed to the patriots' skilful combination of the novel and the familiar in their appeal to the country independents. It was pointed out that in the same session in which the British Riot Act had been passed (1715) a pension bill (from which the present measure had been directly copied) was also enacted: "thus while the crown received in one hand from the parliament an encrease of its power, it gave to that parliament with the other an additional security against the abuse of that encreased power". Forbes allowed his audience to note for themselves the obvious contrast between the government's behaviour in 1715 and that of a government which, having passed a bill to quash "tumultuous uprisings", was now refusing to sanction a pension bill. As in the previous session the country gentlemen's sense of history was appealed to, as Todd Jones disinterred a further precedent in the form of a 1764 motion condemning the pension list of that year (the motion had been lost by "a very small majority").[221]

114

In only two further instances during the remainder of the session did members of the patriot group speak against one another, and on each occasion the instigator of the conflict was Conolly. The patriots' continuing failure to make significant progress and their obvious lack of political prospects seemed to have affected Conolly's morale with particular severity. Near the end of the session he was believed to be "out of humour about politics".[222] To his family he had voiced his disenchantment: ". . . it's plain to see there is *no system* here, nor can there ever be any: the interests of individuals are so contrasted that nothing can be carried on with regularity, and all must depend upon the events of peculiar situations".[223] On 13 March Grattan, apparently by pre-arrangement, cited the existing tithe system as the cause of the Whiteboy unrest and attempted to commit the House to the abolition of the system. Conolly echoed the government's argument that by surrendering to the rioters the House would merely encourage them and demanded that the motion be withdrawn. The confusion caused by Conolly's behaviour was nowhere more evident than in Sir Henry Hartstonge who had seconded Grattan's motion. He arose immediately after Conolly to state that he had changed his mind and would oppose the motion unless it were withdrawn. Doyle, Todd Jones and Curran supported the motion while Newenham, Arthur Browne and Kearney joined Conolly and Hartstonge in demanding its withdrawal. The motion was eventually lost without a division.[224]

The patriots chose to interpret the government's navigation bill as an attempt to smuggle the ill-fated fourth proposition of 1785 onto the statute book under an assumed name.[225]

Mr. Conolly understands it is intended as a resumption of the power over Ireland that England had, and which she gave up in the Duke of Portland's time. Mr. Grattan has never had but one opinion about it, and the change of constitution being a child of his own, will never give it up. Mr. Conolly, you know, never wished for it, but maintains (as he did in the business of the propositions) that since we have got it, we are not going to give it up again for nothing; he would barter it for some very essential good, but not at the pleasure or threat of England.

Conolly's co-operation, and probably the nature of the issue itself, enabled Grattan, Corry, Ogilvie and Curran to support each other unreservedly. The Castle's failure to convincingly rebutt the patriot interpretation of the bill caused the level of support for the opposition to rise to 52 (against the government's 127) in the division.[226]

The quarter sessions had depleted both sides of the House by the time (30 March) the Castle got around to introducing the most beneficial aspects of the Dublin Police Act to the provinces. Both Corry and Grattan were absent (or inexplicably silent) for most of the passage of this measure. This factor may have underlain Conolly's successful attempt in the first debate (30 March) to seize the reins of the patriot group. In the apparent absence of more prominent members, the attack was led by Stewart and supported by Todd Jones and Wolfe who assailed the measure on the familiar grounds that it was really designed to increase government patronage and so was a threat to the constitution, and moved its postponement to 1 May (i.e. until the close of the quarter sessions). Conolly expressed his approval of the bill in principle, but "had some doubts upon it so far as it related to the constitution". He then deliberately moved its postponement to mid-April. To prevent a split vote Stewart, in the moments before the division, withdrew his motion and agreed to Conolly's mid-April date. The proposed postponement was rejected by 81 to 28.[227]

The debate on the proposed committal of the same bill three days later saw an attempt by Conolly — this time unsuccessful — to influence the content of the bill: ". . . if the chief constables to be appointed under the bill were to be made elective in the counties by the grand juries, it would take away every objection he entertained against the bill".[228] It was obvious from the state of the House that the opposition, divided or otherwise, had no hope of succeeding. The other patriots (Brownlow, Stewart and Todd Jones) ignored Conolly and fell back upon their usual arguments. The bill was committed by 110 to 29.[229]

The committee stage of the new police measure, the last significant debate of the session, found the patriots in disarray. Some patriots (Grattan, Arthur Browne) joined the several independent members in trying to secure modifications in individual clauses of the bill, whilst others (Stewart, Forbes, Doyle) continued doggedly to oppose the measure *in toto*. The latter were joined (somewhat surprisingly) by Conolly.[230]

It was something of a tribute to Rutland's system of parliamentary control that the system did not die with him. Despite the manifest displeasure of the new lord lieutenant, the Duke of Buckingham (who, as Earl Temple, had held the viceroyalty in 1782), at the tangled web of "promised" offices bequeathed to him by Orde and the new obstreperousness of the Duke of Leinster (who "waits to be bought"), the Castle maintained a respectable majority in the first divisions of the 1788 session.[231] The patriots, however, were equally optimistic as to the significance of the new administration for them. In an early attempt to secure Grattan's co-operation for a united effort in the coming session Forbes reported that Buckingham had been appointed viceroy because Pitt distrusted him and wanted him out of England; that the new chief secretary, Allyn Fitzherbert, was a manic depressive in the last stages of cirrhosis who, moreover, was "totally ignorant of the business of Parliament, and the internal concerns of these kingdoms".[232]

Despite the now-irritating presence of Lawrence Parsons, the self-appointed successor of Flood in the Irish Commons, and the desertion of the Longfield connection to the government, patriot division figures rose to near fifty.[233] The pattern of patriot activity settled quickly into a well-established mould. Government expenditure was sniped at by Corry,[234] Forbes again brought forward his pension and place bill (and was defeated by 103 to 40),[235] and most of the patriots joined in a deliciously fruitful enquiry into the extravagance and irregularities of the new (1786) Dublin police.[236] With one inexplicable lapse patriot unity held firm.[237]

It was during this session that a social content totally devoid of any possible political advantage began to creep into the patriot policy portfolio. Whereas the government had concentrated on quelling the Whiteboy disturbances through the extension of centralised police control to the provinces, the patriots in 1787 and 1788 suggested that the tithe system was at the root of the unrest and that modification of the system would constitute a healthier preventative approach to the problem. It was true that Grattan's proposed modifications were extensive and that at one point he seemed to favour the abolition of the system.[238] But despite the fact that several members raised the cry "the Church in danger", his motion for an enquiry into possible tithe collection grievances in the provinces drew a relatively impressive 49 votes against the government's 121.[239] The patriots maintained this same figure a week later when the government tried to curtail the police enquiry.[240]

To some extent the patriots had taken up the torch of social reform which had begun to glow in Rutland's grasp before his untimely death. On 15 March 1788, two days after the Castle had consigned Rutland's education scheme to oblivion because the provincial returns on the state of Irish schools were "defective and incomplete", the patriots proposed an enquiry into the administration of the hearth tax.[241] This gesture had not even the ulterior motive of preventing agrarian unrest; Conolly was supported by Stewart, Forbes and Grattan in his belief that "the poor should not be taxed at all" and "that men who receive no benefit from the State, ought not to share in its burden".[242]

(3) November 1788 - January 1801

The strengths and weaknesses of the 1782 settlement were at no time so clearly displayed as during the Regency Crisis. The death or permanent incapacity of George III in 1789 would not have resulted in any major readjustment to the 1782 settlement — merely a change in the personnel at the Castle; so the constitution was not in danger. But although those independent members in whose hands the balance of power in the Irish Commons traditionally rested began to desert the Castle in the uncertain days of January and February 1789, the actual balance of power remained remained with the government. In England the passing of power into the hands of the Whigs depended partly on the possible permanence of the king's malady and partly on their success in gaining support at Westminster for their interpretation of the Prince's succession rights. But in Ireland the very uncertainty of the king's situation seemed to presage an alarming number of desertions to the opposition.

Certainly Buckingham was sufficiently convinced of this prospect so that he avoided meeting parliament until the last possible moment. It was true that money and mutiny bill had to be passed and that Buckingham's respite could only have been temporary. But the crisis itself was only temporary. The fact remained that the lord lieutenant possessed a sufficient degree of executive power to ensure his government's survival in a major political crisis without the sanction of parliament. A considerable loophole in the 1782 settlement, it seemed, was that the executive power in Ireland could still be exploited for narrow party advantage.

Had the fates been kinder to the patriots (i.e. had the king died) their prospects would have been far more promising. Despite their stormy relationship with the British Whigs in 1782-83, the shared experience of hopeless opposition during the '80s seemed to have created a bond of sympathy between the two groups. Admittedly it was a bond prized more by the Whigs than by the patriots: "... you are all so void of principle in Ireland that you cannot enter into our situation", complained Richard Brinsley Sheridan to his Dublin-based brother Charles (who now rarely wrote to him).[243] Even during the affair of the commercial propositions Sheridan had to rely for information about Irish politics on an itinerant Whig merchant, infrequent letters from Corry, and Castle gossip leaked by the treacherous William Eden.[244] But by the summer of 1784 Forbes was a dinner guest at the Sheridans.[245] In 1786 Hardy and Forbes were on friendly terms with Burke.[246] If his son can be believed, Grattan was feted at Carlton House when he visited London in 1788.[247] In fact throughout the crisis neither side appeared in any doubt that the patriots would fill the key posts in Dublin Castle under a British Whig lord lieutenant in the event of the king's death or permanent incapacitation.

Despite the fact that he was in England and apparently welcome at Carlton House, Grattan (perhaps due to the uncertain state of his wife's health) was a poor source of information in the early stages of the crisis: "the papers inform you better than I can", he wrote

118

candidly in early December.[248] In Ireland however, other patriots were busy formulating their attitude to the problems raised by the continuing existence of a king who could not rule. On the vexed matter of whether the Prince of Wales had any right to succeed to the throne while his father lived, Yelverton not unexpectedly took the British Whig view that there was "no difference between a political and a natural demise". However, Yelverton did recognise the dangers of seizing the initiative in the appointment of a regent, even though the Irish parliament had enough status under the terms of the 1782 settlement to reach a decision independently on its right to do so: "... if she [Ireland] may chuse for herself, she and Great Britain may chuse distinct Regents; and so that union between the two crowns, which it was the end and object of the Irish statute [33 Hen. VIII c.1[249]] to preserve and perpetuate, may be dissolved". Although he argued primarily in legalistic rather than in moral or political terms Yelverton was clearly of the opinion that action by the Irish legislature should wait upon and follow the decision then being reached at Westminster. In the matter of the Prince's right to succeed, however, he was prepared to recommend that assistance be given to the British Whigs in their struggle to establish that right. Yelverton suggested a measure not enacting that the Prince be Regent of Ireland, but rather acknowledging his title to that regency — a measure similar to the 1692 Act of Recognition; or, if this was felt inappropriate, an enacting statute "settling the regency on the same ground as the throne".[250]

Forbes had in fact gone to London to hear in person the debates on the Prince's succession rights. The other patriots were not unaffected by Fox's strange new role as champion of hereditary monarchical rights against a prime minister who (however dubious his motives) was upholding the right of parliament to decide the matter. "That he has first claim to the Regency ... I readily admit", wrote Hardy,[251]

but that he has such a *Right* as *must be* acknowledged by Parlt. that both Houses should address him to take the Regency as his *unquestionable* Right, a Right as *entirely precluding* all deliberation on the Subject as his Regular Succession to the Throne would; all this is utterly and entirely new to me, and I do not think it is that Species of Doctrine which the People will very readily acquiesce in.

Yelverton's views were those generally held by Charlemont also.[252] But Yelverton was ignored. The loss of Corry to the Castle (probably due to his straitened circumstances) in 1788 left Grattan the apparently undisputed leader of the patriot group. It may be hindsight but yet perfectly true to point out that he led them ultimately into unnecessary and avoidable defeat. The mass desertions from the Castle ranks which were occasioned by the crisis had provided a glorious opportunity for the patriots to carry through the programme of pension, place and police bills which they had developed during the preceding years. The nature of these bills was such that had they been passed while the tide was still with the patriots in February and March 1789, it would have been difficult to justify their repeal at any future time. But by the time the measures were brought forward the king was recovering and the Castle deserters returning to their old berths. Precedence had been given instead to settling the regency question (insofar as it related to Ireland) before the matter was resolved at Westminster.

The decision to adopt this order of proceeding may have originated in the patriots' understandable if ill-advised optimism that the king would not recover. If one judges by the content of the patriots' arguments in the Commons the chauvenistic determination to prove the extent of Irish parliamentary rights under the 1782 settlement lay at the root of the decision. If this is so then the nature of the patriots' overall motivation is in question.

The possibility that the patriots' ultimate aim was executive power and that their pension, place and police bills were designed with this end in mind has been referred to at an earlier point in this chapter. In view of their behaviour in 1789 and after, this possibility must remain. However, it is true also that the reduction of the pension list, the removal of members not amenable to their constituents' suggestions, and the elimination of corruption and irregularity in the police were all measures conducive to the improvement of the public well-being. Some years ago Dr Denis Kennedy, impressed by the content of the patriots' measures, suggested that their true goal was "responsible government".[253] But to portray the patriots as inspired champions of administrative purity would be as inaccurate as to describe them as machiavellian plotters would be unjust. The truth (insofar as the 1780s were concerned) may lie between the two extremes. Executive power and responsible government are not mutually exclusive concepts. In order to govern Ireland responsibly (or indeed in any other way) it was necessary to possess executive power. However, in the context of the Regency Crisis the patriots' use of their policy programme did have a sinister aspect.

No attempt was made to bring forward the patriots' original programme before 4 March.[254] The recovery of the king had been announced in London on 17 February.[255] In retrospect it does seem as if the patriots during their weeks of triumph had abandoned their long-avowed policies only to revive them again when the shadow of defeat had fallen upon them. The average Castle deserter amongst the opposition would not have had access to the same level of accurate and frequent information which almost certainly flowed throughout

120

the crisis from Carlton House to the patriot nucleus. Hence it can be argued that the patriots exploited the uncertainty — which still persisted in March — regarding the permanence of the king's recovery in order to forearm themselves with pension and place acts against their return to minority opposition in the days ahead.

There is one further possible explanation for the arrangement of affairs during the session. The feverish resurgence of the British Whigs' interest in Ireland during the crisis stemmed from their hope that the patriots' new majority might be used to advance the Whigs' cause at Westminster. Grattan and his supporters could not have been unaware that the coveted posts in the Castle would not come to them automatically but might be secured by co-operation with their future Whig masters. Thus it was that the patriots concentrated for much of the session on bringing the regency issue to the earliest possible solution on lines agreeable to Carlton House. That some hard-and-fast agreement had finally been arrived at between the patriots and the British Whigs is suggested not only by the frenzied to-ing and fro-ing of patriots to London before and even during the session,[256] and the conspiratorial letters,[257] but in particular by Arthur Browne's statement in the Commons on 26 February:[258]

He abhorred the introduction of English party into their house as much as any man. But it was not to be of an English party to coincide in sentiment with a certain body of men there upon certain imperial questions; not questions between the two countries, but questions common to both — the remedying defects in the executive power. Similarity of sentiment is not party. He must coincide with those men who had always the improper influence, and supported the just prerogative of the crown; who had not rested in empty words, but carried these sentiments into effect — witness the contractors bill — the revenue officers bill — the household reform bill — the bill for limitation of pensioners: whose determination did not melt in the heart of the closet, and who were willing, in support of these great principles, to risk both power and popularity with a deluded people.

Between the Regency Crisis and the revival of the Catholic question government and opposition remained in an extreme state of polarisation, a situation for which Buckingham's vindictive behaviour in the aftermath of the crisis was largely responsible. His account of the debate of 20 February which had followed the announcement of the king's recovery was accompanied ominously by a list of "placemen and pensioners (specifying emoluments) in both Houses of Parliament who had voted against the Irish Government".[259] Unlike Rutland who had withheld his wrath (and Pitt's) after the failure of the commercial settlement, Buckingham was sensitive to "the inconvenience, indeed the utter impossibility of suffering many of them to hold some of the most confidential and lucrative departments".[260] The rumour of mass dismissals took hold so quickly that the opposition seized upon the expedient of organised solidarity as a means of stemming the reverse flow of government deserters which had begun almost as soon as the news of the king's recovery arrived. But only thirty-six members of the Commons and twenty Lords put their names to the "Round Robin" signed the following day which threatened the government with systematic opposition if any member was made *"the victim of his vote"*.[261]

Nevertheless, the covenant bore the names of the "four great rats" — Shannon, Loftus, Ponsonby and Leinster — and Buckingham was aware that collectively they commanded 42 votes.[262] Despite his "mortification" he was reluctant to act too hastily lest he "revolt the feelings of Parliament, which, you will easily imagine, will be worked upon in order to raise a popular cry in favour of the martyrs". He was also reconciled to "leaving some culprits in their employments, particularly those who have hitherto returned, and those who first run from the association".[263]

The surviving evidence of opposition behaviour in the early stage of the Regency Crisis provides no clue as to why "the great rats" did not themselves assume leadership of the various opposition groups and individuals but were content merely to follow Grattan. Internal quarrels between the great interests as to which of them should be leader may have been one reason. But a more likely explanation is that, while willing to desert the Castle, they were unwilling to desert it past the point of return. In the event of the king's recovery it would be far easier to desert from the ranks of opposition than from a position of leadership. They may have counted on their personal and political prominence to ensure their unscathed return to the Castle. If this had indeed been their plan it proved a gross miscalculation. The list compiled by Grattan indicates that all the leading interests forfeited their offices along with an uneven number of their followers.[264] These dismissals, however, necessarily committed the government to the creation of a phalanx which would not include the great interests. The years that followed were as much a test of the Castle's capacity to survive without the great interests as of the opposition's ability to win with them.

The understandable anger of those who had had the gates of Eden slammed in their faces can be only a partial explanation of the ferocity of the struggle which was made by the opposition in 1790-91 for control of the Irish Commons. The removal of the great interests from the government benches had placed the balance of power even more firmly in the hands of the country gentlemen and expectant members. The Castle's strength was estimated by the opposition spokesmen at different points during the 1790 session as 144, of whom 104 (or 109) were placemen or pensioners.[265] It was for the "floating" forty votes that opposition exerted itself during both sessions. The divisions in 1790 indicated how fragile the government's credibility would have been in the event of a mass (or even partial) desertion by the forty independents.

Buckingham's creation of a new patronage system, and the expense entailed by its maintenance, provided the opposition with an opportunity to revive with even greater credibility their traditional condemnation of Castle extravagence. As has been suggested earlier, the patriots seemed to believe that independent members would be more responsive to the argument that a government held in power by purchased votes was unworthy of support.[266] The division figures for 1790 indicate that an uneven but undeniable impact had been made by the opposition's arguments. Their support rose from 80 at the beginning of February to 96 by the end of that month.[267] When in mid-February the opposition's support had apparently risen within the space of a week from 81 to 92, the chief secretary Robert Hobart felt obliged to explain:[268]

You will not be alarmed at the majority in favour of government being converted upon this, than on some former questions, when you recollect that this question [Castle extravagance] as a question upon pensions has been repeatedly agitated in various former administrations and that gentlemen had found themselves committed by the part which they had heretofore taken; nor need I observe to you that the question is in itself more popular than any other, and that upon the approach of a general election, such a question must have [a] peculiar effect upon the conduct of many of the members.

The sequence of events, however, showed little artfulness on the opposition's part, but rather a stolid determination to raise the level of their support by sheer force of oratory.

The violent abuse which the patriots and the Ponsonbys heaped upon Buckingham's administration at the start of the session was followed by Forbes's demand for full details of current offices, pensions and salaries.[269] Thereafter the opposition proceeded by way of attempted addresses of compliment to the king, a demand for a committee of enquiry into alleged sales of peerages by the government, attacks on the Castle's proposed renewal of the 1787 Magistracy Act, and with Forbes's usual pension and place bill.

The new element in the opposition's platform was Forbes's responsibility bill, "effectually to secure the responsibility of the servants of the crown in different departments of the executive government of Ireland, to the parliament thereof".[270] This measure represented the opposition's most effective means to counteract the Castle's view that place and pension bills were attacks on the crown's prerogative. The government's argument was based on the procedures

123

of the Irish treasury under which the lord lieutenant, as the king's personal representative, signed warrants by which money was issued. Under the provisions of Forbes's bill such warrants would have to be countersigned by the chancellor of the exchequer, the secretary of state, and several other officers, all of whom would be held personally accountable for the proper expenditure of the money concerned.[271] The effect of the measure, as Hobart pointed out, would have been to transfer the executive power of the crown to the officers designated in the bill.[272] In opposition to Dr Kennedy who has maintained that the achievement of "responsible government" was the sole aim of the opposition in advancing this measure, it is here suggested that the successful nullification of one of the government's most persistent and insurmountable parliamentary arguments was of equal if not greater importance to the bill's sponsors. It was postponed without a division on its second reading.[273]

Despite the fact that the Irish opposition was now popularly believed to have 103 members,[274] and that the Shannon, Leinster and Ponsonby connections (13, 22 and 9 members respectively[275]) were among them, it did not succeed in 1791 either. Their highest division figure of the session was 86, against which the government raised 147 votes.[276] The government's support wavered from 36 to 147 in the various divisions of the session, but the fortunes of the opposition seemed to waver proportionably.

It is clear that a number of those members popularly believed to be followers of the opposition did not invariably cast their votes accordingly. In an appendix to his thesis Dr Kennedy reproduced the names of 103 alleged "opposition" members of 1791. A further analysis of this list based on the assumption that the patriots and the large connections invariably supported all opposition motions indicates that the opposition "party" could count on no more than 53 votes, or almost one half of its reputed strength. To this number can be added a further 12 votes; these were persons who have been listed by Dr Kennedy as members of the Whig Club in 1791[277] but who were not patriots or members of the large connections. The "reliable" opposition strength in 1791 amounted therefore to no more than 65. The names of the 38 members for whose votes the committed opposition competed with the government are listed in Appendix 7 of this work. These were the men who held the balance of power in the Irish Commons in the year before the question of Catholic relief began the inexorable slide towards Union

In terms of policy the opposition approach to the 1791 session had little originality. Accusations that the Castle was trading peerages for votes were followed by the usual attack on the police establishment and by Forbes's forlorn pension, place and responsibility bills.[278] Corry, perhaps the Castle's most valuble acquisition for years, was

124

not named in the opposition's bitter assault on government corruption but was sensitive to the silent accusation of betrayal. "I always supported the pension bill", he began an extraordinary speech of self-justification, "the place bill I do not approve":[279]

The country has resolved itself into two parties, and every man must attach himself to one or the other, attaching himself to either he must accomodate himself to their measures; for my part having attached myself to a party, I think that in all measures, which do not affect the fundamental interest of the country, I ought to go with them; I think in so doing I might be justifiable in deviating from measures which I formerly espoused; but I trust such deviation is not sufficient to make a man an object of public censure; with regard to this measure when tacked to the pension bill, I voted for it, but never since, convinced of the honour and integrity of the Administration under which I hold my office.

The newer element in the opposition's platform in 1791 was tinged with a certain desperation in that it touched upon the sensitive area of Irish foreign policy, an issue fraught with danger to the inter-regnal connection. The debate having been opened by Grattan (who apparently retained his position as leader), it was Sheridan who pointed out that Ireland sent no ambassadors and was dependent on Britain to represent her in matters of foreign policy. The grievance, it was stressed, was not the fact itself but rather the manner in which the representation of Irish interests was being presented abroad. Sheridan implied that the independent status of Ireland was being ignored by its British ambassadors:[280]

England certainly should precede, but Ireland should not follow as a mere *umbra*; here rights should be substantially expressed, and not left to constructive security: But in this convention Ireland is not once named, except where the ambassador (the Right Hon. Allyne Fitzherbert) is called a Privy Counsellor of Ireland: — The people of Ireland are only described under the general expression *British Subjects*, which they are not; and how the court of Spain may construe that expression, is yet unknown;....

The reason for the tactic quickly became clear. The opposition felt that Ireland should be allowed trading with the East within the areas normally monopolised by the East India Company. It was never explicitly stated that the opposition would agree to drop the embarrassing issue of Irish ambassadors if concessions were made in the matter of Eastern trade, but the manner in which both topics were linked in two successive debates does suggest that the opposition was aiming at a *quid pro quo*.[281] George Ponsonby's assertion that the Eastern Trade issue was "the first great public transaction since your free trade and your emancipation" was followed by Grattan's claim that one clause of Yelverton's Act had been framed so "as to

125

keep Ireland beyond danger of misconstruction, perfectly free from the restraint of the charter" (of the East India Company).[282] Hobart's opinion that the opposition, in selecting a trade issue, "have chosen the worst ground" was borne out.[283] The government defeated motions for committees of enquiry by 137 to 78 and 147 to 86.[284]

For the record, the government's opposition to Eastern trading rights for Ireland was founded in reason. At one level it was feared that the docking and unloading of British ships from India in Irish harbours would lead to an increase in smuggling. But a more serious objection was that the College Green parliament was seeking on behalf of Irish merchants rights and privileges which, by the provisions of the East India Company's charter, were denied even to British merchants. Dundas seemed to regard the episode as an attempt by the Irish to readjust the balance created by the 1782 settlement in their favour as regards inter-regnal equality.[285]

The strain which unsuccessful opposition had placed on the alliance between patriots and Whigs in the early 1790s (In April Hobart thought Shannon "a very lukewarm patriot" and ripe for detachment from the alliance[286]) was increased by the Catholic relief legislation. When approached by the Catholic Committee in July 1791 Grattan was "loath to intervene directly" and advised the supplicants to apply to Hobart.[287] The differences of opinion, however, did not surround the 1792 measure, on which the Ponsonbys and patriots seemed to have reached agreement[288] but was related to whether or not the measure was to be the *ne plus ultra*.

The Ponsonbys and the Shannons remained silent when on 18 February Grattan, temporarily in league with the Castle, proposed that Catholics be allowed to take degrees and occupy university posts. The careful strategy was spoiled by Egan who insisted on presenting the petition from unspecified Catholics asking for "a participation in that franchise which will raise them to the rank of freemen", and by Hardy who openly expressed his disagreement with any such proposal. The collision was worsened by Sheridan who demurred at the relief bill's provision to admit Catholics to the Bar. The desperate efforts of Michael Smith, Egan, Grattan and Curran to repair the damage through a series of individual statements approving the bill were then scotched by the Ponsonbys who complained about the manner in which it had been introduced and gave it only grudging and reserved support.[289] Hobart believed that the debate[290]

consisted more in a display of each man's opinion, than in a regular system of support or opposition to the measure; as in both sides of the House several individuals, who concur in their conduct upon the public measures, yet upon this varied in desiring to restrain the objects of the bill, and others to extend them.

The return match was prompted two days later by those members, the Ponsonbys among them, who were unwilling to be associated too unreservedly with the measure. David La Touche's motion that the petition of 18 February be rejected as "it would affect our establishments in church and state" was carried by 208 to 23. Brownlow, Stewart and Hardy were among the patriots who divided with the Ponsonbys and the government. The temporising efforts were made by Arthur Browne who wanted the bill postponed till the next session and by Curran who was in favour of postponing any firm decision on the request contained in the petition.[291]

It was something of a tribute to the flexibility of the Whig Club that between, before and after the debates on the relief bill, the groups allied in opposition firmly closed ranks. Patriots and Ponsonbys supported each other unreservedly on the other issues of the session. George Ponsonby took the lead in suggesting that a fortuitous surplus of revenue over expenditure be devoted to public works,[292] and again in the revival of the demand for trading rights with the East. On the latter issue the government won by 156 to 70, but feared that the sensitive issue would not be dropped and that the opposition "will depart from demand and resort to the principle of negotiation", as they had attempted to do during the previous session.[293] Arthur Browne's complaint that the appointment of a weigh-maker in Cork was a clear example of the undue increase of government influence was not likewise supported by patriots and Ponsonbys.[294] The session did not close without Grattan's usual attack on the inefficiency of the police.[295] The only sign that morale had been slightly lowered was the failure of Forbes's place, pension and responsibility bills to appear on 9 March as scheduled.[296]

On 10 November 1792 Pitt informed Westmorland that the Irish ascendancy need not expect his support if it was their intention to protect their position through the obstruction of "peaceable and constitutional applications from Catholics".[297] A month later he was officially informed of the growing determination of the cabinet that the goodwill of Irish Catholics be retained, even if it meant conceding a degree of franchise.[298] Doubtless the cabinet was relieved to learn from Westmorland that the opposition would probably split on the issue of Catholic franchise in such a way as to leave some of the great interests isolated. Shannon, Conolly and Ponsonby would resist the franchise "if they could see the practicability of success". Leinster and Grattan had "decided for the Catholics and also for a Reform in Parliament". Despite the "disapproval" of Foster and FitzGibbon, Westmorland (at this stage) felt that the measure could be carried.[299]

It is likely that the prospect of achieving a further measure of Catholic relief would by itself have been enough to induce Grattan to part company with both patriots and great interests. But to forestall

127

the consequences of any possible compromise the cabinet, via Lord Loughborough, held out to Grattan personally an offer to concede certain of the patriots' desired measures in exchange for their co-operation in the passing of the relief bill. In the extraordinary care taken by the cabinet in making this offer they seemed blind to the fact that Grattan's personal following in the Commons without the great interests was negligible, and had been so demonstrated as recently as the previous session when he had found himself in a minority of 23.[300] The possibility cannot be ignored that the offer was made with a view to driving a permanent wedge between members of the Whig Club.

Loughborough's letters on the transaction were vague but he seemed to hint at some far-reaching political settlement, or as Henry Grattan the younger was to term it, *"an incipient union"*. However, whether due to Grattan's obvious willingness to agree to any such proposal, or the persistent uncertainty of Pitt in the matter, the actual terms of the agreement reached by both sides in February 1793 were probably much more modest. The key words of Loughborough's letter were not, as Grattan the younger was to suggest, "the permanent connected establishment of Ireland, both internally, and relatively to England", but rather:[301]

We have marked with attention, and without jealousy, the progress of your improvement; we must be weak and short-sighted, indeed, not to observe that the Administration must be adapted to the change of situation, and must be founded on the firm basis of public confidence and esteem; that to be respectable, it must be responsible, and cannot subsist by favour and protection from any external support.

It has not appeared to me that any of the ideas which have gained the favour of respectable men in your country, are bad in their outline; but they will require great care, and much temper, in filling up that outline.

In any case Grattan entered the parliamentary fray in 1793 prepared to co-operate with the Castle in regard to the relief bill on the understanding that certain concessions would be made on patriot measures. Again, outside the area of Catholic relief, the fellowship of the Whig Club held firm during the session of '93. On matters such as the libel action taken by the government against the printer of the *Hibernian Journal*, the proposed augmentation of the army, parliamentary reform and the postponement of the militia bill, the various sections of the Whig Club supported each other.[302]

The only potentially serious internal collision was W.B. Ponsonby's attempt on 14 January to wrest the leadership of the opposition away from Grattan. Conolly was the first to support Ponsonby on this occasion and perhaps spoke for both of them when he hinted that he might be prepared to agree to the intended Catholic relief bill

128

if Ponsonby's demand for parliamentary reform was conceded. Grattan avowed his own intention to introduce such a reform measure, asserted his willingness to be led in the matter by Ponsonby ("it is my humble office to follow on this subject, and to applaud"),[303] but then tried to divert the House's attention by proposing a committee on enquiry on government corruption. Corry (for government), in a gesture designed to appease the opposition and yet protect the Castle from a Grattan-inspired committee, suggested instead the appointment of a committee "to enquire into the state of the representation". Corry was in fact using an old trick learned while in opposition; the House could not be reformed until it was clear where the need for reform lay, and Ponsonby would appear unreasonable were he to reject a proposed committee of enquiry. Grattan, with an incredibly skilful movement, then confirmed the quashing of Ponsonby and re-asserted his own position as leader:[304]

all must be reform: but if the House wish to confine themselves to a part of my motion for the present, that is, the state of the representation: I will rejoice that they pledge themselves so far, and shall not hesitate to adopt the amendment, and thank the member who suggested it.

Grattan confirmed the position on 5 February when, unsupported but also challenged by Ponsonby, he proposed an address to the king asking for a none-too-clearly specified measure of parliamentary reform. Having made his point he just as effortlessly dropped the proposal upon a member's appeal for more time to consider it.[305]

On the day the Catholic relief bill passed its final reading in the Commons (7 March) it became clear that the patriot measures which the cabinet had offered in February to concede were Forbes's cherished place, pension and perhaps also the responsibility bills. When Forbes followed the final reading of the Catholic bill with a proposal that his place bill be committed, th government tried to have it postponed "for a distant day". Grattan suggested that the Castle was not meeting its commitments: "we have made great grants, and have a right to expect an equivalent return". Ponsonby's support for Forbes's bill was likewise laced with accusations of government treachery. Despite the firm support of the Castle members Hobart was sufficiently sensitive to these accusations to eventually allow the committal of Forbes's bill for mid-April. He was at pains to stress that it was not a "government" measure but that "as it seemed a measure necessary for the security of the country, it had the most cordial support of Government".[306]

The "distant day" was sought by Hobart not with a view to renaging on the February agreement but rather to give the Castle servants enough time to develop enough administrative machinery to enable them to control the consequences of the new measures. It is not clear whether the bill for parliamentary reform espoused by Ponsonby and Conolly in March, and Grattan's bills to abolish the police and disfranchise revenue officers had formed part of the February agreement, but it seems unlikely.[307] With regard to Forbes's place and pension bills, Westmorland assured Pitt "that the less efficacious or instructive either are made, the more satisfactory to the generality of people here, who are not disposed that the king's power should be laid at the mercy of an aristocracy or of Mr. Grattan at the head of the mob". The responsibility bill was "too ridiculous to pass". The interesting element of this letter was its clear indication that the Castle servants were developing the administrative machinery referred to above without detailed consultation with the lord lieutenant. Westmorland "never could understand why the king's servants should model a reasonable responsibility for the opposition". It is likely that this activity on the part of the Castle servants was connected not with "half-patriotism", as Westmorland thought, but with the growing realisation that the cabinet in London was unwilling, and the lord lieutenant unable, to protect their monopoly of executive power.[308]

"Self-protection" for the Castle took the form of an Irish Treasury Board for the more effective supervision of government expenditure.[309] The foundations on which the new board was to be built were laid before the Commons on 10 June and provided a justification for the abandonment of Forbes's place bill, and later for the postponement of the pension bill (brought forward in fact by W.B. Ponsonby).[310] Neither the debates nor the Castle's "situation reports" on its level of support give any indication that one or other of the great interests had returned to the government benches in the latter half of the 1793 session (although the Shannons had abandoned opposition by 1794[311]). But the opposition's performance in divisions was definitely in decline. Forbes lost the attempt to retain his place bill by 110 to 41. Grattan's police bill was rejected by 86 to 30, and his opposition to the convention bill was rendered worthless by 128 to 27.[312]

Opposition behaviour during the 1794 was relatively unremarkable. Unity was disturbed only by the strange desertion of Henry Duquery, Curran, Egan and Browne to support Parson's proposal that treaties between Britain and foreign powers be laid before the House "on the ground of the right of the Irish parliament to investigate the motives and conduct of the war". Grattan and George Ponsonby were among those who helped government to defeat the motion by 128 to 9.[313] The Whig Club appeared to be united on Grattan's proposed equalisation of import tariffs between the two kingdoms, and on Ponsonby's parliamentary reform measure. Grattan's somewhat nervous refusal to divide the House over the import duties seemed

130

justified when, a fortnight later, Ponsonby's reform bill was rejected by 142 to 44.[314]

The personal and political conflicts which split the British Whigs over the formation of the coalition with Pitt in 1793-94 had no obvious counterparts in Ireland. The leadership tussle between Ponsonby and Grattan had not been serious enough to shatter the Whig Club, and the opposition seemed (publicly at least) not particularly concerned with the rightness or wrongness of the war. Thus, when the split occurred in London, the Irish opposition moved with apparent effortlessness into the Portland camp and onto the gravy train which by August 1794 they knew to be imminent.[315] Only Conolly was later to disown his former allies because of the coalition with Pitt (and this disclaimer came suspiciously late in the day).[316]

The disappearance of the Whig Clubmen from the opposition benches in January 1795 with the appointment of the Whig Earl Fitzwilliam to succeed Westmorland left a vacuum which long-term rivals such as Parsons, and those who may have lost out in the rush for places, such as Duquery,[317] were quick to fill. There is no evidence that Parsons and Duquery acted in concert initially, but their separately-expressed grievances were identical. Grattan and his colleagues proved as reluctant to advance time-honoured patriot policies in 1795 as they had been during the Regency Crisis. Parsons demanded to know what had become of the proposed abolition of sinecures, exclusion of placemen, parliamentary reform, equalisation of commercial advantage and other patriot ideals.[318] Oblivious to the incongruity, Grattan and Ponsonby responded with examples of how effectively Westmorland's treasury board was reducing the pension and place lists.[319] When Duquery suggested that a projected tax on leather would be oppressive to the poor and that the government pensioners should be taxed instead, he was bluntly told (by Grattan) that the pension list was now largely composed of "persons who are objects of compassion" and "persons who already pay a tax of 4s[hillings] in the pound as absentees".[320] But the brevity of Fitzwilliam's sojourn in Ireland renders it difficult to arrive at any positive conclusion as to patriot/Whig intentions.[321] As in 1782 (and perhaps with less reason) Grattan refused to accept office.[322] He continued to press for the repeal of the police act and Forbes seemed bent on further reform of the Castle's accountability through the medium of the treasury board.[323] These measures had been brought forward before 26 February 1795, the day on which rumours of Fitzwilliam's dismissal began to circulate.[324] Despite the fact that the truth behind the rumour had become obvious by 2 March, and had caused the desertion of Michael Smith and Arthur Browne, Parsons could still conjure up only 24 votes on that day against the Castle's 146 on his proposal for a short money bill.[325]

As during the Regency Crisis, patriot measures to disfranchise revenue officers and to directly increase the accountability of the Castle for its expenditure came only with the shadow of defeat.[326] When on 21 April Grattan finally decided to take stock of the position he found that not only had his older friends regrouped behind him in the face of Pitt's alleged "betrayal" but that the division figures had returned to their 1794 position. In his proposal for a committee on "the state of the nation" he was supported by the Ponsonbys, Curran, Browne, Egan and Hardy, and was defeated by 158 to 48.[327] A week later Grattan conceded defeat and allowed the Castle to take over the reform of the police.[328]

The general air of disturbance brought about by the Fitzwilliam affair did, however, bring some small victories to the Whig Club. Fitzwilliam's successor, Lord Camden, evidently tried to avoid alienating too many members by shattering too abruptly the Fitzwilliam arrangements. The government *did* agree to reform the police and part of Forbes's plan to further regulate the treasury board *was* adopted.[329] Castle administrators displaced by Fitzwilliam were reinstated, but not without reservations. Camden felt the reinstatement of Cooke to be "an act of justice to which he had a claim but that circumstance unless his abilities were eminently useful to Government would not alone have determined me to adopt this measure".[330] At the end of April Grattan's demand for the equalisation of import duties was supported strongly by the Ponsonbys.[331]

The Whig Club as an institution survived 1795[332] but by the opening of the 1796 session its parliamentary support had sunk to 14, as the government mustered 122 votes against Grattan's attempt to revive the equalisation of duties.[333] A month later Grattan was reported to be "not well, and not in the House. Neither of the W. Ponsonbys were there either".[334] Conolly, although still in opposition, had also ceased to attend.[335] The absence of detailed accounts of parliamentary proceedings for most of this period obscures the ebb and flow of the patriot/Whig connection, but this was the point at which Henry Grattan the younger stated that "Opposition ... had vanished with Lord Fitzwilliam, and never again rallied".[336] Curran's motion in January 1796 for an enquiry into "the state of the peasantry and the prices of labour" was quashed by 127 to 16.[337]

The picture painted by Grattan's son of the opposition's futile attempts to act as a brake upon a government bent on coercion may have been over-simplified. But the fact that Grattan's pro-Catholic motions of October 1796 were supported by the Ponsonbys does suggest that the latters' views on Catholics had altered.[338] Patriots and Ponsonbys struggled in vain against the government's proposed suspension of the Habeas Corpus Act, attracting only 7 votes against the Castle's 137.[339] The fear of a popular uprising was clearly having a marked effect upon many former critics of the government. On 17 October a number of those who normally supported pro-Catholic measures helped to defeat Grattan by 143 to 19 on the pretext that his motion[340] had been brought forward "rather to distress Govt. than to alliviate the Catholics".[341] By March 1797 the "great fear" had found its way to Egan who abandoned his old comrades on the issue of General Lake's celebrated proclamation and cited them as "the Seven Wise Men who opposed every measure which tended to save the country".[342]

In such a situation effective parliamentary opposition was no longer possible. The active alliance with the Foxite Whigs, renewed evidently on the Irish opposition's initiative, attracted support at the highest level of the Foxite connection,[343] but drowning men cannot save each other. Two months after Egan's desertion Grattan, the Ponsonbys, and their few remaining followers, "finding their labours useless", withdrew from the Commons.[344]

The shift in the balance of power between the British and Irish legislatures included, as we saw in Chapter 2, one reservation in Britain's favour; the power of the British privy council to halt Irish bills was preserved. However, in view of the fact (which emerged in the course of the present chapter) that the fulcrum of the balance of power rested in the hands of a varying number of independent and "expectant" members, it seems worthwhile to examine the extent to which the British privy council used its advantage.

The British privy council papers which survive for the period 1782 to 1800 indicate an apparently intense reluctance to halt Irish bills. In fact only four Irish bills were interfered with by the British privy council. In 1785 a bill "for granting bounties on gunpowder the manufacture of this kingdom Ireland exported", and a bill "for preventing doubts concerning the parliament, Privy Council and officers civil and military on the demise of the Crown, and for confirming letters patent in certain cases" were both "thought proper to respite".[345] No reason was given, but the date (1785) suggests that it may have been a manifestation of Pitt's anger at the failure of the propositions. The failure of the bills to return was not remarked upon by the opposition.

In 1788 a bill "for more effectually preventing deceits and frauds in the manufacturing of cordage for shipping and to prevent the illicit importation of foreign-made cordage" was "thought to be in many respects so objectionable" that its return to Ireland was postponed. The "objectionable" aspects in fact arose from poor research by the draftsmen, the effect of which was that "the Irish trade to our Colonies will be more beneficial ... than it can be exercised by his Majesty's British subjects".[346] Despite the obvious potential flashpoint

133

contained in this postponement the Irish opposition apparently did not respond, and the following year the British privy council agreed to the return of the bill.[347] It is worth noting, however, that while the failure of the bills to return was not remarked upon by the opposition at the time, the incidents had not gone completely unnoticed. In a 1797 pamphlet Grattan included the respited gunpowder bill in a list of "popular" grievances.[348]

It will have been noticed that the non-return of the sheep-stealing bill of 1788, considered by E.M. Johnston to be an example of how the British privy council continued the practice of retaining Irish bills after 1782,[349] has not been referred to. Professor Johnston used as her source for this matter a private letter edited and published by the Historical Manuscripts Commission. In the edited version the sentence — "It is good to keep up the practice of rejecting in the English Privy Council, and this Bill is an extraordinary instance of every absurdity and illegality in the enacting clauses" — is included.[350] A comparison of this version with the original of an official letter on the same bill among the Home Office papers revealed similar sentiments but also the following crucial sentence:[351]

no power is given to the magistrates to convict for the offence, which the Bill professes to punish, and that the words "being convicted of the same" refer in fact to the sentence which immediately precedes it, and by this means the Bill is a strange medley of unconstitutional and ungrammatical inaccuracy.

Whatever Buckingham's personal views on the power of the British privy council may have been, the sheep-stealing bill was in fact halted purely on grounds of technicality.

The Government (2): The Regency Crisis in Ireland, 1788-9

Although the first news of the king's illness had reached the Irish public by 25 October 1788, bad weather conditions prevented Buckingham and Fitzherbert from receiving official or private word until early November.[1] At this point, Buckingham, like Pitt, did not foresee the crisis soon to develop, though his naturally pessimistic nature focussed immediately on the possible consequences of the king's death.[2] By the end of the first week of November the situation had altered dramatically. Pitt's inconclusive meeting with the Prince of Wales on 8 November was followed, in the light of the king's failure to improve significantly, by the cabinet decision to invest the Prince temporarily with royal powers.[3]

The possible consequences in Ireland of the expected death of the king are not reflected in the relatively sparse evidence relating to the early part of the crisis, partly no doubt because they were obvious. The immediate dismissal of the existing governments in Ireland as well as in England is anticipated in Grenville's assurance to Buckingham that he would "enter into no engagements with a view to any new government" without "knowing your sentiments".[4] The remoteness of the Irish repercussions was probably increased by the other obvious fact that if matters indeed came to the worst, Ireland would no longer be Pitt's problem. Buckingham, his burden eased by the concurrent prorogation of the Irish parliament and by the absence from Ireland of individual Patriots, prepared to "meet the question of a demise, which operates very differently in the two kingdoms. In this, *all* commissions except those for life, and mine under the Great Seal of England, are *void*".[5]

In fact Buckingham's first reaction to the possibility of a regency was a curious mixture of incomprehension and wishful thinking. Clearly, regency would be but a short interlude preceding the death of the king and would not affect Ireland:

In this kingdom no immediate difficulty can occur, for we are prorogued to the 20th January; and if we were not, I am competent to every act of kingly power which may be necessary to keep the executive department perfect, till our Parliament should interfere; but in what manner *that* is ultimately to be done must be very doubtful, until we see your proceedings.

But this hint that the Irish parliament would adopt the form of regency agreed upon at Westminster was overshadowed by Buckingham's obvious relief that the king's death would forestall any such event. The lord lieutenant discussed the possible forms of regency in total detachment from its Irish context and continued to worry about the details of the procedures to be adopted in Ireland in the event of the king's death.[6] The legal basis of Buckingham's belief that a regency would bring no Irish problems in its wake evidently lay in Poyning's Law "which pledges Ireland to acknowledge as her sovereign the Prince who shall be the King *de facto* in England".[7]

That Buckingham held such ideas is less surprising in view of the fact that his brother in London also believed the king to be dying and that an English regency bill "should be passed *verbatim* in the Irish Parliament. Some opinions here seem to doubt the necessity of this; there has, however, been very little discussion upon it".[8] Buckingham felt that "I must be guided by your ideas, for here I can consult no one".[9] But it was Buckingham who first recognised the dangers inherent in such a proceeding and who wondered "how it would be possible to convince Mr. Grattan that this is not a resumption of internal legislation". He had already warned Grenville against the execution of any act involving Ireland by the proposed regent, even the revocation of the lord lieutenant's commission, before obtaining the Irish parliament's recognition of the regent.[10]

As November ended without a solution Buckingham's fears turned to positive alarm. To be turned out of office by the successor of a king whom he had served loyally and well would be an Act of God and entail no dishonour. But to extend the prorogation of the Irish parliament for no other purpose than to keep Pitt in office in the faint hope of the king's recovery would expose the Irish economy to ruin and Buckingham to censure in both kingdoms. Although he had the power to prorogue parliament to 1 February or later if necessary, Buckingham knew that any further delay would jeopardise the passage of the necessary money and mutiny bills by 25 March. He could not have been unaware also that the loss of hope consequent upon the king's continuing illness would in the event of further delay cause desertions from the government ranks in parliament. The government ranks had shown signs of strain in the face of a rumour that Ireland might be included without its parliament's permission or agreement in a British regency settlement.[11]

In addition Buckingham feared that the legal difficulty surrounding his recall would oblige him to do the bidding of a regency cabinet composed of men whom he had no desire to serve, or alternatively to attempt to guide essential measures through a hostile parliament. His anxieties were mirrored by those of Fitzherbert who was directly responsible for assembling the government's majority:[12]

he expresses the strongest doubt and unwillingness to meet our Parliament unless it is clear that we are to remain, as he is very jealous that the Ponsonby connexions will endeavour to make any meetings very unpleasant to us. This, you will observe, proceeds on his belief, which he now strongly entertains, that Mr. Pitt will be out of office as soon as the Prince can compass his arrangements; and he fears that we may be left in the very unpleasant situation of appearing to add to the confusion and difficulty by abandoning the government, or, of remaining here after our friends are out of employment in England.

Fitzherbert would have been acutely aware that his power to form a solid parliamentary phalanx was limited, since in the prevailing situation peers could not be created nor army officers commissioned.[13]

Grenville could not accept as serious the possibility that the Irish parliament might refuse to accede to the British regency settlement. He argued simply that the consequences attendant upon such a refusal would be sufficient to prevent its occurrence: "... no measure taken in parliament here can possibly affect Ireland any otherwise than as a precedent, which every Irishman must think himself bound to follow, who does not wish to separate the two countries".[14] But he understood the legal difficulty relating to the vacating of Buckingham's commission and he felt that no alternative was left to the lord lieutenant but to meet parliament and obtain its recognition of the regent. At this point Grenville expected the regent to be appointed in England by mid-January:[15]

I think your line clear and that you have nothing to do but to sit still saying or doing nothing till our measure passes. You then ask the Prince of Wales whether he chooses that you or any Lords Justices should meet parliament; and if he directs you to stay, you have nothing to do but to express to anybody that asks you, your wish that the English measure should be precisely followed. Whatever, under the circumstances, is the conduct of the Irish parliament, you cannot be responsible for it unless you make yourself so.

Although Buckingham seems to have agreed with this latter statement he still preferred not to meet parliament unless it was made a matter of duty.[16] Less than a month after he had received "every assurance" of Irish willingness to accept whatever regency would be adopted in England, his parliamentary prospects bristled with uncertainties:[17]

very respectable person with whom I converse confirms me in the assurance that the question is only understood in this kingdom as a personal struggle between Mr. Pitt and Mr. Fox, and that the generality of the House of Commons will only look to the profit which they make upon the decision.

The correspondence between Buckingham and Grenville during November and December was not related to the question of whether the proposed regent should have powers to dismiss the current ministry. It was partly concerned with the familiar issue of ensuring that Ireland was not included inadvertently in the formulatin of a British act of parliament. The king's illness affected the Irish administration through the suppression of the higher patronage arrangements through which the Castle exercised control of its members in the Irish parliament.

This failure to control parliament would amount to a constitutional crisis only if the Irish refused to adopt the British regency settlement. It was not this which Buckingham feared but rather a defeat on some unspecified issue should it prove necessary to meet parliament with the British arrangements unresolved. But there was no obvious reason why the Irish parliament should refuse to accept the British regency provided its introduction was not accompanied by any overtones that such acceptance was obligatory. Buckingham's vanity was such that he tended to confuse personal and constitutional crises.

But the policy of procrastination pursued by the ministry after 10 December and the tandem policy of a restricted regency involved Buckingham in a double-crisis.[18] The failure to settle the matter in England would leave him short of means to ensure a majority, and the uncertainty created by the state of the king's health would probably operate against him in parliament. In addition his obligation to pursue a policy of restrictions would bring the regency crisis into the Irish parliament in a manner which would lead to conflict with those who would copy the Foxite position. It would also alienate others who would view the government's policy as an attempt to impose a British-born settlement upon the parliament.

"In no case could I, or could any man, be mad enough to meet our mischievous parliament, before our government is finally settled", he wrote shortly before Christmas. He was now prepared to extend the prorogation to 10 February if necessary.[19] But Buckingham was unable to obtain the cabinet's agreement for this move. Pitt was determined that the policy pursued by his minister in Ireland should be not seen to deviate from that advanced by the government in London:

We [that is Pitt and his friends] hold and have persuaded parliament to declare that, in such a case as the present, the right of providing for the emergency rests in the two Houses, not as branches of the legislature, but as a full and free representative of all the orders and classes of the people of Great Britain. Now the moment we admit this, we do it on the ground of this being a case unprovided for. If it is so in England, it is unquestionably equally unprovided for in Ireland; and the right of making such provision must of necessity rest in the same manner in the Lordsd and Commons of England.

138

In Ireland parallel procedures should be adopted wherever possible: "the two Houses should themselves decide, and not any individual for them, whether it is expedient or not to proceed to any business". In short, the lord lieutenant should not exercise his powers as the king's representative while the king himself was incapcited. This policy emerged not from legality but from expediency. Pitt was clearly anxious that the behaviour of Buckingham should not compromise him at Westminster. The obvious legality of Buckingham's powers of prorogation was ignored, as was the liklihood that his meeting parliament under prevailing conditions would lead to worse embarrassments. He was advised that the best course to pursue was to meet parliament, lay before it the examinations of the king's physicians as conducted before the British privy council, and to procure an adjournment "on the ground of its not being known . . . what form will be adopted here". In short, Buckingham was being thrown back on his abilities as a manager of politicians, the situation which above all he wished to avoid.

The cabinet seemed oblivious to the possibility that the Irish parliament might refuse to accept the medical reports of a foreign legislature, or that it might regard the proposed grounds of adjournment as notice of an attempt to impose upon Ireland a foreign regency settlement. Grenville's belief that adjournment "must extremely fall in with the wishes of the party who are looking to the government immediately after the passing of the English Bill" was untroubled by the possibility that the Irish members might view the proposal as an effort to silence them.[20]

Buckingham was in fact receiving early signals that his managerial abilities might be insufficient. Charlemont, not unexpectedly, was "a convert to the right divine". Conolly, despite his continuing cordiality with the lord lieutenant,[21] "pauses" and "wavers"; Buckingham was convinced that "he will ultimately vote against us". Even the "steadiness" of the ten "independents" who jointly "agreed to support Pitt's claim of parliamentary right against the hereditary claim" was to be doubted.[22] The normally loyal Lord Earlsfort chose this moment to take advantage of his partial leadership of the Irish Lords to obtain a higher-salaried office. Buckingham, faced with the possible defection of half of the Irish peers, swallowed "a most bitter pill" and gave in to the demand.[23]

From Lord Mornington and from Grenville himself came disturbing tales of Irish opposition members' intrigues in London.[24] Charles Sheridan, employed by government since his defection from opposition politics in the early 1780s, felt sufficiently confident of his future to personally inform Buckingham that the latter's days were numbered once the new cabinet was installed.[25]

But aside from these doubts other circumstances coalesced to make prorogation a necessity. The untimely death of the Speaker of the British Commons had caused delays which made it even more difficult for Buckingham to construct a coherent and up-to-date assessment of either the king's health or of the progress of the regency matter. His efforts to accurately assess his parliamentary support were hampered by heavy snowfalls which had marooned a number of Irish members in their country estates. The opening of the session was postponed until 5 February 1789.[26]

At this point communications, while not actually breaking down, were directed into slightly unorthodox channels. While Buckingham officially requested the Secretary of State to endorse his intended prorogation to 5 February, Fitzherbert simultaneously suggested to the Under-Secretary, Evan Nepean, that it might be necessary to prorogue further, perhaps to 12 February.[27] In the event the cabinet, acting explicitly on Fitzherbert's suggestion, permitted Buckingham to prorogue to 12 February.[28] This was done apparently in the belief that the extra week would improve the Castle's prospects of victory. It was for the latter reason, as well as due to the probable insufficiency of time available for the passing of routine measures, that Buckingham refused the offer.[29] For by the close of January the nadir of government support had been reached. Leinster, Shannon and Ponsonby had all avowed their intentions to vote against government in any division relating to an address to the Prince.[30]

When Buckingham finally opened the session on 5 February his only tactic was one of delay. His opening speech was "purposely guarded to give them no information, but to compel them to seek for it . . .".[31] But the manoeuvre was too transparent to be effective. The clause of the proposed address of thanks which expressed the House's agreement to accept the evidence (as it had been laid before the British parliament) was assailed as an attack upon the 1782 settlement. Grattan claimed that "the pretence of such a form being necessary was designed to cut out the free agency of the Irish Parliament; it was meant as the ground for wanton delay . . ." But it was clear that this argument, if proceeded with, would end with the dispatching of Irish doctors to Kew and the success of the Castle's delaying tactic. Therefore Grattan avoided the trap by agreeing to accept the evidence on the understanding that "it was not with an eye of servile acquiescence". In practice, it was stated, this meant that the opposition would demonstrate the independence of the Irish parliament by striking an attitude on the regency issue before a solution was determined upon at Westminster.[32]

Buckingham later asserted that the division of 6 February over the date of the proposed enquiry into the physicians' evidence had been deliberately induced by the Castle in order to learn its true standing in the House. However, this division, in which the government was defeated by 128 to 74, was more probably brought about by Fitzherbert's clumsy wording of the motion. The government's proposed date (16 February) had been fixed "on the ground that no system of Regency could in all probability be settled by Great Britain before that time".[33] The opposition's date (11 February) was then carried without a division.[34] Buckingham thereafter avoided all divisions until 20 February — three days after the king's recovery had been announced in London.[35]

The opposition seemed fearful of a Castle attempt to create delay during the passage of the supply bills. The Chancellor's anguished protests that it would take 28 days to process the bills was brushed aside (it was claimed that the supply bills had been passed in three days during an emergency in 1775) and the measures were postponed until after the enquiry into the king's health.[36] Nor was any opportunity given to the government to procrastinate during the enquiry. The enquiry was effectively cancelled because as soon as the clerk began to read the evidence "the House soon became very inattentive and disorderly".[37] The government did not venture to oppose Grattan's motion (based apparently on little other than common knowledge) that the king was incapacitated.[38] To some extent the regency proceedings in the Irish parliament mirrored those at Westminster. Fitzherbert's proposal that the House proceed to appoint the Prince of Wales Regent by act of parliament may have been recognised as an attempt (should the bill have succeeded) to influence the course of events in London:[39]

... nothing could be more completely operative on the mind of a statesman in England bringing forward a plan to carry the regency into effect, than the apprehension that Ireland might not adopt his plan ... from particular motives in the British parliament, unless it appeared to be above all factious or party designs whatever. If it did not approve of the plan, a disagreement between the countries might indeed take place, and perhaps the prospect of such a disunion, would make that ambition halt in its progress, ...

The Patriots' arguments, however, tended rather to parallel those of their British Whig friends. It was asserted that, since the king was monarch of both countries, the parliament of Ireland could not legislate in the absence of the third estate any more than could the parliament of England. "We propose", declared Grattan, to make an efficient third estate in order to legislate, not to legislate in order to create the third estate". The act of creation was to take the form of an address to the Prince asking him to assume the title of Regent of Ireland. But even Grattan was aware that the legality of his proposed address was a trifle dubious, for "though the address shall, on this occasion, have all the force and operation of law, yet still that force and operation arise from the necessity of the case, and are

141

confined to it". The dubiousness of the legality was further diluted by modelling the address on the address of the Convention Parliament to the Prince and Princeness of Orange. The difference in circumstances was held to be of little real consequence:

the principle of your interference is established by the Revolution, the operation of that principle limited by the contingency, the power of the Houses of Parliament in the one case extended to remedy a defect in the personal capacity, but in both cases it is the powers of the Houses of Parliament called upon to interfere by their own authority when the ordinary course of law has made no provision, and where the three estates cannot supply the defect.

The executive was not considered to have a role in this proceeding and was explicitly attacked, as in 1782, as an unconstitutional body: "The Lords and Commons of Ireland, and not the Castle, should take the leading part in this great duty. The country gentlemen who procured the constitution, should nominate the regent".[40] The address, moved by Conolly, represented the British Whig position that the regency should be unrestricted. The Prince was to be allowed "to exercise and administer, according to the laws and constitution of this kingdom, all royal powers, jurisdiction and prerogatives to the Crown and government thereof belonging".[41]

Government counter-arguments were grounded on an appeal to opposition and independents not to bring about a separation of the two kingdoms by allocating powers to the regent perhaps different to those to be granted to him in England,[42] and upon subtle legalism. The legal argument arose from a loophole in Yelverton's Act. Under the wording of this Act bills from Ireland had to be certified into *England* and returned under the English great seal. If the prince was appointed Regent of Ireland before being appointed Regent of Great Britain he would have no access to the great seal of England and therefore would still be unable to take part in the legislative procedures of Ireland.[43] Against this Curran argued that "the crown of Ireland was annexed to, not merged in the crown of England" and that therefore[44]

no law could be law here by virtue of the seal of England, but by virtue only of the royal assent, by a real third estate, given in full parliament; and that the king of England, as such, affixed the seal of England, but that he gave the royal assent as king of Ireland.

The government's view did not fundamentally conflict with Curran's statement and was grounded largely on a detail of procedure, but it was difficult to refute. The opposition retreated to the "probability" that the Prince would have become Regent of Great Britain by the

142

time he would be called upon to take part in the Irish legislative process.[45]

Grattan was ungently reminded that he had been one of the architects of Yelverton's Act:[46]

If the right honourable gentleman's act had run thus: That no bill should pass unless it was returned under the great seal of England, and that a commission should pass under the great seal of Ireland for giving the royal assent, then the law would have been what he now stated it ought to be; but if there is a defect in the law, on his head be it. He might have had the great seal of England as a proof that the bill had passed under the consideration of his majesty in council, and he might have had the great seal of Ireland as an authority for passing the bill into a law.

The following day (12 February) the address was carried without a division and sent to the Lords.[47]

Buckingham's despatches on these debates differ in the intensity of their tone from those sent by Fitzherbert. While not concealing any relevant facts the lord lieutenant seemed to emphasise the more personal aspects of Grattan's attacks on him and gave little credit to the clear superiority of the opposition's oratory.[48] Buckingham need not have worried that his performance would be criticised in London where the domestic political crisis had banished Ireland from serious consideration:[49]

I find that people here, those at least with whom I converse, are indifferent about the success of the measure in Ireland, but are much exasperated at the madness and folly of the people who are endeavouring to stir fresh questions of separation between the two countries.

Pitt wrote twice to assure Buckingham that "you have done everything which depended on you".[50] The cabinet considered his actions "in every respect proper and judicious".[51] It was nevertheless at this point (i.e. about 11 February) that Buckingham sent an undated letter of resignation to Grenville for transmission to the Prince if Pitt's government was dismissed.[52] It is, however, clear from the tone of Grenville's exhortations that Buckingham was pressing for immediate release.[53] On 18 February Grattan carried a resolution approving the presentation of the address to the lord lieutenant for transmission to the Prince.[54]

Even before the session had begun Buckingham had decided to refuse the address should it be presented to him. The situation had now come to the worst. The government had failed to divert the House's energies into an enquiry on the king's health. The opposition had secured the indefinite postponement of the money and mutiny bills. The Castle's plan to appont the Prince of Wales Regent of

Ireland by bill "restricting His Royal Highness as in Great Britain from granting peerages or offices or pensions for life", had been defeated in favour of a premature address of doubtful legality and uncertain efficacy.[55]

On the day on which he refused to transmit the address Buckingham had still not received official cabinet approval for his action,[56] but doubtless he found encouragement in Pitt's private assurance that "Whatever you may have decided on the spot will, I dare say . . . have been right".[57] Because the opposition had recognised him as the right and proper person through whom the address should be presented, Buckingham did not have to enter into a possibly contentious definition of his own position and role in order to justify his refusal. The address was deemed by the lord lieutenant's legal advisers to be illegal because it implied that the Irish parliament had the power to "suspend the prerogatives of the Crown without the consent of the third estate; that consent certified under the authority of the Great Seal of Great Britain, controlled by the laws and by the executive power of Great Britain".[58] The purveyors of the address were not contradicting any existing law but were attempting to act in accordance with a law that did not exist. Thus it was that Buckingham saw fit to reject the assertion that the Prince could assume the Regency of Ireland "before he shall be enabled by law so to do".[59]

It was perfectly true that no statute existed which could have rendered the address legally valid, but Buckingham did not explicitly challenge the opposition's theory that their address was cut in the same general mould as that of the Convention Parliament. However, the opening sentence of the draft refusal ("My allegiance to the King and my duty to the Prince of Wales oblige me to decline transmitting this address")[60] together with scattered references to his oath of office seem to suggest that Buckingham would, if necessary, have rested his case upon the differing circumstances of the two addresses.[61]

The news of the king's recovery[62] reached Buckingham on 20 February and was "sent into" the Commons[63] near the close of an inconclusive and somewhat repetitive debate which followed a motion by Grattan that delegates be appointed to carry the address directly to the Prince.[64] For the first time since the start of the session the government divided the House. Even before the division individual members began to desert the opposition. Bushe coupled his approval of the delegates with a warm defence of Buckingham's refusal to transmit the address, "his royal highness being not yet our regent".[65] Kearney also defended the lord lieutenant's refusal and explained that "he had voted for the address as a mark of respect to his royal highness, but he could not support the present resolution".[66] The House agreed to the appointment of the delegates[67] by 130 to 74,[68] showing that the state of the Commons had scarcely altered since the start of the session. But a further motion by Grattan condemning Buckingham's refusal as "ill-advised", "unwarranted and unconstitutional" saw the desertion of Sir Frederick Flood who had supported the address and the delegates.[69] A government attempt to amend the motion was lost but their numbers rose to 78 while opposition fell to 119. When Grattan's original motion was put the figure had shifted yet again; the government divided 83 against the opposition's 115.[70]

Buckingham, however, perhaps due to his understandable desire to relinquish his post[71] was not disposed to be over-optimistic. He felt that while the king's continuing recovery "certainly induces many individuals to act with more caution", "the numbers, that form the majority of both Houses, are composed of persons connected with what are termed great followings in the country, the divisions will not much fluctuate".[72] The fluctuation of members in the direction of government depended on confirmation of the king's recovery. The opposition, doubtless sensing the imminence of unpredictable fluctuation, did not apparently oppose the adjournment which was proposed and carried on 23 March.[73] By the time parliament reconvened on 13 April it had become clear that the king was well on the way to recovery. A week later the Castle defeated opposition motions by 148 to 93 and 132 to 78.[74] In Ireland the Regency Crisis was over.

The Irish Policy of William Pitt

One of the major problems of evaluating William Pitt's attitude to any matter over any significant period of time is simply lack of material. Those closest to him in his cabinet and one of those to whom his private papers had been bequeathed saw fit to destroy his letters.[1] But in any case Pitt was not the best of correspondents.[2] Many essential communications would have been made orally. But then again Pitt was an uncommunicative man. His aloofness, especially toward those with whom he was not closely acquainted, was well known. When he did communicate, particularly with regard to Ireland, he tended to engage the persons concerned in long (sometimes very long) conversations the precise point of which was not always clear to them.[3] On one occasion (at least) Pitt's expression of his views on Ireland was followed immediately by an official instruction quite contrary to those views.[4] It must also be remembered that the time and attention which Pitt could devote to Irish matters would necessarily have been limited by his many other commitments.[5] It should be pointed out also that much of the actual government of Ireland, particularly internal affairs, was the business of the lord lieutenant and chief secretary. Only matters which were of inter-regnal significance, or Irish measures which might establish British precedents (e.g. tithe reform), were likely to become the direct concern of the cabinet in London.

But having listed all these "mitigating" circumstances it is worth emphasising that no measure originating in government could become law in the face of Pitt's disapproval. To this considerable extent he had control over the decision-making process in Ireland. The effectiveness of that control rested only partly in the quality of the relationship between the Southern Department in London and Dublin Castle. To an incalculable degree Pitt's influence over the making of Irish policy depended on the depth of "understanding" which existed between him and the lord lieutenant. In this area Pitt's luck was uneven. His best relationship was with the Duke of Rutland, who was his first appointee in Ireland, but who expired sadly of alcohol poisoning in his fourth year of office in 1787. His successor, the Duke of Buckingham, was an unpopular choice, and a man who preferred to communicate with the cabinet via his brother, William

Grenville, rather than through Pitt. Westmorland, who succeeded Buckingham in 1789, maintained a close correspondence with Pitt but no rapport seemed to develop between them. He ultimately fell under the exclusive influence of the Castle administrators, Beresford, FitzGibbon and Foster. His misguided lack of trust in Pitt resulted in behaviour which rendered himself equally untrustworthy and necessitated his eventual removal. Even had Fitzwilliam survived in office in 1795 it is likely that due to the presence of the Duke of Portland as secretary of state, control of Irish affairs would have remained in the Whig "half" of the remodelled cabinet and thus have slid further out of Pitt's control. Westmorland's successor Camden also succumbed to the suffocating influence of Castle officialdom and embarked upon a headstrong security policy which effectively transformed an elitist insurrection into one of the most violent peasant uprisings of the century.

The commercial propositions having been dealt with at an earlier stage we may now consider those areas and policies with which Pitt was most directly involved. These were the restoration of public calm in the heady aftermath of the Renunciation Crisis; the less-than-well-defined attempt to reform the Irish parliament; and the long and agonised interconnection of Catholic relief and Union.

The restoration of public calm was *de rigeur* for any minister who intended to pursue an Irish policy without risk of restraint by what were described as "unconstitutional forces". The forces in question were of course the Volunteers. By December 1782 the patriot members who had promoted the settlement of the previous summer were hoping that having "reaped the benefits of having armed the people" they could now "avoid the inconveniences of it".[6] In England it was felt that as a deterrent to invaders the Volunteers were too few and "weakened by their part-time status", "but more dangerous to the State than they would be to an invading enemy".[7] The Castle considered that the real danger presented by the Volunteer Companies was less that of their unity on a national basis than the fact that "they each had the means of resisting the execution of any law they disliked in their own places of residence".[8] This absence of control over Volunteer behaviour had been lamented by the lord lieutenant (Earl Temple) during the previous summer when they had abandoned their efforts to assist in the recruitment of the seamen voted by parliament to the imperial service.[9]

It was in the suppression of the Volunteers more than in respect of any other of his measures that Pitt could be said to have continued the policy of his predecessors. But neither the method employed by Shelburne nor that by the coalition had been successful. In the clear absence of any means to outlaw the Volunteers (in June 1782 the government's infantry strength was down to 7,555) Shelburne had suggested replacing them with provincial regiments or fencibles in order to restore "to the Crown the sole exercise of the sword".[10] Despite the secrecy which enshrouded the background to the recruitment operation the government's intention was recognised almost from the outset.[11]

By October official circles in London as well as in Dublin were aware that the fencibles were becoming "an eternal bone of contention".[12] Thomas Conolly's wife was convinced that Ulster opinion was "set against them". The decision to separate the fencibles from the rest of the army both by title and description "has raised the suspicion that it is a scheme to defeat the Volunteers".[13] By the close of the year the experiment, in terms of replacing the Volunteers, was effectively at an end. Complaints, memorials and affidavits, all critical of the new corps, arrived on Charles Sheridan's desk in the military office of the Castle at the rate of almost a hundred a week:[14]

the opposition they met with is scarcely to be credited; innumerable disputes between them and the Volunteers, townspeople and all manner of people; magistrates refused to attest or to billet them, townspeople would not let them lodge in their houses, country people would sell them nothing to eat, old women pelted them with rotten eggs, and the young ones swore that no Fencible should ever get between their legs.

Despite the obvious defeat of the scheme's main purpose the government refused to admit its error. The requisite number of recruits were scraped together and the fencibles kept in being.[15] But as late as April 1783 the Kilkenny corps came under attack from local Volunteers assisted by a stone-throwing mob.[16] For the greater part of 1783 the government, perhaps in the hope that the fencibles experiment would yet yield dividends, adopted a low-key approach to the Volunteers. Moreover it was obvious that, whatever the muted misgivings of the parliamentarians, the Volunteers subsisted also on their extra-parliamentary popularity. But the growing involvement of the Volunteers in activities which threatened the basis of the representation put down a challenge to the Irish politicians which they could not afford to ignore. As the Volunteers' "reform" convention of November 1783 approached, the chief secretary of the day (Thomas Pelham) reported to London that "every man is afraid of them, wishes to see them disbanded but does not dare own it".[17] Even the normally optimistic Fox wanted "words to express to you how *critical* ... I conceive the present moment to be: unless they dissolve in a reasonable time, government ... must be at an end".[18]

That the Irish Commons was no longer prepared to condone the Volunteers' unsolicited interference in its affairs was further demonstrated as the convention got under way. Two motions advanced by the Volunteers' "representative" in parliament, Henry Flood, demanding the reduction of the army establishment as a gesture of confidence in the Volunteers, were crushingly defeated.[19] The belief that fear of the Volunteers had finally driven opposition members into the arms of government was fully borne out.[20] When the convention, through the medium of Flood, presented to the Commons a parliamentary reform bill the government pressed home its defensive attack, a number of members adverting to "the necessity of resisting the interference of an armed body of men in propositions of legislation". Even the four members whose principles or constituents would not allow them to oppose the measure itself expressed their disapproval of Volunteer interference.[21] The desertion of Henry Grattan, hitherto one of the Volunteers' most reliable parliamentary supporters, was answered predictably by the dismissal of that worthy member from the command of the Dublin Volunteer Corps.[22]

But no recriminations could adequately restore the Volunteers' loss of self-confidence. Pelham gleefully reported that they were "very much disconcerted".[23] As the coalition ministers moved through their last weeks of office the Volunteers subsided into an indecisive quiescence. Flood, far from leading them against either the Castle or College Green, committed the ultimate folly of seeking succour at Westminster.[24] Radicalism for Flood, as for the Volunteers, stopped short of rebellion.

Thus it was that Pitt on entry to office was not faced by an immediate crisis regarding the Volunteers. The initial picture drawn by Rutland was that of the Volunteers in decline. An attempt to improve the flagging membership of the corps had gone badly awry. In one of several efforts "to revive the spirit of arms", several hundred "of the lowest class of the people were paraded through the streets in conjunction with some of the Volunteer corps" to the disgust of veteran Volunteers.[25] To this disgust was added intense alarm several weeks later when the Dublin Liberty Corps of Volunteers, itself composed largely of tradesmen, recruited some two hundred "low mechanics", most of whom were Catholic.[26] The summer reviews of Volunteers bore out the government's hopes. The Leinster Corps' membership had fallen from 2,400 to 870.[27] In Belfast where the "dangerous folly" was reportedly slower to fade, the review turned up sixteen to seventeen hundred men but was yet believed to be "much inferior" to previous occasions.[28]

The ending of the American war in response to which the Volunteers had originally arisen, the absence of Flood and of a "popular" issue were all taking their toll. The Volunteers failed for instance to react decisively to the popular clamour for protective duties which arose in the spring of 1784. But from the government viewpoint their decline into insignificance was not enough. Their continuance in defiance of official disapproval represented a source of possible unrest in future disputes between government and parliament. If they continued to exist they could be exploited. The cabinet's proposal in June 1784 to further reduce the army in Ireland by five regiments gave the matter a degree of urgency.[29] Throughout the summer Rutland's dreams had been filled with shadowy French agents and Catholic plots to separate the two kingdoms, all set against a backdrop of Volunteer blue and buff.[30] In October Rutland warned that "the people are at rest *with arms in their hands*; and, until they are either *deprived* of those arms or hold them by a legal commission from the Crown, certain and permanent tranquillity will never be established".[31] Orde followed this with expressions of how depleted the reduction of regiments had left the kingdom's military resources and of the need to "keep up at least the appearance of strength to prevent the progress of evil machinations". Thus it was that although the actual solution to the Volunteer problem was to originate with Rutland, the requisite conditions were created by actions of the cabinet in London. The solution was scarcely original. A militia was to be brought into being by act of parliament for the ostensible purpose of replacing the withdrawn regiments, but really as "the best way of getting quit of these associations".[32] Pitt was impressed and in response to his request for further details Rutland forwarded the suggestion that a further act be passed prohibiting all future paramilitary manifestations.[33] Rutland found encouragement also in the reactions of the various "persons of confidence" with whom he had discussed the proposal.[34]

However, when Orde visited London at the end of November he discovered that the plan had still not been discussed by cabinet members other than Sydney and Pitt to whom it had been originally communicated.[35] A week later Orde reported more ominously that while the proposal "appears still to be of the most desirable consequence", Pitt was unprepared to accept immediately Rutland's recommended mode of proceeding.[36] Concealed beneath Pitt's pious wish to thoroughly investigate, discuss and settle Rutland's largely well-reasoned proposal lay a clash of priorities between the two men. Letters between Dublin and London for several weeks following Orde's visit display Rutland's determined efforts to keep the militia plan before a prime minister who seemed equally determined to forget about it. While the general desirability of the proposal was not lost on Pitt he obviously feared that it would jeopardise his personally-favoured commercial plan. Indeed the opportunistic nature of Irish opposition politics was such that support for one issue might be withheld against the abandonment of the other should the two plans be presented simultaneously.[37] Clearly the best means of securing both measures was to present them in single file. Rutland, less interested in commercial schemes (the details of which he may never fully have grasped), viewed the removal of the Volunteers as the necessary prelude to all further inter-regnal devices and wanted the militia bill to be first in the queue. Despite his assurance to Pitt in mid-December 1784 that he would maintain a primarily defensive policy it was clear that Rutland was gathering his parliamentary supporters for some anti-Volunteer gesture.[38]

But since the actual decision in the matter the militia rested with the cabinet it was hardly surprising that when the proposal came before the ministers on 10 January 1785 the victory went to Pitt. The only firm decision reached was that the proposed militia should be composed only of Protestants. No consideration seems to have been given to the problem of recruiting in counties populated largely by Catholics.[39] In particular no timetable for action on the issue was laid down. Rutland was told simply to formulate the details and submit the plan for approval.[40] But any suggestion that he was being given *carte blanche* on the format of the plan was banished the following day when Pitt warned him against trying to quash the Volunteers before the militia plan had been successfully carried through parliament. This gem of military common sense was followed by Pitt's stated belief that "Important and necessary as [is] the object, it may be endangered, or at least embarrassed, if too soon brought forward". More to the point Pitt felt that the achievement of the commercial plan together with a measure of parliamentary reform would render unnecessary any coercive measures towards the Volunteers.[41]

Rutland, realising that events were slipping out of his grasp, represented to Pitt the "universal discontent" which prevailed in regard to certain aspects of his commercial plan. He contrasted this with the more likely prospects of carrying the militia bill and abolishing the Volunteers, matters toward which "Mr Daly and Mr Grattan, in speeches perhaps the finest and most decisive ever delivered within the walls of the Irish parliament, have paved the way".[42] However, in his belief that he thus had the support of the entire patriot group Rutland was mistaken. Half a century later Grattan's son was to claim that the patriot policy at this time was not to abolish the Volunteers but rather to "keep them in the background".[43]

Nor could Rutland have lived long in the hope that it would be otherwise. When on 14 February the Castle as part of the annual supply bill requested from parliament funds to outfit a yet-non-existant militia, attention was drawn to the fact that the proposed militia would be under the control of the government. Upon this "the members of the opposition began to apprehend ... the annihilation of the

151

Volunteers". Clearly torn between their desire to be rid of the Volunteer "shadow" and their anxiety at the prospect of any increase in the executive's power, members' speeches tended to be "animated and inflammatory". The patriot group split on the issue, with Grattan, Daly and Arthur Wolfe supporting government, and Forbes, Westby, Curran, Arthur Browne, Hartstonge, Hardy and others opposing what they claimed was an ungrateful assault on the saviours of the constitutions. As dawn broke the government won by a majority of 76 in a depleted house.[44] The debate convinced Rutland that it was "absolutely necessary" to bring on the bill "without delay".[45] His alarm was in fact unjustified. The inclusion of the militia's clothing allowance in the supply bill signified that the militia itself had been conceded in principle. All that really remained was the question of whether the Volunteers would co-exist with the militia or be replaced by it.

It was not government but opposition that brought on the crucial debate five days later. The most curious aspect of this debate was the opposition's unpreparedness. A motion complimentary to the Volunteers, moved by Brownlow, was so vaguely worded that the leading government spokesman (Gardiner) was able to add to it without obvious compromise. Brownlow was thereupon attacked for his mildness and vagueness by another opposition member with such violence that some of the latter's remarks had to be withdrawn under threat of censure. The attorney-general (FitzGibbon) felt sufficiently stimulated to openly threaten the Volunteers with proscription if they "did not follow the hint now given them by parliament". Flood's efforts to salvage matters with a motion supportive of the Volunteers' right to bear arms was lost by nearly a hundred votes. Conolly and Ponsonby divided with the government.[46]

Leave was given for the introduction of the militia bill and five members appointed to draft it, but the bill never appeared. A draft was apparently sent to London in September 1785.[47] And although Pitt himself had pondered as late as January 1786 on the wisdom of coupling it with an anti-Volunteer measure the matter was consigned to the same limbo which by then also held the commercial propositions and parliamentary reform.[48] It had long been Orde's opinion that Rutland had been "a little too rapid about the wish of knocking down the Volunteers".[49] For months the lord lieutenant continued to fear that the Volunteers would again become the tools of faction. But by January 1786 even he was recommending that they be allowed the old soldiers' opportunity of simply fading away.[50]

There had been no obvious change of policy by Rutland or Pitt. What had happened was that the opposition, in its unco-ordinated attempt to protect the Volunteers from government "insult", had provoked a parliamentary repudiation of them that had exceeded the government's wildest expectations. After February 1785 the militia bill and the more nebulous anti-Volunteer measure lost much of their urgency. In time they became unnecessary. For the Volunteers did indeed fade away. In a welter of accident, inertia and policy the "unconstitutional force" had been removed from Irish life and Pitt was free to pursue more positive goals.[51]

Pitt's earliest proposal with regard to Ireland paralleled one of his English policies — parliamentary reform. It was clear from the beginning, however, that Pitt intended this measure to be government-inspired. Even before he became prime minister he had been careful to offer no encouragement to the Volunteer-appointed Committee of Correspondence which sought his opinion on the issue.[52] Despite the fact that the popular reform bill when finally introduced by Flood in March 1784 was designed to "restore the constitution" and "not to introduce novelties" (which closely resembled Pitt's own view of reform[53]), the cabinet in London and the lord lieutenant in Dublin planned its defeat.[54] Rutland did not in fact arrive in Dublin until 24 February 1784. However, his advice to the cabinet on 4 March that government should withhold its opposition until the second reading as a gesture of lip-service to the many county petitions in support of the bill does seem to suggest that the basic decision to oppose had been already made in London with Rutland's concurrence.[55]

Pitt's personal opinion of Flood's bill has not survived, but even had it been favourable he would have experienced great difficulty in promoting it in the face of Rutland's belief that the measure was "unpleasant and distressing", and Sydney's feeling that "so crude and undigested a proposal" would be "ruinous to the prosperity of Ireland".[56] Pitt's refusal may have been based partly also on his belief that Catholics should be excluded from the franchise.[57] But underlying the decision to reject the bill was almost certainly the fact that its provisions would commit the cabinet to the passage of a similar type of measure for England. Significantly, the Irish parliamentary attack on Flood's measure was grounded less on imperfections in the detail of the bill but rather on the principle of the constitution's perfection:[58]

That the general system would be an innovation upon the constitution; that the evils complained of were imaginary; that the constitution of these kingdoms is superior in excellence to that of any other country in the globe; that the past conduct of parliament proved how securely the interests of the people may be entrusted to the assembly constituted as it is; that so important a change as that proposed should not be attempted but on a moral certainty of advantage; that the contrary was justly to be apprehended; that the design would in effect but shift the patronage into other hands; that rights of corporations would be sacrificed; that their privileges would be thrown into the lowest rank of the people, whose morals would be vitiated by continual temptations to corruption and perjury, to the utter destruction of industry, virtue and happiness.

That Pitt's own plan for parliamentary reform in either kingdom was doomed from the outset was partly due to the peculiar implications of such reform in Ireland. In Ireland would almost necessarily involve the extension of the franchise to a section of the Catholic population. Such a concession would be viewed by the Irish Protestant ascendancy as the thin end of a very unattractive wedge and by Pitt's Westminster supporters as a plot to separate the two kingdoms. In the immediate sense such a move would compromise Rutland's administration by compelling him to introduce to a parliament filled with Protestants a measure which he could have no hope of carrying (Flood's measure had been crushingly defeated). Moreover, despite the fact that the measure would be initiated by government, the almost-necessary similarity of the proposed reform to that demanded by the Volunteer Convention would invest it with the mantle of a concession to popular pressure. This would in turn militate against government's prior commitment to restore public order and might even have the disastrous appearance of recognising the Volunteers as a legitimate organ of popular discontent.

Due to the exigencies of his position in Dublin it is difficult for us (and was probably more so for him) to separate Rutland's private opinion of the principle of reform from the policy he would be forced by circumstances to impress upon the cabinet in London.[59] Rutland, fearing the probable effect a successful English reform bill would have on the punctured reform campaign in Ireland, voiced his disapproval of all such measures. Pitt was warned in June 1784 that it "would greatly tend to increase our difficulties. . . . In England it is a delicate question, but in this country it is difficult and dangerous in the last degree. The views of the Catholics render it extremely hazardous". Buoyed up perhaps by information that Pitt's English reform proposals "had no sort of chance . . . let him exert, even in earnest, every power of government", Rutland tempered his opposition with cautious approval of the more innocuous Irish provisions.[60] During the summer of 1784 Rutland was kept in a state of constant alarm by reports from his chief secretary Thomas Orde in London who refused to attend the debates on the Sawbridge proposals, fearing "misconstruction upon my conduct, in whatever way I may direct it, if it ever found its way into a Dublin newspaper". Orde expressed "a serious alarm about the consequences which may immediately ensue from it [the Sawbridge motion] in Ireland, where your Grace's government may feel the effects".[61] To Pitt's clear disgust Rutland's Westminster informants voted with the majority

154

on 16th June when reform was shelved for the remainder of the session.[62]

While the details of Pitt's Irish reform proposals have not survived, it is clear from a reference by Rutland to "a certain proportionable addition of county members" that the prime minister's scheme had assumed a definite format.[63] That this format included some measure of Catholic franchise is also clear from the forthright manner in which Orde begged him to "Consider only the very circumstance of Roman Catholics and Independent Dissenters; recollect their nature, their views, and their interests. What can serve them all; what can prevent confusion, what can preserve the uniformity of government but — *to do nothing*?"[64] Rutland continued to emphasise to both Pitt and Sydney the unpopularity of Catholic voting rights in respectable Irish circles.[65]

But by the autumn it was obvious that the June defeat of Sawbridge had had no deleterious effect on Pitt's determination to press forward with an Irish reform bill. He responded to Rutland's advice that no respectable Irish member would consider the idea by telling him to talk to some members who would. The prime minister, in his earliest surviving remarks on Irish reform, simply ignored the detailed and uncompromising condemnation of the proposal which he received from Orde almost certainly on the same day on which he penned the remarks.[66] These remarks are worthy of close examination because in terms of purely Irish policy they do not make complete sense. Pitt presented reform as the second instalment of a two-part plan under which Ireland would first be allowed to participate in a commercial agreement mutually beneficial to both kingdoms.[67]

And having, by holding out this, removed, I trust, every temptation to Ireland to consider her interest as separate from England, to be ready, while we discountenance *wild and unconstitutional attempts, which strike at the root of all authority*, to give real efficacy and popularity to government, by acceding (if such a line can be found) to a *prudent and temperate reform of parliament*, which may guard against or gradually cure real defects and mischiefs, may show a sufficient regard to the interests and even prejudices of individuals who are concerned, and may unite the Protestant interest in *excluding the Catholics from any share in the representation* or the government of the country.

So, despite all the dire warnings from Rutland and Orde, Pitt insisted that the Irish administration would gain "efficacy and popularity" from reform; his suggestion that reform would combat "*real* defects and mischiefs" seems to imply that he was prepared to accede to popular demands which he nevertheless believed to be imaginary. Although he linked reform with the commercial package there was no obvious connection between the two issues. In the

155

broader context of the restoration of public calm the reform gesture would have been counterproductive. The question thus remains as to why Pitt so determinedly proposed a line of action which was at variance with another of his Irish policies; which would risk the embarrassment of his Irish minister and the consequent repercussions on his own position in London. The evidence, sketchy though it may be, seems to suggest that Pitt's Irish parliamentary reform proposal did not represent an Irish policy at all but rather was a means by which he hoped to obtain the passage of reform in England.

Pitt began to probe for information as to the source of the Irish hunger for reform. In response Orde told a story of popular insincerity, of the many deluded by the few, of general misconception of the results of the proposed reform, "and perhaps the greatest cause of all ... is, the constant rage of imitation of anything of that sort started in England". He concluded with a warning that a successful English reform bill would precipitate an Irish measure of a similar nature.[68] Back in London in December Orde was favoured with "a long conversation" with Pitt on the subject but "met with nothing unexpected in his partial adherence to his original ideas, and his delicacy on the point of consistency".[69] Orde also heard "from indisputable authority" that Richmond was the source of pressure on Pitt to reform the Irish parliament.[70] Just previous to this conversation Pitt had informed Rutland that the latter's resistance was pointless and that reform "*must* sooner or later be carried in *both countries*".[71] Ten days later on the eve of a cabinet meeting on Irish affairs he was still convinced that "the substance of it [reform] cannot be finally resisted". But it was then clear that his colleagues would not countenance its extension to Ireland until the English reform proposal was settled.[72] Whether or not this represented a victory for Richmond, Pitt had succeeded in again focussing cabinet attention on the prospect of English parliamentary reform.

That the promotion of an English reform bill may have been the main motive underlying Pitt's advocacy of Irish reform is further suggested by his dramatic reversal of tactics following a further cabinet meeting on Irish affairs in January 1785. Officially Rutland was instructed by Sydney to obtain a postponement of any reform measure should such arise from the Irish parliament before the settlement of an English reform bill. Pitt's refusal in the autumn of 1784 to prosecute or otherwise harass the Irish purveyors of popular reform was now further manifested by the cabinet decision to seek a type of reform which "would be agreeable to the greatest number" of Rutland's Irish supporters.[73] Rutland received similar advice from Pitt who still professed his certainty "that if any reform takes place here the tide will be too strong to be withstood in Ireland". The

156

official reason was that the raising of a major issue such as reform might jeopardise the commercial propositions which were due for introduction to the Irish parliament early in February 1785, and the safe passage of which was of central importance in Pitt's efforts to regulate Anglo-Irish relations.[74]

But conclusive proof that Pitt manipulated the uncertainties of Anglo-Irish politics in order to revive his colleagues' interest in English reform has not survived. Indeed the necessarily solitary nature of such a pursuit suggests that it may never have existed on paper. The curious form of irrational optimism he displayed in the face of Rutland's obvious reluctance to introduce reform in Dublin may have represented a stratagem but it was also one of the most infuriating aspects of Pitt's character. His similarly groundless optimism on the more intractable areas of the commercial propositions was later to hinder those delicate negotiations. His apparent acceptance of Richmond's advice that an Irish reform would emasculate the Volunteers does his judgement little credit.[75]

He had promised Rutland that, pending the completion of the commercial arangement and the successful persuasion of hostile Irish members, Irish reform would be revived.[76] But by the time the commercial propositions had failed so also had Pitt's proposed English reform bill. With the introduction of the commercial propositions to the Irish parliament early in February 1785 the word "reform" vanished from the otherwise solid and well-explained objects of Pitt's Irish policy.

The apparent conflict between Pitt's espousal of an union at irregular intervals over a fifteen-year period and his persistent failure to put his supposed "wish" into practice has led to confusion as to the precise nature of his long-term Irish policy which even recent studies have left unresolved. Thus it was that Bolton, in a specialised account of the passing of the Act of Union could find no evidence to suggest that the act was being seriously contemplated even by 1792. Even on 1 and 2 June 1798, the dates on which an union was allegedly first discussed as a serious proposition, the evidence for this discussion is (on Bolton's own admission) no more than "indirect but suggestive".[77] However, E.M. Johnston in a general history of the century which post-dated Bolton by nearly a decade was clearly more impressed by the evidence of Pitt's periodic sighs for union. She felt it "not improbable that the foundations of Pitt's Irish policy were laid during the viceroyalty of the Duke of Rutland, 1784-7".[78]

While my main object is to resolve the apparent conflict between Pitt's words and actions, this can only be done in the light of a proper understanding of his attitude to the Catholic community in Ireland. The obvious connection between the issues of union and Catholic Emancipation raises the question as to which issue was uppermost in Pitt's mind, and why. It is probably true that in the event of Catholic Emancipation the Irish Protestant ascendancy could have preserved its political status only within the framework of a united parliament. Thus, if Pitt's object in obtaining an union was to protect the ascendancy and satisfy the Catholics, then it can be said that the union was not an end in itself but a necessary step on the road to Catholic Emancipation. Yet there is no evidence to suggest that any prospect existed (or that Pitt believed it to exist) of a change in the king's attitude — an attitude which he had expressed with uncompromising bluntness at the time of the Fitzwilliam controversy in 1795:[79]

letters from the lord lieutenant of Ireland, which to my greatest astonishment propose the total change of the principles of government which have been followed by every administration in that kingdom since the abdication of King James II . . . venturing to condemn the labour of ages, and wanting an immediate adoption of ideas which every man of property in Ireland and every friend to the Protestant religion must feel diametrically contrary to those he has imbibed from his earliest youth.

Though no evidence remains to suggest that Pitt tried to soften the king's viewpoint after 1795 he apparently continued to believe emancipation to be a feasible proposition.[80]

But the closer one examines Pitt's attitude to the union the more untenable becomes the notion that the Act represented in his mind a solution to the constitutional difficulties created by the independent status of the Irish parliament. The arguments used by Pitt on 31 January 1800 in his justification of the projected union do not stand up to close scrutiny. While it was true that the separation of the legislatures increased the difficulties of co-ordinated defence tactics in time of war, it was not entirely clear what mutual advantage would lie in stripping the Irish representatives of the right to decide in their own interests. While it was true that the members of the Irish parliament represented a minority from which the bulk of the Irish population had become alienated, it was far from clear how this situation would be improved by transferring the focal point of odium to Westminster. Both of these arguments suggested that union was but one instalment of a two-part solution and that it was being sought with a view to facilitating the arrival of Catholic Emancipation.[81]

But even allowing for the obvious political necessity to guard his intentions carefully, his apparent belief that the king's intransigence could be overcome suggests a miscalculation of unprecedented magnitude in Pitt's dealings with the monarch. The roots of the miscalculation lay only partly in the intricacies of Pitt's relationship with George III. The conviction that he could successfully carry such an unpopular Irish policy against the manifest disapproval of the

158

Protestant establishments in both islands represented at once the exhaustion of a policy which Pitt had pursued since 1784 and the culmination of an idea which had been developing during the same period.

One of the difficulties of evaluating Pitt's Irish policies is that they have too often been treated in isolation from his attitude to similar issues which had occurred in an English context. To make matters worse, those very issues have escaped the attention of even the most attentive biographers. The Irish angle to Pitt's English parliamentary reform drive of the early 1780s has gone almost unnoticed.[82] The London police bill, on which Pitt suffered a defeat at Westminster in 1785 and on which the successful Irish police act of the following year was based, is barely referred to in any biography.[83] Similarly the background to the government's decision to introduce the English Catholic relief bill of 1791 has never been investigated.[84]

It would be unrealistic to assume that Pitt's attitude to Irish Catholics, whose numbers and geographical location presented him with a serious political problem, was similar to his view of their English co-religionists. Certainly his early impressions cannot have been favourable. The extreme fears expressed by Rutland and Orde throughout 1784 that Catholics were intriguing with French and Spanish agents to promote the violent separation of the two kingdoms were groundless and probably originated in the mind of the Irish attorney-general John FitzGibbon.[85] But without any alternative source of information other than the wild but unfortunately corroborative letters of the violent radical Sir Edward Newenham, Pitt was inevitably seduced into the belief that Irish Catholics represented a serious threat.[86]

Although the prospect of political concessions for Irish Catholics disappeared along with the parliamentary reform scheme, Pitt evidently did not despair of healing the religious divisions of Ireland. The plan for the chartering of Maynooth which came to fruition in 1795 had its origins in a conversation between Pitt and Orde a decade earlier, when Pitt raised no objection to a proposal that Catholic priests should be trained in Ireland.[87]

However, the initial move for a further measure of relief for Catholics came not from the Irish Catholic Committee but from its British counterpart (between which bodies there was apparently no contact).[88] The precise sequence of events is unclear, but by the end of May 1787 Lord Petre, a leading British Catholic peer, was in a position to thank John Mitford, a talented and rising member of parliament, for agreeing to sponsor a relief measure at Westminster. At this point Henry Dundas had been given a copy of the proposed bill and had almost certainly discussed it with Pitt. Petre was at pains to emphasise "that the toleration granted by it will not exceed what

159

the Catholics now enjoy in Ireland, and every French Catholic in England under the fifth clause of the commercial treaty, and even not so extensive as in Ireland, the Catholic bishops being there recognised by law".[89]

No record has survived of Pitt's attitude to the proposed measure, but the fact that a solicitous memorial based on the bill was drawn up and presented to him by William Fermor of the Catholic Committee would seem to suggest that the Committee had been given some positive sign.[90] The memorial was presented to Pitt (apparently in person) on 25 February 1788. However, by early May Fermor, in spite of "frequent communications", had received no reply from Pitt and had taken to writing to William Grenville instead.[91] Within a few days the cabinet had decided to proceed with the measure, subject to some alterations. The alterations insisted upon included an oath of allegiance, and hard evidence as to the opinions prevailing amongst Catholic clergy and universities on "the existence or extent of the Pope's dispensing power". The oath was potentially divisive and the acquisition of the required evidence would involve a survey covering large tracts of Europe. Fermor's "very candid" letter to Grenville in late July indicates his awareness that the cabinet was stalling on the issue (Pitt had not even responded to a suggested format for the foreign universities survey). The letter openly accused Pitt of discourtesy to the Catholic Committee and claimed that "we are apprehensive of not being able to procure the information wanted previous to the meeting of parliament".[92]

Fermor and his colleagures were correct in their apprehension. A further year was to pass before the Committee was again in a position to advance the measure. But by the summer of 1789 the Protestant bishops, led by the Archbishop of Canterbury, were of the "unanimous opinion that the extent to which the bill goes is very alarming, and likely to produce such impressions on the minds of the people as may tend to disturb the public peace". Pitt and Mitford were simultaneously informed of their views.[93] Following a discussion with Grenville, Mitford managed to persuade the Catholics to postpone the issue until the following year.[94] The details of this discussion have not survived, and Petre was fobbed off with the excuse that the Catholics' application was causing intractable difficulties with the Dissenters. Petre was indignant but helpless.[95]

But by December 1790 Mitford was being heavily pressed by the Catholic Committee. His plea to Grenville for advice elicited no response and Grenville was "out" when Mitford called on him in person a month later. Within a few days however, on 16 January 1791, Grenville conveyed to Mitford the cabinet's agreement to proceed with the relief bill.[96] But with regard to the reasons for the long delay between Pitt's acceptance of the Committee's memorial and the decision to concede the measure the government, and probably Mitford also, had been less than frank with Petre. Several years after the passing of the Irish relief acts Fermor recalled a conversation with Grenville in which the latter "was pleased to say that you did not see any difficulty in government enabling the English Roman Catholics to do so [i.e. vote at elections], but that it was a great political question with regard to the Irish of that description [freeholder], who certainly in consequence would demand a removal of the same obstructive laws".[97]

Buckingham, who was lord lieutenant at the time of Pitt's acceptance of the English memorial, was evidently not informed. It was over Westmorland's head that the storm broke in February 1791 in the form of a demand from the Catholic Committee of Ireland that the king and parliament "relieve them from their degraded situation and no longer suffer them to continue like strangers in their native land".[98] It was to Westmorland that Grenville was to assert that "it does not by any means follow that what is right and expedient to be done here, will be expedient to be done in Ireland under circumstances so extremely different". The whole question of Catholic relief, he claimed, was "a matter of expediency, not of right, except as far as relates to toleration only, strictly so called".[99]

It seems that a certain lack of realism had begun to affect the behaviour of Pitt and his colleagues. Catholic relief acts in England in 1778 and 1782 had been followed by similar measures in Ireland. In both cases the successful passage of the measures was due to some extent (more so in 1778 than in 1782) to government pressure.[100] From the previous October Westmorland had expected the Catholics to apply for further concessions, but it is probable that his expectations in this regard related to the smoldering tithe dispute; he showed no sign that he knew of the imminent English Catholic relief bill.[101] In July 1791 he referred to the English measure as the cause of "very great mischief" in Ireland.[102]

The striking feature of the spring and summer of that year was the silence of Pitt and his colleagues on the issue. They, like Westmorland and the Irish administration, clearly hoped that the split in the Catholic Committee in Ireland and the obvious reluctance of the Irish opposition to become involved would jointly exhause the Catholics' determination.[103] The shift in policy which began in Dublin following a second approach by a Catholic deputation in July, and which was agreed to by Pitt in October, did not represent a concession to popular pressure or a surrender to any imminent threat. Rather, it was a decision taken with a view to preventing matters from deteriorating to the point where demands damaging to the Anglo-Irish connection would either have to be conceded or else resisted in blood. The conservative nature of the Irish relief bill of 1792

161

reflected the conservative intentions of its sponsors.

Thus it was that when in mid-October 1791 Hobart personally explained to Grenville the risk (which Westmorland had long suspected[104]) of an alliance between the Catholics and the increasingly unruly Dissenters of Belfast, the lord lieutenant was told of the cabinet's "very great anxiety that such measures may be taken as may effectually counteract" that risk. But the cabinet was not unaware that the Irish relief measure, which placed Irish Catholics on an equal footing with their English counterparts, would inevitably lead to an Irish Catholic demand for political status commensurate with their professional and civil standing.[105] It was in this context that the prospect of an union began to take on the outlines of a serious possibility.

Due to the unsatisfactory nature of the system which had emerged from the 1782 settlement and the probable inadequacy of the old "Townshend" arrangements (i.e. if legislative independence were to be repealed) union had throughout the Pitt years been an attractive solution to the problem of governing Ireland. As early as 1784 Rutland had advised that "without *an Union* Ireland will not be connected with Great Britain in twenty years longer".[106] When the Irish opposition humiliated Pitt over his commercial plan in August 1785 the feared Volunteers were in decline and so were no longer a threat. When the Irish opposition baited his lord lieutenant and plotted Pitt's own downfall during the Regency Crisis the Volunteers were no more. The instability of the Irish governing system was brought home to Pitt every year as his lords lieutenant looked forward to each approaching session with urgency and trepidation and a sense of near-helplessness which could only have underlined the humiliating nature of the 1782 settlement for Britain. The extent of the disadvantage at which Britain had been placed by the settlement was further manifested by the anxiety which had surrounded the necessary correction of clerical errors in two Irish bills in 1788. Despite the fact that the power of the British privy council to reject Irish bills had been retained under the terms of the 1782 settlement, neither the Irish nor British administrations felt confident that it could be used even on rare occasions without elaborate justification.[107]

A further effect of the settlement was to increase the degree to which the lord lieutenant depended upon the support of leading members of the Castle administration.[108] The extent to which these persons exerted their influence over Rutland is clear from his exaggerated fears of Volunteers, reformers and Catholics. But the more serious implications of this tendency did not become fully apparent until the autumn of 1791 when the Castle administrators, having set their face against Catholic relief, persuaded Westmorland to represent *favourably* their opposition to the stated policy of the cabinet which had appointed him.[109]

It was this last episode that revealed the urgency of the Irish problem. To prevent the Catholics from joining in an unholy alliance with the Francophiles of Belfast and thus posing a formidable threat to the safety of Britain and the empire, it was necessary that they should be bought off with some measure of the political status which they craved. In December 1791 Dundas had declared in the most uncompromising terms that if such a choice was forced upon the cabinet by the intransigence of the Irish ascendancy, then that ascendancy *would* be sacrificed.[110] By the end of the following year the realisation had begun to impress itself upon the main protagonists that any further adjustment to the 1782 settlement would render it unworkable: "Protestants frequently declare they will have an Union, rather than yield the franchise to the Catholics. The Catholics will cry out for Union rather than submit to their present state of subjection".[111]

It was in response to Westmoreland's suggestion that "the violence of both parties might be turned on this occasion to the advantage of England" that Pitt delivered his clearest espousal of Union before 1800:[112]

The idea of the present fermentation gradually bringing both parties to think of an Union with this country has long been in my mind. I hardly dare flatter myself with the hope of its taking place, but I believe it, tho' itself not easy to be accomplished, to be the only solution for other and greater difficulties. The admission of Catholics to a share of suffrage could not then be dangerous. The Protestant interest, in point of power, prosperity, and church establishment, would then be secure because the decided majority of the supreme legislature would necessarily be Protestant; and the great ground of argument on the part of the Catholics would be done away, as compared with the rest of the Empire, they would become a minority.

But unlike Westmorland who felt that the opportune moment had arrived,[113] Pitt was no more prepared for union in 1793 than he had been in 1785 or 1789. Far more revealing than the November letter quoted above was Pitt's conversation with Hobart the previous June, when he referred to the need for "a permanent system which they could stand upon", but that he wished "to see how far the present system was maintainable", and how this might be best accomplished. Pitt and Dundas, optimistic to the last, "seemed to assent to an idea which I [Hobart] threw out, of the probability of the present system in Ireland continuing as long as the system of Popery, which every hour was losing ground, and which once annihilated put an end to the question". In Hobart's view the British determination to support the Irish ascendancy "seemed to have been Pitt's from the beginning and Dundas's ultimately".[114] In a somewhat confused memorandum

163

of a conversation he had held with Pitt and Dundas in January 1793, Edward Cooke reported that the two ministers "by no means wished to give the Catholics the right of sitting in parliament".[115] The truth of the matter was that Pitt's speculations on union had arisen from the uncertainty that the Catholic relief measures would pass the Irish parliament. The successful passage of the measure had made union an unnecessary expedient. Afterwards Westmorland himself "always imagined all thoughts even of Union" even amongst the ascendancy "were destroyed by the late relaxations to Catholics".[116]

But it soon became clear that neither Westmorland nor Hobart nor Cooke nor any member of the Irish administration was any longer the repository of Pitt's confidence. He could not forget the manner in which his best intentions had been opposed by those who owed their positions to him. The appointment within a year of Sylvester Douglas as chief secretary represented one of Pitt's final attempts to recapture from the Castle the ultimate direction of Irish affairs. To reduce the influence of the Castle administrators upon a future lord lieutenant Douglas was, in defiance of recent practice, to remain in office even after the replacement of Westmorland. Hence it was that Douglas was afforded the most thorough briefing on record of a newly-appointed Irish chief secretary, having not one but three conferences with Pitt and two with Dundas.

Pitt asserted that "Ireland had hitherto been, and must yet continue, a government of expedients"; he "wished, rather than had any specific hopes of, a general remodelling of the political frame of that country. He desires to keep back if possible concessions which may at a convenient opportunity be purchased by some sort of union — which, however, he seems to despair of ever seeing accomplished". Only now did Pitt reveal that he regarded Protestant fears that Catholics in parliament would seek to reverse the Tudor, Stuart and Cromwellian confiscations as "very cheap", "not real" and "brought forward to induce government to protect them in the monopoly of power and emolument". Both Pitt and Dundas felt that "the Catholics, being the majority of the inhabitants, must in justice and policy be admitted by degrees to a full participation of all the advantages now held exclusively by the Protestants. . . . Mr Pitt thinks, truly, that such a monopoly is unjust and cannot long be maintained but . . . that it would be impolitic, and also even in some degree unjust to wrest it from them with violence". The transfer of monopoly from Protestant to Catholic was to be accomplished "by degrees . . . and must be done as it were insensibly to the Protestants". His last instruction to Douglas was that the policy they had discussed "must not be avowed in Ireland".[117]

The most recent study of Fitzwilliam's period of office by E.A. Smith included a close examination of the existing evidence that

Portland, and ultimately Fitzwilliam, believed themselves entitled to mould and initiate Irish policy in isolation from their coalition partners. While the academic value of such an exercise is not in question, its relevance to the overall issue of why Fitzwilliam acted as he did is in doubt. In the weeks previous to the fateful meeting of 15 November 1794 Pitt had made it clear to both Windham and Grattan that he was not amenable to any significant alteration in existing Irish political arrangements. At the November meeting, in the presence of Portland, Spencer, Windham and Fitzwilliam himself, agreement was reached with Pitt that no changes were to be made in the higher personnel of the Castle and that any government move on further Catholic demands was to wait upon specific instructions from London. Fitzwilliam's later suggestion that some misunderstanding had surrounded these points does not stand up to close inspection. Had any such doubts really existed, or had Pitt made any attempt to deceive his Whig colleagues, Portland and the other Whigs who had attended the meeting would have supported Fitzwilliam's assertion. But as it turned out, all the participants appeared to have understood the position except Fitzwilliam.

The seeds of Fitzwilliam's destruction lay in his isolation from sources of sound advice after his arrival in Dublin. The nature of the coalition agreement, and probably Fitzwilliam's own attitude, made it impossible to retain Douglas in the post of chief secretary as had been originally intended. George Damer, the secretary chosen by Fitzwilliam, was too inexperienced to be of any real assistance. Even if the Castle administrators had sufficiently overcome their suspicions of Whig viceroys to offer him advice and assistance, the curt dismissals of Beresford, Sackville-Hamilton and Cooke would have borne out their worst fears. The vacuum was quickly filled by the ill-natured advice of Thomas Lewis O'Beirne and the stark opportunism of Grattan and others. Fitzwilliam's certainty that he had been the victim of at best a misunderstanding and at worst a trick was contrived, though perhaps not consciously so. His personality was such that it was far easier for him to accept martyrdom with all its attendant political consequences than to face the fact that he had been a dupe and a fool.[118]

Pitt's refusal to countenance a radical alteration in Irish political arrangements had been forced to the surface by the Fitzwilliam affair and was again proven to be unshakable. However, it was doubly regrettable that the incident should have revealed to the Catholics Pitt's obvious reluctance to grant them the right to sit in parliament in the foreseeable future. The degree to which this revelation served to alienate middle-class Catholics has not been measured but may have been considerable. The appointment of Camden as lord lieutenant in 1795 led to the final victory of the Castle administrators and the effective end of Pitt's control over events in Ireland.

Despite the confused efforts to rid Irish society of the Volunteers, at parliamentary reform and commercial agreements, two inter-locking lines of consistency are visible in Pitt's attitude to his Irish responsibilities. Firstly, he accepted the system laid down by the 1782 settlement and was prepared to work within it. Secondly, this acceptance was carried to the point where he made strenuous efforts to assist in the self-reformation of the settlement with a view to ensuring its survival. The passing away of the Volunteers in the mid-1780s had left the way clear for him to repeal the unwieldly settlement if that had really been his wish. When provoked by the failure of the propositions in 1785 and by the dangerous situation brought about by the Regency Crisis he reacted not with an hasty union but with a determination to try again. I tend to agree with Professor Johnston's point that the union was the product of "exhaustion rather than of evolution".[119]

Whatever the inconveniences of the system Pitt would have been acutely aware that it represented (in theory at least) the legally-expressed will of the Irish voters. The humiliations of the propositions and of the regency affair would have made less impression on him than the information from Westmorland after the Catholic relief act of 1793 that union was "generally talked of by Protestants with a sort of acquiescence", when "two years ago a man would have been insulted for the mention".[120] He would have been even more impressed by the opinion of an aged commentator in 1797 (which was almost certainly brought to his attention) that "the people have lost all confidence in the parliament and have entirely ceased to have the least expectation from it".[121]

Pitt's Irish policy is to be found in his actions rather than in his words. That policy was one of respect for the independence of the Irish parliament; those actions testified not to a sincere desire for its demise but rather to the recognition that it embodied the will of the Irish people. He worked consistently for its preservation and survival. Only when it became clear that it no longer possessed that confidence and that its existence was in conflict both with the security of the empire and the progress of toleration did he seek its abolition.

Conclusion

The Politics of Confrontation in Eighteenth-Century Ireland

In 1692, the beginning of Ireland's political eighteenth century, the English government and the Anglo-Irish ascendancy faced each other in Chichester House in an atmosphere of frank hostility which in the ensuing decades was to pass through several phases, but never to disappear. The active conflict with the Catholics had ended, but the numerical imbalance between them and the colonists, and the apparent indifference of the English government to that situation had combined to place the colonists in a defensive posture that was to become permanent. The tale (for it is not necessarily a myth) of the "abandoned people" which plays so large a part in Ulster Unionist politics even in the late twentieth century may have originated with the Treaty of Limerick. The disastrous parliamentary situation which defeated Sydney was alliviated from 1695 by a series of compromises which lasted in effect until 1770. The compromises collectively shifted the balance of power considerably, though not decisively, into the hands of the undertakers. But the long-term effect of the shift was to deflect the heat of the confrontation which had existed between the colonists and the English ministers to the undertakers — who naturally fought amongst themselves for the largest slices of the patronage cake.

Only occasionally, in unusual circumstances such as those surrounding the Wood's Halfpence and the 1753 incident, did the original underlying conflict re-assert itself. On both occasions, and also during the Lucas controversy, the undertakers displayed a willingness to exploit the situation in the hope of shifting the balance of power a little further in their individual (if not collective) directions. By 1770 it had become clear that the continued allocation of patronage to the undertakers, particularly in the revenue department, had resulted in a transfer of legislative power so substantial as to leave the government at a serious disadvantage. The removal of the undertakers as a distinct power-bloc in 1770 and their return to the arena of general parliamentary opposition signified a reversion to the polarised positions of 1692; government and opposition again confronted each other. The absence of internecine strife amongst the undertakers caused opposition attention to focus on the constitutional grievances which had for the most part remained an undercurrent of parliamentary conflict. In general the issues which came to be known as grievances reflected the colonists' fundamental belief that their rights were being treated as a matter of secondary consideration by the British government. Specifically they concentrated on the balance of legislative power — the only means by which their rights could be maintained. The various mechanisms by which the British government retained ultimate superiority in that power-balance — "sole right", *habeas corpus*, mutiny acts — were assailed as grievances. But the grievance at the centre of the conflict concerned the Irish privy council — a body which had arrogated to itself power to alter and suppress Irish legislation on its way from parliament to England. The patriots' refusal, for reasons explained in Chapter 2, to assail the similar exercise of power by the English privy council curtailed the visible achievement of 1782. But the unseen effect was to remove from the arena the main focal point of the conflict. Between 1782 and 1800 the British government and its small coterie of Castle administrators confronted the opposition in what became an increasingly naked and expensive struggle for control of the balance of power — the balance which now lay solely in the hands of that nebulous group, the "independent" country gentlemen.

Even without the French War and its violent Irish consequences, the unending tug-of-war in College Green was putting a considerable strain on the Anglo-Irish constitutional framework. The British government which had held the upper hand in the contest throughout the period eventually resolved it to its own advantage. The Act of Union abolished the Irish parliament as an institution; henceforth the Anglo-Irish ascendancy would be compelled to pursue its rights through the Westminster legislature where it could pose no threat to the British government. But the removal of the Irish parliament from the arena, while it relieved an immediate problem, activated a confrontation between the British government and the Catholic Irish which had lain dormant since 1690. For a century or more the Anglo-Irish had stood between Britain and this last major struggle (even as the English had once saved the colonists from James II). But their political demise in 1800, their economic decline after 1815, their religious subordination in 1829 — each signified a stage in the intensifying struggle between the British government and the Catholic Irish for control of political, social, economic and cultural resources.

One further conclusion has emerged during the course of this study. Public opinion has long been believed by historians to have acted as a primary factor in determining the course of events in eighteenth-century Ireland. The importance of pamphlet literature in shaping public policy, highlighted most memorably by R.B. McDowell, was reiterated as recently as 1978.[1] However, a determined search in the papers of leading politicians of the 1782-1800 period for conclusive

168

evidence of the influence of such literature came up empty. The sources indicate that government and opposition were influenced by circumstances and arrangements peculiar to the parliamentary arena in which their most public relationship was normally conducted. They feared public opinion only in the armed form of the Volunteers (while they lasted) and even the patriot members failed to respond positively to popular manifestations — such as the mob incursion into the Commons in 1784 — except to make use of them in a crudely exploitive sense. Occasionally members would publish pamphlets espousing a cause but it is not clear that these were directed at a truly popular audience. Throughout the period the contending groups vied for the support of the country gentlemen; these were far more likely to have been the objects of members' literary endeavours. Elections were infrequent and in the intervals even the county members were not above affecting a certain deafness to their constituents' voices.[2] It cannot be doubted that the political literature of the day did have a genuine popular readership and it is equally certain that popular views were brought to the attention of individual members. But thereafter the connection failed. The achievements of 1782 did indeed reflect the opinions and demands set out by numerous anonymous or little-known pamphleteers. But a close examination of the political preliminaries to the settlement has revealed sets of motives none of which can be indisputably termed a response to public opinion. The same is true of the other political events of the 1780s and early '90s. Throughout these years the stock responses by both government and opposition to literary or mob manifestations was similar to those which prevailed earlier in the century: if the pamphlet was too outspoken the printer or the author (or both) would be prosecuted; if the people protested too loudly in the streets the militia was summoned. This had been the case with the fourth *Drapier's Letter* and with the unruly artisans in 1784. Petitions were taken up and cynically exploited by members if their sentiments could be of material assistance to the members' current political gambit, but otherwise would be left to "lie upon the table". Further studies of the supposed relationship between public opinion and government policy in regard to incidents of the early and mid-eighteenth century may well correct the generality of this conclusion; but with specific regard to the later decades of the century I believe it to be correct.

This leads us on to some concluding reflections on the *actual* determinants of political behaviour. The single most difficult problem in relation to the patriots' political behaviour is that of their motivation. It is perhaps doing them a great injustice to suggest that the men who laboured to achieve Irish legislative independence did so merely as the first step in a naked power struggle between them and the Castle; a struggle for possession of those high administrative offices which by their very nature formed an integral part of the executive power in Ireland. But uncritical acceptance of sentiments voiced in tactical debate has for too long formed the basis of historiographical conclusion with regard to this period. For two centuries historians have responded to the patriots with that unstinting credulity which the latter struggled for so many years and with so little success to elicit from the country gentlemen and "expectant" members of the Irish parliament.

Detailed examination of the patriots' interaction with each other and with the government between 1779 and 1782 has not substantiated but rather has shattered the illusion of comradeship and consistency with which that campaign has traditionally been interwoven. The struggle which ended with Grattan on 16 April 1782 had begun with Yelverton the elected leader of the only known extra-parliamentary patriot body of the period (the Monks of the Screw), of which Grattan was a mere member. While both men pursued separate aspects of the same settlement, neither aspect was complete in itself nor did they complement each other. Neither man lent unqualified support to the other while any hope remained that they could succeed separately. Even after their support had been put on a mutual footing the agreement was never other than tentative and temporary. At a critical stage in early December 1781 Yelverton preferred to deal with the chief secretary rather than to proceed by pure opposition.

The departure of the Irish and British administrations from the roles traditionally allotted them during the crisis was less total but was nonetheless devastating in its effect. North and his cabinet colleagues certainly lived up to their image as crotchety imperial governors doggedly defending the *ancien regime* in Ireland, as they saw it, by blunt and uniformed refusals to make even trivial concessions. It was, indeed, the cabinet's refusal to pay proper attention to the developing Irish crisis that facilitated the dramatic policy reversal by Carlisle and Eden in December 1781. It was not unknown (or indeed particularly unusual) for Irish administrators to take the initiative in policy matters. But it was quite unheard-of for that initiative to depart so radically from the known sentiments of the British cabinet as to amount to a reversal of a policy which had been pursued at least since 1720. The Irish government in 1781 was not overcome by the alleged spread of patriotism amongst the Irish members; it conceded voluntarily and apparently out of conviction. Similarly, the 1782 settlement was delivered ultimately not by an enlightened Whig government, but by a set of ministers harassed by lack of time, poor information, pressed by other urgent concerns, and at odds with each other.

The 16 April 1782 represented less a popular victory than the culmination of Eden's policy mingled with the ill-circumstanced ineptitude of Portland. It is not my intention to suggest that the patriots and the Volunteers were of no significance in the making of 1782 but rather that without the government manoeuvre of 3 December 1781 their impact would have been considerably less. The constitution of 1782 was primarily the product of government policy and a set of political circumstances over which neither the patriots nor the Volunteers had any direct control.

The commercial propositions affair and the Regency Crisis represented attempts by one (or more) of the participants in the new power-sharing experiment to reinterpret the conditions created by the 1782 settlement in a manner which would result in a further shift of legislative power in that participant's favour. In the case of the commercial propositions both the Dublin and London administrations co-operated in an effort to obtain from the Irish parliament agreement to a commerce-based treaty. The significance of the propositions as a factor intended to transform the relationship between the two kingdoms lay not in their individual financial provisions but in their collectivity, the nature of which seemed to imply a fresh interpretation of the role of each participant in the making of Irish policy — an interpretation which was seen to conflict with that set down by the 1782 settlement. The conflict of interpretations lay not in the letter but rather in the spirit of the propositions. Hence their impact (had they been successful) would have been psychological rather than actual. That the advantage sought by the London administration (which was more active on this occasion than its partner in Dublin) was psychological rather than actual suggests that *actual* legislative superiority was not a primary motivating factor in William Pitt's conception of the inter-regnal relationship. The ultimate rejection of the propositions by the members of the Irish parliament stemmed from their recognition that the interpretations were in conflict and from their consequent refusal to acquiesce in the loss of an advantage which they also recognised to be primarily psychological.

The propositions represented Pitt's effort to secure the consent of the Irish parliament to the withdrawal of political recognition in return for a more generous measure of recognition of English-"Irish" equality on the economic level. That he failed was due to the conviction of the Irish members that their security for such recognition of such equality as had been given them by England on the economic level (i.e. in 1779-80) was dependent on the co-existence of their recognised political equality. A further reason underlying the failure was that Pitt's motives in suggesting the agreement were not in accord. At one level (the commercial) he wished to raise England's recognition of its economic relationship with Ireland from subordination to equality. But on the political level he wished to lower England's recognition of its relationship with Ireland from the equality agreed upon in 1782 to one of subordination. This conflict of motives itself stemmed from the British government's failure to view its connection with Ireland in other than monolithic terms, whereas the Anglo-Irish community tended to see the connection in a pluralist, multi-faceted sense. To the British government there seemed no reason why a largely-implicit measure of political subordination could not be exchanged for a tangible and substantial measure of economic equality. To the Irish the two levels of experience were interdependent and inseparable.

In the more immediate sense the propositions may have failed because the manner of their treatment fell into a rather unfortunate pattern. Firstly, they were introduced and passed in the Irish parliament. Secondly, they were duly transmitted to England for ratification by the British parliament. Thirdly, the propositions were (as it seemed) subjected to substantial alterations in Britain. Fourthly, the "altered" propositions were returned to the Irish parliament for acceptance or rejection and in circumstances which suggested that no further alterations could be made. The similarities between this pattern and the system which had prevailed before the 1782 settlement seem not to have been commented on at the time, but must have been blatantly obvious.

A point of importance shared by the Regency Crisis and the Fitzwilliam affair was the revelation of how the Irish opposition might have behaved once power was in their hands. The duration of both incidents was too brief to afford us more than a fleeting glimpse of what the "alternative" 1790s might have held in store. But the glimpse revealed the opposition to be slow in putting into practice the policies they had avowed in days of powerlessness, and swift to wreak revenge upon their opponents of those days. However, the disturbing illusion that the battle was for possession of Castle offices obscures two important realities. Firstly, the object of the battle for Castle positions was not simply about the personal security and well-being of the victors. It had become increasingly clear that the men who controlled enough patronage to negotiate *effectively* with the "expectant" members of the Irish parliament were also the men who controlled the exercise of legislative power in Ireland. It was for this "effectiveness" that the opposition struggled. Secondly, it is an unsubtle but all-too-true comment upon the nature of "power" that those who do not obtain it can never hope to benefit from its exercise. Patriot policies, however sincere the feelings which may have underlain them, had to be moulded into political weapons and used accordingly in order that the power to realise those policies might be obtained.

It is difficult not to detect a fundamental cleavage between the

172

intentions, motives, and even the identities of the patriots who were once Monks of the Screw, and those of the great interests who later joined the patriots to form the Whig Club. It is perhaps over-simplistic to portray the distinction as one between patriots who regarded themselves as Irishmen with exclusively Irish interests, and "Irish Whigs" who viewed themselves as Englishmen with Irish interests. Coming so soon after the 1798 rebellion, the behaviour of individual patriots and Whigs during the union debates cannot be considered as a manifestation of true feelings or beliefs. It is worth remembering that although Leinster and Shannon deserted the Whig Club in the mid-1790s, the Ponsonbys stayed with the patriots to the end. It is worth remembering that a number of patriots, including Grattan, thought it no "betrayal of self" or betrayal of their country to continued their struggles in a United Parliament.

Appendixes

Appendix 1

Heads of Irish Bills suppressed by the Irish and British Privy Councils,
1773-82

Year	Total number of Heads considered	Heads suppressed by councils	
		Irish	British
1773-4	67	7	6
1775-6	48	10	4
1777-8	58	7	1
1779-80	63	5	4
1781-2	90	1	0

Heads of Bills "respited" by British Privy Council:

1773-4	A bill for the better securing the liberty of the subject A bill for amending public roads A bill to regulate the trials of peers A bill for quieting titles and possessions
1775-6	A bill for the further promotion of trade Judges Commission bill Barrack bill A bill for establishing a militia
1777-8	A bill for paving and lighting the city of Dublin
1779-80	A bill for the general quiet of the subjects against all pretence of concealment whatsoever A bill to regulate partnerships and promote trade
1781-2	Nil

Heads of bills "postponed" by British Privy Council:

1773-4	A bill to prevent litigation amongst the poor A bill relative to tryals by *nisi prius*

1775-6	Nil
1777-8	Nil
1779-80	A bill for the better securing the liberty of the subject
	A bill for the making commissions of judges to continue *quam diu se bene gesserint*
1781-2	Nil

Appendix 2

Text of the Declaratory Act, 1720

An act for the better securing the dependency of the kingdom of Ireland on the crown of Great Britain:

Whereas the House of Lords of Ireland have of late, against law, assumed to themselves a power of jurisdiction to examine, correct and amend the judgments and decrees of the courts of justice in the kingdom of Ireland; ... be it declared ... that the said kingdom of Ireland hath been, is and of right ought to be, subordinate unto and dependent upon the imperial crown of Great Britain, as being inseparably united and annexed thereunto, and that the king's majesty, by and with the advice and consent of the Lords spiritual and temporal, and Commons of Great Britain in parliament assembled, had hath, and of right ought to have full power and authority to make laws and statutes of sufficient force and validity to bind the kingdom and the people of Ireland.

And be it further enacted and declared ... that the House of Lords have not, nor of right ought to have, any jurisdiction to judge of, affirm or reverse any judgment, sentence or decree, given or made in any court within the said kingdom, and that all proceedings before the said House of Lords, upon any such judgment, sentence or decree, are, and are hereby declared to be utterly null and void to all intents and purposes whatsoever.

Text of the Repeal of the Declaratory Act, 1782

An act to repeal an act, made in the sixth year of his late majesty King George the first, entitled, an act for better securing the dependency of the kingdom of Ireland upon the crown of Great Britain:

Whereas an act was passed in the sixth year of his late majesty King George the first, entitled, *An act for the better securing the dependency of the kingdom of Ireland upon the crown of Great Britain,* ... be it enacted ... that from and after the passing of this act, the above-mentioned act, and the several matters and things therein contained, shall be, and is, and are hereby repealed.

176

An act to regulate the manner of passing bills, and to prevent delays in summoning of parliament:

Whereas it is expedient to regulate the manner of passing bills in this kingdom, be it enacted by the king's most excellent majesty, by and with the advice and consent of the lords spiritual and temporal and the Commons in this present parliament assembled, and by the authority of the same, That the lord lieutenant, or other chief governor or governors and council of this kingdom, for the time being, do and shall certify all such bills, and none other, as both houses of parliament shall judge expedient to be enacted in this kingdom, to his Majesty, his heirs and successors, under the great seal of this kingdom, without addition, diminution, or alteration.

And be it further enacted by the authority aforesaid, That all such bills as shall be certified to his Majesty, his heirs and successors, under the great seal of this kingdom, and returned into the same under the great seal of Great Britain, without addition, diminution, or alteration, and none other shall pass in the parliament in this kingdom; any former law, statute, or usage to the contrary thereof in any wise notwithstanding.

And be it further enacted, That no bill shall be certified into Great Britain, as a cause or consideration for holding a parliament in this kingdom, but that parliaments may be holden in this kingdom, although no such bill shall have been certified previous to the meeting thereof.

Provided always, That no parliament shall be holden in this kingdom until a license for that purpose shall be first had and obtained from his Majesty, his heirs and successors, under the seal of Great Britain.

Appendix 3

An act for extending certain of the provisions contained in an act entitled, An act confirming all the statutes made in England:

Whereas by an act of parliament made in this kingdom in the tenth year of the reign of his late Majesty King Henry the seventh, entitled, *An act for confirming all the statutes made in England,* all such statutes therefore made in England, as concerned the common weal of the realm were confirmed in this kingdom: and whereas after that time, and particularly upon occasion of the rebellions which subsisted in this kingdom in the years one thousand six hundred and forty-one, and one thousand six hundred and eighty-eight, divers statutes were made in the parliament of England, and since the union in the parliament of Great Britain, for settling and assuring the forfeited and other estates in this kingdom, and for the regulation of trade, and other purposes: and whereas it is at all times expedient to give every assurance, and to remove every apprehension concerning the titles of lands: and whereas it is the earnest and most affectionate desire, as well as the true interest of your Majesty's subjects in this kingdom to promote, as far as in them lies, the navigation, trade and commercial interests of Great Britain as well as Ireland; and whereas a similarity of laws, manners, and customs, must naturally conduce to strengthen and perpetuate that affection and harmony which do, and at all times ought to subsist between the people of Great Britain and Ireland: be it enacted by the King's most excellent Majesty, by and with the advice and consent of the lords spiritual and temporal, and commons in this present parliament assembled, and by the authority of the same, That all statutes heretofore made in England or Great Britain, for the settling and assuring the forfeited estates in this kingdom, and also all private statutes made in England or Great Britain, under which any lands, tenements, or hereditiments in this kingdom, or any estate or interest therein, are, or is holden or claimed, or which any way concern the title thereto, or any evidence respecting the same; and also all such clauses and provisions contained in any statutes made as aforesaid, in England or Great Britain concerning commerce, as import to impose equal restraints on the subjects of England and Ireland, or of Great Britain and Ireland, and to entitle them to equal benefits; and also all such clauses and provisions contained in any statutes made as aforesaid, and equally concerning the seamen of England and Ireland, or of Great Britain and Ireland, save so far as the same have been altered or repealed, shall be accepted, used, and executed in this kingdom, according to the present tenor thereof respectively.

Provided always, That all such statutes, so far as aforesaid, concerning commerce, shall bind the subjects of Ireland only, so long as they continue to bind the subjects of Great Britain.

And be it further enacted by the authority aforesaid, That all such statutes made in England or Great Britain, as concern the style or calendar, and also all such clauses and provisions contained in any statutes made as aforesaid, as relate to the taking any oath or oaths, or making or subscribing any declaration or affirmation in this kingdom, or any penalty or disability for omitting the same, or relate to the continuance of any office, civil or military, or of any commission, or of any writ, process, or proceeding at law or in equity, or in any court of delagacy or review, in case of a demise of the crown, shall be accepted, used, and executed in this kingdom, according to the present tenor of the same respectively.

Appendix 4

Text of the commercial resolutions as presented to the Irish Commons on 7 February 1785

1. That it is the opinion of this committee, that it is highly important to the general interest of the British empire that the trade between Great Britain and Ireland be encouraged and extended as much as

possible; and for that purpose, that intercourse and commerce be finally settled and regulated on permanent and equitable principles, for the mutual benefit of both countries.

2. That it is the opinion of this committee, that towards carrying into full effect so desirable a settlement, it is fit and proper that all articles, not the growth and manufacture of Great Britain or Ireland, should be imported into each kingdom from the other reciprocally, under the same regulations, and at the same duties, if subject to duties, to which they are liable when imported directly from the place of their growth, product or manufacture; and that all duties originally paid on importation into either country respectively, shall be full drawn back on exportation to the other.

3. That it is the opinion of this committee, that for the same purpose it is proper that no prohibition should exist in either country against the importation, use or sale of any article, the growth, product or manufacture of the other; and that the duty on the importation of every such article, if subject to duty in either country, should be precisely the same in one country as in the other, except where an addition may be necessary in either country, in consequence of an internal duty on any such article of its own consumption.

4. That it is the opinion of this committee, that in all cases where the duties on articles of the growth, product or manufacture of either country are different on the importation into the other, it would be expedient that they should be reduced in the kingdom where they are highest to the amount payable in the other; and that all such articles should be exported from the kingdom into which they shall be imported as free from duty as the similar commodities or manufacture of the same kingdom.

5. That it is the opinion of this committee, that for the same purpose it is also proper that in all cases where either kingdom shall charge articles of its own consumption with an internal duty on the manufacture, or a duty on the material, the same manufacture, when imported from the other, may be charged with a farther duty on importation to the same amount as the internal duty on the manufacture, or to an adequate to countervail the duty on the material; and shall be entitled to such drawbacks or bounties on exportation as may leave the same subject to no heavier burden than the home-made manufacture; such farther duty to continue so long only as the internal consumption shall be charged with the duty or duties to balance which it shall be imposed, or until the manufacture coming from the other kingdom shall be subjected there to an equal burden, not drawn back or compensated on exportation.

6. That it is the opinion of this committee, that in order to give permanency to the settlement now intended to be

established, it is necessary that no prohibition, or new or additional duties, should be hereafter imposed in either kingdom on the importation of any article of the growth, product or manufacture of the other; except such additional duties as may be requisite to balance duties on internal consumption, pursuant to the foregoing resolution.

7. That it is the opinion of this committee, that for the same purpose it is necessary farther, that no prohibitions, or new or additional duties, should be hereafter imposed in either kingdom on the exportation of any article of native growth, product or manufacture, from thence to the other, except such as either kingdom may deem expedient from time to time upon corn, meal, malt, flour and biscuit; and also except where there now exists any prohibition which is not reciprocal, or any duty which is not equal in both kingdoms, in every which case the prohibition may be made reciprocal, or the duties raised so as to make them equal.

8. That it is the opinion of this committee, that for the same purpose it be necessary that no bounties whatsoever should be paid or payable in either kingdom on the exportation of any article to the other, except such as relate to corn, meal, malt, flour and biscuit, and such as are in the nature of drawbacks, or compensation for duties paid; and that no bounty should be granted in this kingdom on the exportation of any article imported from the British plantations, or any manufacture made of such article, unless in cases where a similar bounty is payable in Britain on exportation from thence, or where such bounty is merely in the nature of a drawback, or compensation of, or for duties paid and above any duties paid thereon in Britain.

9. That it is the opinion of this committee, that it is expedient, for the general benefit of the British empire, that the importation of articles from foreign states should be regulated from time to time in each kingdom, on such terms as may afford an effectual preference to the importation of smaller articles of the growth, product or manufacture of the other.

10. That it is the opinion of this committee, that for the protection of trade, whatever sum the gross hereditary revenue of this kingdom (after deducting all drawbacks, repayments, or bounties granted in the nature of drawbacks) shall produce annually, over and above the sum of £[not initially specified], should be appropriated towards the support of the naval force of the empire, in such manner as the parliament of this kingdom shall direct.

Appendix 5

Text of the fourth and twentieth commercial propositions as agreed to by both Houses of the British parliament on 18 July 1785

4. That it is highly important to the general interests of the British empire, that the laws for regulating trade and navigation should be the same in Great Britain and Ireland; and therefore that it it essential, towards carrying into effect the present settlement, that all laws which have been made, in Great Britain, for securing exclusive privileges to the ships and mariners of Great Britain, Ireland, and the British colonies and plantations, and for regulating and restraining the trade of the British colonies and plantations (such laws imposing the same restraints, and conferring the same benefits, on the subjects of both kingdoms), should be in force in Ireland, by laws to be passed in the parliament of that kingdom, for the same time, and in the same manner, as in Great Britain.

20. That the appropriation of whatever sum the gross hereditary revenue of the kingdom of Ireland (the due collection thereof being secured by permanent provisions) shall produce, after deducting all drawbacks, repayments, or bounties, granted in the nature of drawbacks, over and above the sum of £650,000, in each year, towards the support of the naval force of the empire, to be applied in such manner as the parliament of Ireland shall direct, by an act to be passed for that purpose, will be a satisfactory provision, proportioned to the growing prosperity of that kingdom, towards defraying, in time of peace, the necessary expenses of protecting the trade and general interests of the empire.

Appendix 6

Members of the Irish House of Commons who were also "Monks of the Screw"

Barry Yelverton
Arthur Browne
Denis Daly
Henry Duquery
Francis Hardy
Dudley Hussey
Sir Edward Newenham
George Ponsonby
Charles Francis Sheridan
Lord Viscount Kingsborough
W. Tankerville Chamberlayne

John Philpot Curran
Walter Hussey Burgh
Robert Day
John Forbes
Sir Henry Hartstonge
Richard Martin
George Ogle
Arthur Wolfe

Robert Johnson
Isaac Corry
John Doyle
Henry Grattan
Richard Herbert
Peter Metge
Charles O'Neill
Sir Michael Smith

Appendix 7

The "less than reliable" supporters of opposition in 1791

H. Alcock
T. Bligh
H. Cane
N. Clements
A. French (Jnr.)
G. Hatton
W. Knott
C.J. Moore
Sir W.G. Newcomen
C.B. Ponsonby
F. Saunderson
C. Stewart
N. Westby

Sir J. Blackwood
J. Bourke
R.S. Carew
E. Cooper
J. Finlay
G. Jackson
W. Lackey
A. Montgomery
W.M. Ogle
W. Richardson
R. Sheridan
B. Stratford

J. Blennerhasset
H.V. Brooke
J. Chetwood
W. Flood
H. Harman
E. King
C.P. Leslie
G. Montgomery
C. O'Hara
W.P. Ruxton
H. St. G. Smyth
E. Tighe

Notes and References

Introduction

1 J.C. Beckett, "Anglo-Irish constitutional relations in the later eighteenth century", in Beckett, *Confrontations* (1972), 123.

2 J.R. Fisher, *The end of the Irish parliament* (1911); Sir James O'Connor, *History of Ireland 1798-1924*, Vol. 1 (1925); M. McDonnell Bodkin, *Grattan's Parliament: before and after* (1912).

3 Patrick Rogers, *The Irish Volunteers and Catholic Emancipation* (1934); Rosamund Jacob, *The rise of the United Irishmen 1791-4* (1937).

4 T.M. O'Connor, "The more immediate effects of the American Revolution on Ireland, 1775-85" (unpub. M.A. thesis, Queen's University, Belfast, 1938); M.E. Clune, "The Irish parliament, 1776-83" (unpub. M.A. thesis, University College, Dublin, 1943); T.V. O'Neill, "The Irish parliament 1798-1800" (unpub. M.A. thesis, University College, Dublin, 1943).

5 R.B. McDowell, *Irish Public Opinion, 1750-1800* (1944).

6 Solid evidence of the extent to which this attitude prevailed may be found in the Irish government's refusal to preserve intact the relics of Grattan's life and career. The contents of his home in County Wicklow were auctioned in October 1943 and scattered. In may cases the items were disposed of for mere pittances. See *Irish Press* of 14 October 1943 for details.

7 Sir Henry McNally, *The Irish Militia 1793-1816* (1949); T.H.D. Mahony, *Edmund Burke and Ireland* (1960); Brian Fitzgerald, *Emily, Duchess of Leinster, 1731-1814* (1949), and *Lady Louisa Conolly, 1743-1821* (1950); S. Gwynn, *Henry Grattan and his times* (1939); J.A.G. Whitlaw, "Anglo-Irish commercial relations, 1779-85" (unpub. M.A. thesis, Queen's University, Belfast, 1958).

8 M.R. O'Connell, *Irish politics and social conflict in the age of the American Revolution* (Philadelphia, 1965).

9 E.M. Johnston, *Great Britain and Ireland, 1760-1800* (Edinburgh, 1963).

10 Beckett in *Confrontations* (the paper was originally published in *Irish Historical Studies* in 1964).

11 G.C. Bolton, *The passing of the Irish Act of Union* (Oxford, 1966); A.P.W. Malcomson, *John Foster; the politics of the Anglo-Irish ascendancy* (Oxford, 1978).

12 This was the conclusion reached by Richard Koebner, "The early speeches of Henry Grattan", in *Bulletin of the Institute of Historical Research*, Vol. 30, 1957. My more reserved views may be found in "The Grattan Mystique", *Eighteenth-Century Ireland*, Vol. I, 1986.

Chapter 1

1 J.G. Simms, *The Treaty of Limerick (Dundalk, 1966)*, 14; *J.G. Simms, The Williamite Confiscation, 1691-1703*, 62.

2 Simms, *Williamite Confiscation*, 60.

3 ibid., 62-3.

4 It will be obvious from this that I don't accept as adequate the explanation

put forward by James Maguire, "The Irish Parliament of 1692", in T. Bartlett and D.W. Hayton (eds.), *Penal Era and Golden Age*, 3.

5   J.L. McCracken, *The Irish Parliament in the eighteenth century* (Dundalk, 1971), 5.

6   Maguire, "Irish Parliament of 1692", 11.

7   ibid., 17.

8   ibid., 20.

9   Isolde L. Victory, "Colonial Nationalism in Ireland, 1692-1725: From Common Law to Natural Right" (unpub. Ph.D. thesis, Trinity College, Dublin, 1985), 15-16.

10 Maguire, "Irish Parliament of 1692", 24-5.

11 This incident may have been the origin of the dispute over judges' tenure which is dealt with in Chapter 2.

12 Victory, "Colonial Nationalism", 21-2, 24-5.

13 T.W. Moody and W.E. Vaughan (eds.), *A New History of Ireland, IV: Eighteenth-Century Ireland* (Oxford, 1986), 14.

14 ibid., 14-15.

15 F.G. James, *Ireland in the Empire, 1688-1770* (Harvard, 1973), 82.

16 Victory, "Colonial Nationalism", 79-121; *New History*, p 11. For interesting echoes of the 1709 affair see Chapter 3.

17 James, *Ireland in the Empire*, 99-101.

18 Joseph Griffin, "Parliamentary Politics in Ireland during the reign of George I" (unpub. M.A. thesis, University College, Dublin, 1977), 179.

19 ibid., 182.

20 James, *Ireland in the Empire*, 101-7.

21 Michael Ryder, "The Bank of Ireland, 1721: Land, Credit and Dependency", *Historical Journal*, Vol. 25, No. 3, 1982.

22 *New History*, 111-14; Victory, "Colonial Nationalism", 190-221.

23 *New History*, 114; James, *Ireland in the Empire*, characterised the period as "Hibernia non movere".

24 *New History*, 62-3, 114-18.

25 J.C. Sainty, "The Secretariat of the Chief Governors of Ireland, 1690-1800", in *Proceedings of the Royal Irish Academy*, Vol. 77. No. 1, 1977, 14.

26 See Declan O'Donovan, "The Money Bill Dispute of 1753" in *Penal Era* for an expert critique of this incident.

27 Thomas Bartlett, "The Townshend Viceroyalty, 1767-72" in *Penal Era*, 109.

28 David Lammey, "Anglo-Irish relations between 1772 and 1782, with particular reference to the Free Trade dispute" (unpub. Ph.D. thesis, Queen's University, Belfast, 1984), 55.

Chapter 2

1   I am indebted to Prof. R.B. McDowell for his guidance in this matter.

2   Lists of Irish bills which indicate the various stages of their progress in England have survived for the period 1773 to 1798 in P.R.O., P.C.1/43/A148. See Appendix 1.

3   *Commons Journals (Ireland)*, 1773, pp 63, 75, 118; 1775-6, pp 225, 227, 244-5, 248-9, 252-3; 1777-8, p 498.

4   ibid., 1775-6, 278; 1777-8, 468.

5   Lord President to Duke of Bedford (Ld. Lieut.), 3 Feb. 1758, P.C.1/31/78.

6   Granville (Ld. President) to Bedford, 1 April 1758, P.C.1/31/78.

7   Granville to Bedford, 14 April 1758, P.C.1/31/78.

8   Ld. Pres. to Ld. Lieut., 1 May 1760, P.C.1/31/78.

9   Winchilsea to Ld. Lieut., 19 April 1766, P.C.1/31/78.

10 Ld. Pres. to Bedford, 25 March 1760, P.C.1/31/78.

11 Ld. Pres. to Ld. Lieut., 1 May 1760, P.C.1/31/78.
12 Ld. Pres. to Halifax, 6 April 1762, P.C.1/31/78.
13 Ld. Pres. to Hertford, 14 May 1766, P.C.1/31/78.
14 ibid.
15 Gower to Townshend, 2 May 1771; Ld. Pres. to Hertford, 14 May 1766, P.C.1/31/78.
16 Ld. Pres. to Ld. Lieut., 13 Dec. 1765, P.C.1/31/78.
17 Ld. Pres. to Hertford, 14 May 1766, P.C.1/31/78.
18 Ld. Pres. to Buckinghamshire, 12 June 1778, P.C.1/31/78.
19 [Ld. Pres.] to Ld. Lieut., 7 Dec. 1759; Granville to Ld. Lieut., 5 Dec. 1761; Winchilsea to Hertford, 10 Dec. 1765, P.C.1/31/78.
20 ibid., 10 Dec. 1765.
21 J.C. Beckett and A.G. Donaldson, "The Irish parliament in the eighteenth century", *Proceedings of the Belfast Natural History and Philosophical Society*, second series, IV, 1951, 30.
22 ibid., 32-7.
23 A.G. Donaldson, "The Application in Ireland of English and British Legislation made before 1801" (unpub. Ph.D. thesis, Queen's University, Belfast, 1952), 220-1, 234, 250-1.
24 See James, *Ireland in the Empire*, chapter iv and *passim*.
25 Beresford to Robinson, 22 Nov. 1779, W. Beresford (ed.), *The Correspondence of the Rt. Hon. John Beresford* (1854), Vol. I, 87-8.
26 Sir J. Irwine to Germain, 8 Dec. 1779, *H.M.C. Stopford-Sackville MSS*, Vol. I, 263.
27 Waite to Germain, 13th Dec. 1779, ibid., I, 263-4.
28 Reports of the 1779-80 debates used here are taken from R.V. Callen, "The Structure of Anglo-Irish Politics during the American Revolution: Cavendish's Diary of the Irish Parliament, October 12, 1779 to September 2, 1780; Edition of the Partial Text and a Critical Essay" (unpub. Ph.D. thesis, Notre Dame, 1973), pp 340, 362, 337-8.
29 ?[Dublin] to North, 9th Jan. 1780, *H.M.C. Abergavenny MSS*, 27-8.
30 Buckinghamshire to Hillsborough, 10 Feb. 1780, P.R.O., S.P. 63/468, f 221.
31 Callen, 263-4.
32 Beckett and Donaldson, 34-6.
33 G.J. Hand, "The Constitutional Position of the Irish Military Establishment from the Restoration to the Union: An Introductory Note", *Irish Jurist*, iii, 1968, 332.
34 Lois G. Schwoerer, *No Standing Armies* (Baltimore, 1974), 190.
35 G.O. Sayles, "Contemporary Sketches of the Members of the Irish Parliament in 1782", *Proc. of the Royal Irish Academy*, Vol. 56, No. 3, 1954, 285.
36 Buckinghamshire to Hillsborough, 17 Feb. 1780; Hillsborough to Buckinghamshire, 22 Feb. 1780, quoted in Henry Grattan (Jnr.), *Memoirs of the Life anf Times of the Rt. Hon. Henry Grattan* (1839), Vol. II, 20-2. The bill "was received with general dissatisfaction"; see Buckinghamshire to Hillsborough, 21st Feb. 1780, S.P. 63/468, f 288.
37 Buckinghamshire to Hillsborough, 19 April 1780, S.P. 63/469, ff 101-2; quoted in *Grattan*, II, 45-7. For Carysfort's role see Buckinghamshire to Hillsborough, 2 March 1780, S.P.63/468, ff 332-3.
38 Lieut. Gen. Cunninghame to Germain, 20 April 1780, *H.M.C. Stopford-Sackville MSS*, 269-70; Lifford to [Buckinghamshire], 29 April 1780, S.P. 63/469, ff 173-6.
39 Buckinghamshire to Hillsborough, 19 April 1780; Sir Richard Heron to Sir Stanier Porten, 8 April 1780, quoted in *Grattan*, II, 47, 71-3.
40 Buckinghamshire to Hillsborough, 22 April 1780, S.P. 63/469, ff 107-8, quoted in *Grattan*, II, 74.

41 Buckinghamshire to Hillsborough, 8, 21 May 1780, quoted in *Grattan*, II, 85-91.

42 Buckinghamshire to Hillsborough, 28 May 1780, quoted in ibid., 93-5.

43 *Debates in the House of Commons of Ireland on a Motion whether the King's most excellent Majesty, and the Lords and Commons of Ireland, are the only power competent to bind or enact laws in this kingdom. By a Gentleman* (Dublin, 1780), 7-9, 20, 25.

44 Carysfort to Charlemont, 10 July 1780, *H.M.C. Charlemont MSS*, Vol. I, 374; Heron to Porten, 11 July 1780, S.P. 63/470, f 81.

45 *Grattan*, II, 98; Malcomson, *Foster*, 44.

46 Heron to Porten, 9 August 1780, quoted in *Grattan*, II, 99-100, 125-6; Buckinghamshire to Hillsborough, 17 August 1780, S.P. 63/470, f 267.

47 H. Grattan, *Observations on the Mutiny Bill* (Dublin and London, 1781), 29-30, 11, 13-14, 19, 13, 19-20, 31.

48 *The Parliamentary Register, or History of the Proceedings and Debates of the House of Commons of Ireland, 1781-97* (Dublin, 1782-1801), Vol. I, 52, 69, 55-7, 60 78-9, 113-20; Carlisle to Hillsborough, 14 Nov. 1781, 63/477, ff 80-1.

49 M.R. O'Connell, *Irish Politics*, 219-23, 247-8.

50 ibid., 248.

51 Buckinghamshire to Hillsborough, 26 Jan. 1780, S.P. 63/468, f 110.

52 *Parl. Reg.*, I, 135-53.

53 [Eden] to Hillsborough, 15 Sept. 1781, B.L. Add. MS. 34, 418 (Auckland Papers), ff 103-4.

54 *Grattan*, I, 136n tells of Grattan's reaction to a speech at the Temple by George Grenville in 1769 on Britain's "indisputable" right to tax America: "It impressed on my mind a horror of this doctrine; and I believe it was owing to this speech of George Grenville's, that I became afterwards so very active in my opposition to the principles of British government in Ireland".

55 *Baratariana* (Dublin, 1777 edition), 43-4.

56 ibid., 41.

57 ibid., 225-6. Yelverton's argument when the Poynings' Law issue was resurrected in October 1781 closely resembled that employed by Grattan and his co-authors almost a decade before, and was peculiar in that it identified the English privy council (especially the attorney-general) as the source of the evil: "at the present *our constitution* was the *constitution of England inverted*. Bills originated with the British minister and with this House it only remained to *register* or *reject* them". The sugar bill was cited as an example of the misuse of the power of altering bills. *Parl. Reg.*, I, 15.

58 Scott to Robinson, 13 Oct. 1779, *Beresford*, I, pp 63-4; see also the *D.N.B.* entry on Yelverton.

59 See note 29 above.

60 Buckinghamshire to Hillsborough, 17 Feb. 1780, S.P.63/468, ff 251-2.

61 Callen, p 323. The only lapse in this regard was necessarily the pretext stated for the demand for a short money bill on 19 Feb. See Sir James Caldwell to Germain, 19 April 1780, *H.M.C. Stopford-Sackville MSS*, p 268.

62 Buckinghamshire to Hillsborough, 21 April 1780, *Grattan*, II, 55.

63 Buckinghamshire to Hillsborough, 27 April 1780, S.P.63/469, f 135.

64 Buckinghamshire to Hillsborough, 29 April 1780, *Grattan*, II, 78-80; Raymond J. Barrett, "A Comparative Study of Imperial Constitutional Theory in Ireland and America in the Age of the American Revolution" (unpub. Ph.D. thesis, Trinity College, Dublin, 1958), 16-17.

65 Barrett, 157-8.

66 C.F. Sheridan, *Observations on the doctrine laid down by Sir William Blackstone*

respecting the extent of the power of the British Parliament, particularly with relation to Ireland (Dublin, 1779), 33-4.

67   *ibid.*, 34-6.
68   *ibid.*, 45-6.
69   *ibid.*, 48-9.
70   *ibid.*, 54-5.
71   *ibid.*, 56-7.
72   *ibid.*, 62.
73   *ibid.*, 64.
74   *ibid.*, 65n.
75   *ibid.*, 66, 70-1.
76   *ibid.*, 82.
77   [C.F. Sheridan], *A Review of the Three Great National Questions relative to a Declaration of Right, Poynings's Law, and the Mutiny Bill* (Dublin and London, 1781). In a letter to Eden dated 14 May 1781 Isaac Corry explains that although Sheridan had been brought into parliament by Lord Muskerry, he no longer felt obliged to follow Muskerry's lead once the latter had been raised to the peerage. Corry is clearly seeking some government favour for Sheridan: "I have always known him to be a warm supporter of the party he sincerely espouses, and a man of principle". Eden's reply was non-committal. B.L. Add. MS. 34,417 (Auckland Papers), ff 347-8.
78   [Sheridan], *Review*, p 29.
79   *ibid.*, 37.
80   *ibid.*, 61.
81   *ibid.*, 63.
82   *ibid.*, 67-8.
83   *Parl. Reg.*, I, 182.
84   For two conflicting views of this phenomenon, see A. Aspinall, "The Cabinet Council, 1783-1835", *Proc. of the British Academy*, xxxviii, 1952, pp 237-42, and I.R. Christie, "The Cabinet in the reign of George III to 1790" in *Myth and Reality in late eighteenth-century British politics* (Berkeley and Los Angeles, 1970), 84 and *passim*.
85   *Baratariana*, 225-6; [Sheridan], *Review*, 63; see note 56 above.
86   William Jephson to Flood, 12 Feb. 1780, P.R.O.N.I., Rosse Papers, C/1/14: "The most that can be done by the moderate party (my party) is to retain that part of it [Poynings' Law] which gives the King and Council of England a power altering, etc.; but the other part, which relates to the interference of the Council of Ireland, will and ought to be destroyed".
87   See E.M. Johnston, *Great Britain and Ireland*, pp 89-103, for an account of the roles of the two privy councils.
88   *Parl. Reg.*, I, 187.
89   *ibid.*, 268-9, 278, 279, 283.
90   *ibid.*, 316-17; Donaldson, 256-76.
91   *Parl. Reg.*, I, 266-9.
92   *ibid.*, 333-46. *Speeches of the Rt. Hon. Henry Grattan, with prefatory observations* (Dublin, 1811), lxxxi-xc.
93   Parl. Reg., I, 329.
94   R.B. McDowell, *Ireland in the Age*, 270.
95   Pery to Buckinghamshire, 28 March 1780, *H.M.C. Emly MSS*, p 157.
96   *Grattan*, II, 20-2.
97   Buckinghamshire to Germain, 5 Feb. 1780, *H.M.C. Stopford-Sackville MSS*, 266-7.
98   Hillsborough to Buckinghamshire, 28 March 1780, *Grattan*, II, 30-1.
99   Buckinghamshire to Hillsborough, 2 April, 21 May 1780, *ibid.*, pp 43-4, 90-1.

100   Beresford to Robinson, 14 March 1780, *Beresford*, I, 130.

101   Buckinghamshire to Germain, 22 April 1780, *H.M.C. Lothian MSS*, 363-4.

102   Callen, 267-8. Buckinghamshire to Germain, 2 March 1780, *Grattan*, II, 25-6. *Debates*, 12-13. I.R. Christie, *The end of North's ministry* (1958), 241-2.

103   Buckinghamshire to Germain, 5 Feb. 1780, *H.M.C. Stopford-Sackville MSS*, 266-7.

104   *Debates*, 20.

105   Burke to ? [ante 19 April 1780], J.A. Woods (ed.), *Correspondence of Edmund Burke*, IV (Cambridge and Chicago, 1963), 231.

106   *Debates*, 26.

107   *The Last Journals of Horace Walpole*, II p 305, tells of a cabinet disagreement on this issue: May 1780 - "The mutiny bill carried with a high hand in Ireland. The Chancellor firm against submitting to it. Wedderburn, probably in opposition to the Chancellor, for submitting to it. The Irish softened the preamble even beyond what they owned they meant, to keep some decency".

108   John, Bishop of Ossory [Dr. Hotham] to Germain, 26 August 1780, *H.M.C. Stopford-Sackville MSS*, 272; *Grattan*, II, 140-1.

109   North to George III, 5, 7, 18 Sept. 1780, J. Fortescue (ed.), *The Correspondence of King George III*, V (1928), 115, 117, 123; Hillsborough to Buckinghamshire, 14 Sept. 1780, *Grattan*, II, 139.

110   [Eden] to [North], 19 August [1780]; Carlisle to Eden, 19 August 1780; Loughborough to Eden, 27 August 1780; Eden to [North], [2 Sept. 1780]; Eden to North, 5 Sept. [1780]; Eden to North, 14 Sept. 1780, B.L. Add. MS. 34,417 (Auckland Papers), ff 134-6, 137, 147-8, 158, 174, 190.

111   Eden to Hillsborough, 15 Nov. 1780, ibid., ff 250-1.

112   Carlisle to Gower, 30 June 1781, *H.M.C. Carlisle MSS*, 509-10.

113   *ibid*. Also Carlisle to Hillsborough, 10 Nov. 1781, S.P. 63/477, ff 76-7.

114   Carlisle to Gower, 11 Oct. 1781, *ibid*., 521.

115   Eden to [Loughborough?], 19 July [1781], B.L. Add. MS. 34, 417 (Auckland Papers), ff 396-7.

116   [Carlisle] to Hillsborough, 15 Sept. 1781, B.L. Add. MS. 34, 418, ff 103-6.

117   [Carlisle] to Hillsborough, ibid. Also Hillsborough to Carlisle, 21 Oct. 1781, S.P.63/476, ff 275-6.

118   Hillsborough to Carlisle, 29 Sept. 1781, B.L. Add. MS. 34,418, ff 124-5. See also S.P.63/476, ff 180-3.

119   See Appendix 3.

120   *Parl. Reg.*, I, 124-34.

121   [Carlisle] to Hillsborough, 10 Nov. 1781, B.L. Add. MS. 34,418, f 164.

122   Eden to [Hillsborough], 5 Dec. 1781, ibid., f 203. Carlisle to Hillsborough, 5 Dec. 1781, S.P.63/477, ff 159, 165 (two letters).

123   [Eden] to Hillsborough, [3 Dec. 1781], B.L. Add. MS. 34,418, f 228.

124   Hillsborough to Carlisle, 3 Dec. 1781, ibid., ff 199-200. See also S.P.63/477, f 134.

125   Adam Ferguson to [Eden], 3 Jan. 1780, B.L. Add. MS. 34,417, f 11.

126   [Carlisle] to Hillsborough, 10 Nov. 1781; Eden to North, 23 Nov. 1781; Eden to]Hillsborough], 23 Nov. 1781; Eden to [Loughborough], 24 Nov. 1781, B.L. Add. MS. 34,418, ff 163-4, 182, 184, 187.

127   Christie, *End of North's ministry*, 276-7.

128   Eden to Col. Ross [early March 1782 - this letter has been misdated Dec. 1781], B.L. Add. MS. 34,418, f 204.

129   *Parl. Reg.*, I, 266-78, 306-7, 312-13, 316-19.

130   Carlisle to Hillsborough, 3 March 1782, S.P.63/480, ff 296-300; Eden to [Loughborough], 18 March 1782, B.L. Add. MS. 34,418, f 367.

131   Loughborough to Eden [early March 1782 - this letter has been misdated

Dec. 1781], B.L. Add. MS. 34,418, ff 206-7.

132 Hillsborough to Carlisle, 12 March 1782 (two letters); Hillsborough to [Eden], 12 March 1782; Cooke to Eden, 15 March 1782; Loughborough to Eden, 16 March [1782], B.L. Add. MS. 34,418 ff 347, 349, 350, 359, 361-2.

133 Carlisle to Hillsborough, 27 March 1782, S.P.63/480, f 426.

134 Much of the Irish material in Rockingham's papers at Sheffield City Library relates to this dispute. See also T.F. Moriarty, "The Irish absentee tax controversy of 1773: a study in Anglo-Irish politics on the eve of the American revolution", *American Philosophical Society Transactions*, cxviii, 1974, pp 370-408; and J.E. Tyler, "A letter from the Marquess of Rockingham to Sir William Mayne on the proposed absentee tax of 1773", *Irish Historical Studies*, viii, 1953, 364-9.

135 [Bristol] to [Rockingham], 24 Jan. [1778?], Sheffield City Library, Rockingham Papers, R.78/46.

136 Text of motion of 11 May 1779, S.C.L., Rockingham Papers, R.1020a.

137 Rockingham to [Denham?], 11 May 1779; William Denham to Rockingham, 17 May 1779; Rockingham to Denham, 26 May 1779, ibid., R1/1020b, R1/1021, R1/1022.

138 Rockingham to Keppel, [Nov. 1779], Earl of Albemarle, *Memoirs of the Marquis of Rockingham and his Contemporaries*, II (1852), pp 388-9.

139 *The Parliamentary History of England from the Norman Conquest to 1803* (1806-20), xx, 1156-78, 1197-1242; *Speeches of the Rt. Hon. Charles James Fox in the House of Commons*, I (1815), 211-21.

140 Shelburne to Rockingham [27th Nov. 1779], S.C.L., Rockingham Papers, R1/1217/55.

141 *Parl. Hist.*, xx, 1284-5.

142 Forbes to Adair, 6 Feb. 1780, B.L. Add. MS. 53,802 (Adair Papers), ff 1-3 (unbound).

143 ibid., ff 3-4, 6; see also Fox to Leinster, 4 Jan. 1780, *H.M.C. Charlemont MSS*, I, 369-70.

144 Richmond to Thomas Conolly, 23 Nov. 1780, A.G. Olsen, *The Radical Duke* (Oxford, 1961), pp 185-6.

145 *Parl. Hist.*, xxi, 1292.

146 *Speeches of Fox*, I, 308-16. Fox somewhat confusingly framed the latter objection as a motion to add a clause to the British act in order to counterbalance the omission of "Ireland".

147 Rockingham to George III, 1 April 1782, *Corr. of Geo.III*, V, 437. No mention of Ireland appears on the three sheets among the Rockingham Papers which set out briefly the stipulations put by the Marquis to the King before he agreed to take office. R1/1217/73, R1/1217/60, R166/40.

148 Charles Sheridan to R.B. Sheridan, 27 March 1782, T. Moore, *Memoirs of the Life of the Rt. Hon. R.B. Sheridan*, I (1825), 372.

149 H.M.C. Charlemont MSS, I, 58-9; *Grattan*, II, 226-7. The Irish parliament was in recess from 14 March to 14 April 1782.

150 Lord John Russell (ed.), *Memorials and Correspondence of Charles James Fox* (1853), I, 312.

151 Fitzpatrick to Grattan, 10 March 1785, *Grattan*, II, 277, 233-4.

152 The decision as to the use of the king's message may have been the outcome of the cabinet meeting on Ireland which took place on 8 April 1782; see C. Price (ed.), *The Letters of R.B. Sheridan* (Oxford, 1966), I, 142-3. *Speeches of Grattan* (1811 edition), lxxxviii.

153 *Parl. Reg.*, I, 341-4.

154 Portland to Shelburne, 16 April 1782, P.R.O., H.O. 100/1, ff 74-81.

155 Buckinghamshire to Germain, 31 August 1780, H.M.C. Stopford-Sackville

MSS, I, 274; *Grattan*, II, pp 148-9.
156 P.D.H. Smyth, "The Volunteers and Parliament, 1779-84", in *Penal Era*, 118.
157 *ibid.*, 119-20, 125.
158 Lucan to Pery, 3 April 1782, H.M.C. Emly MSS, 164.
159 Grattan to Robert Day, 11 May 1782, *Grattan*, II, 271.
160 Portland to Shelburne, 24 April 1782, H.O. 100/1, ff 133-9.
161 Fox to Fitzpatrick, 20 April 1782, B.L. Add. MS. 47,580 (Fox Papers), f 93.
162 Grattan to Fox, 18 April 1782, quoted in *Memorials of Fox*, I, p 404-9.
163 Portland to Fox, 28 April 1782, ibid., 415-16.
164   Fox to Fitzpatrick, 20 April 1782, B.L. Add. MS. 47,580 (Fox Papers),
     f 94; Portland to Shelburne, 6 May 1782, P.R.O., H.O. 100/1, ff 178-82.
165 Fox to Fitzpatrick, 11 May 1782, *Memorials of Fox*, I, 417-18.
166 Portland to Shelburne, 24 April 1782, quoted in Lord E. Fitzmaurice (ed.),
     *Life of William, Earl of Shelburne (1876), III, 141-2; Fitzpatrick to Fox, 17th
     April 1782, Memorials of Fox*, I, pp 398-9.
167 *Grattan*, II, 252. For evidence of Shelburne's awareness of Irish grievances
     see Fitzmaurice, 56-8.
168 Shelburne to Portland, 29 April 1782, Fitzmaurice, pp 144-5.
169 Portland to Shelburne, 6 May 1782, P.R.O., H.O. 100/1, ff 178-82.
170 Pery to Shelburne, 6 May 1782; Shelburne to Pery, 18 May 1782, H.M.C.
     Emly MSS, pp 166-7, 168.
171 Grattan to Day, 22 April 1782, *Grattan*, II, 249-52; Fitzmaurice, 146.
172 The Duke of Grafton was ill during the crucial week of 12 to 17 May, but
     recorded that the cabinet perused Portland's despatches informally on 24 April
     and in formal session the following day. His diary is amongst the Grafton
     Papers, West Suffolk Record Office, Bury St. Edmund, HA 513/4/3.
173 Shelburne to [Rockingham], Saturday [11 May 1782]; Portland to
     Rockingham, 11 May 1782, S.C.L. Rockingham Papers, R2/154, R1/1170.
     Shelburne to George III, 13 May 1782; Shelburne to George III, 14th May
     1782; George III to Shelburne, 14 May 1782; Minute of Cabinet, 15 May
     1782, Corr. of George III, VI, 16, 19, 21, 22, 23, 24. Present at the crucial
     cabinet meeting on 15 May were the Lord Chancellor, Lord President, Duke
     of Richmond, Rockingham, Lord Keppel, Lord Ashburton, General Conway,
     Lord John Cavendish, Fox, Shelburne.
174 Unless amongst the Shelburne Papers at Bowood, to which I was refused
     access.
175 *Speeches of Fox*, II, 60.
176 *ibid.*, 62.
177 *ibid.*, 64.
178 *ibid.*, 62, 63-4.
179 *ibid.*, 65.
180 *ibid.*
181 *Parl. Hist.*, xxiii, 39-43, 47.
182 *ibid.*, 43.
183 Sheridan to Fitzpatrick, 20 May 1782, Letters of Sheridan, I, 144.
184 Shelburne to Portland, 18 May 1782, P.R.O., H.O. 100/1, ff 213-22.
185 [Rockingham] to Portland, [25th May 1782]; [Rockingham] to Charlemont,
     17 June 1782, S.C.L., Rockingham Papers, R1/1177, R131/13.
186 Portland to Shelburne, 6 June 1782, P.R.O., H.O. 100/2, ff 34-5. This letter
     is misdated 6 July in *Grattan*, II, 291-2.
187 Shelburne to Portland, 9 June 1782, *Grattan*, II, 291-2.
188 Portland to Shelburne, 22 June 1782, ibid., 293-4. In 1800 Fitzpatrick told
     Grattan that William Ogilvie had been the author of the plan — Fitzpatrick
     to Grattan, 28 Jan. 1800, ibid., pp 297-8.

189 *Parl. Reg.*, I, 360, 390, 358. See also P. Jupp, "Earl Temple's Viceroyalty and the Question of Renunciation, 1782-3", *Irish Historical Studies*, xvii, 1971. Also P. Jupp, *Lord Grenville* (Oxford, 1985), 16-39.

Chapter 3

1 See A.S. Foord, "The Waning of 'The Influence of the Crown'", R. Mitchison (ed.), *Essays in Eighteenth-Century History* (1966), 171-94.

2 J. Ehrman, *The Younger Pitt: The Years of Acclaim* (1969), p 198; McDowell, *Ireland in the Age*, 330; for Smith's opinions on Ireland see I.A. Simpson (ed.), *The Correspondence of Adam Smith* (Oxford, 1977), 239-44.

3 Portland's abortive plan for a set of commissioners to fix the extent of Irish legislative independence was set out in an official despatch, P.R.O., H.O. 100/1, ff 178-82, to which Pitt would almost certainly have had access.

4 Rutland to Pitt, 15 August 1784, *Correspondence between the Rt. Hon. William Pitt and Charles Duke of Rutland* (1890), 36; Rutland to Pitt, 13 Sept. 1784, H.M.C. *Rutland*, III, 142.

5 Orde to Nepean, 24 April 1784, P.R.O., H.O. 100/12, ff 377-80; *Windham Papers* (1913), I, 37.

6 Rutland to Sydney, 14 May 1784, P.R.O., H.O. 100/13, ff 69-70.

7 *ibid.*

8 Rutland to Sydney, 20 May 1784, ibid., f 75.

9 Mornington to [Rutland], 31 May 1784, *H.M.C. Rutland*, III, 99-100.

10 Orde to [Rutland], 5 July 1784, ibid., 120.

11 Rutland to Pitt, 16 June 1784, *Pitt-Rutland*, 17.

12 Orde to Pitt, 15 Sept. 1784, P.R.O. 30/8/329 (Chatham Papers), f 133.

13 Malcomson, *John Foster*, 49-50.

14 Pitt to [Orde], 19 Sept. 1784, National Library of Ireland, MS. 16,358 (Bolton Papers), p 2 of a paginated letterbook.

15 Jean Dawson, "Pitt and Ireland", 16a. This unpublished paper made constructive use of the voluminous Bolton Papers now in the National Library of Ireland. As will be seen here and below the paper has been quoted from in three instances only; my efforts to locate the originals of the letters referred to by Miss Dawson were regrettably unsuccessful. I am grateful to Miss Dawson for allowing me to read this paper and to Mr John Ehrman for his assistance in obtaining it.

16 Pitt to [Orde], 19 Sept. 1784, N.L.I., MS. 16,358, 2-3: "The matter of naval strength is of the utmost importance".

17 Pitt to Orde, 25 Sept. 1784, ibid., 12.

18 Pitt to Rutland, 7 Oct. 1784, *Pitt-Rutland*, 42-3.

19 Orde to [Pitt], 10 Oct. 1784, N.L.I., MS. 16,358, 39.

20 [Orde] to [Pitt], n.d., ibid., 45.

21 *ibid.*, 42.

22 Sydney to Rutland, [17] Oct. 1784, P.R.O., H.O. 100/14, ff 144-5; *H.M.C. Rutland*, III, p. 143.

23 Dawson, 16a.

24 Pitt to Rutland, 4 Nov. 1784, *Pitt-Rutland*, 49.

25 Quoted in Malcomson, *John Foster*, 50.

26 Rutland to Pitt, 14 Nov. 1784, *H.M.C. Rutland*, III, 147.

27 *ibid.*

28 [Rutland] to Sydney, 25 Oct. 1784; Rutland to Pitt, 17 Nov. 1784, *H.M.C. Rutland*, III, 145, 148.

29 Rutland to Pitt, 14 Nov. 1784, ibid., 149; Orde to Sydney, 29 Nov. 1784, P.R.O., H.O. 100/14, f 244.

30 Pitt to Rutland, 4 Dec. 1784, *Pitt-Rutland*, 51. There is some doubt as

to whether Rutland received this letter until mid-December. Pitt, writing on 14th December, referred to the enclosure of a letter "of ten days ago", Pitt-Rutland, 53.

31   Orde to [Rutland], 30 Nov. 1784, *H.M.C. Rutland*, III, 152.

32   Pulteney to [Rutland], 17 Oct. 1784; Orde to Rutland; 30 Nov. 1784, *H.M.C. Rutland, III*, 145, 153.

33   Orde to [Rutland], 30 Nov. 1784, ibid., 152; Pitt to Rutland, 4 Dec. 1784, Pitt-Rutland.

34   Orde to [Rutland], 6 Dec. 1784, *H.M.C. Rutland*, III, 157.

35   Pitt to Rutland, 14 Dec. 1784, *Pitt-Rutland*, 54.

36   Sydney to Rutland, 6 Jan. 1785, P.R.O., H.O. 100/16, ff 11-16.

37   *ibid.*, ff 16-17.

38   Pitt to Rutland, 6 Jan. 1785, *Pitt-Rutland*, 56-7. Also Richard Atkinson to George Rose, 21 Dec. 1784, P.R.O. 30/8/321 (Chatham Papers), f 205: "As to the Irish trade with the British Plantations. They already enjoy it upon an equal footing with Great Britain, and so it ought to be continued. But it should never be forgot that they hold this privilege by the favour of Britain; and when therefore their pretensions are advanced to limit the trade of those very Colonies to which they themselves only trade by favour, it is manifest that such an incroachment [*sic*] cannot be too decisively withstood".

39   Pitt to Rutland, 6 Jan. 1785, *Pitt-Rutland*, 60.

40   *ibid.*, 62.

41   *ibid.*, 69.

42   *ibid.*, 66.

43   *ibid.*, 58.

44   *ibid.*, 71.

45   *ibid.*, 58.

46   *ibid.*, 72.

47   *ibid.*, 67, 69.

48   Rutland to Sydney, 13 Jan. 1785, P.R.O., H.O. 100/16, f 41.

49   *ibid.*

50   *ibid.*, f 43.

51   *ibid.*, f 43.

52   "Hints and precautions to be made use of", 14 Jan. 1785, *H.M.C. Rutland*, III, 164.

53   Rutland to Sydney, 13 Jan. 1785, P.R.O., H.O. 100/16, f 43.

54   Orde to Sydney, 19 Jan. 1785, *ibid.*, ff 59-60.

55   Pitt to Orde, 12 Jan 1785, *Pitt-Rutland*, 87.

56   Rutland to [Sydney], 23 Jan. 1785, *H.M.C. Rutland*, III, 165-6.

57   Rutland to Pitt, 23 Jan. 1785, *ibid.*, 166.

58   *ibid.*, 167; Rutland to Sydney, 25 Jan. 1785, P.R.O., H.O. 100/16, ff 84-5.

59   Pitt to Orde, 12 Jan. 1785, *Pitt-Rutland*, 87-8.

60   Foster to Grattan, 28 Jan. 1785, *Grattan*, III, 236-7.

61   [Sydney] to Rutland, 19 Jan. 1785, 27 Jan. 1785, P.R.O., H.O. 100/16, ff 58, 80-1.

62   Rutland to Pitt, 6 Feb. 1785, *H.M.C. Rutland*, III, 175-6.

63   Sydney to Rutland, 1 Feb. 1785, P.R.O., H.O. 100/16, ff 90-2. The letter referred to in the text seems not to have survived, so I am deducing its contents from Sydney's reply to it.

64   *ibid.*, f 92.

65   *ibid.*, ff 93-5.

66   *ibid.*, f 99.

67   *ibid.*, ff 97-8.

68   Lord Ashbourne, *Pitt: Some aspects of his Life and Times* (1898), 103-6.

69   Rutland to Sydney, 7 Feb. 1785, P.R.O., H.O. 100/16, ff 138-42.
70   Sydney to Rutland, 1 Feb. 1785; Rutland to Sydney, 7 Feb. 1785, ibid., ff 103-4, 139-42.
71   *ibid.*, f 141.
72   Rutland to Sydney, 12 Feb. 1785, ibid., ff 153-7. Orde to [Pitt], 12 Feb. 1785, P.R.O. 30/8/329 (Chatham Papers), f 206.
73   *ibid.* (H.O.).
74   *ibid.*
75   *ibid.*
76   ibid., ff 145, 160.
77   See pp 71-2 above.
78   Orde to Nepean, 12 Feb. 1785, P.R.O., H.O. 100/16, ff 166-8.
79   Dawson, 30; Orde to [Rose], 27 Feb. 1785, N.L.I., MS. 16,358, 83-6.
80   J. Holland-Rose, *Pitt and the National Revival* (1911), 253.
81   This proved to be untrue. On the strength of the understanding that the propositions would be agreed to by the British parliament, new taxes of £140,000 were voted in Ireland. Rutland to [Sydney], 25 Feb. 1785, *H.M.C. Rutland*, III, 184; Rutland to Sydney, 25 Feb. 1785, P.R.O., H.O. 100/16, ff 212-16; *Grattan*, III, p 244.
82   Sydney to Rutland, 24 Feb. 1785, P.R.O., H.O. 100/16, ff 189-202.
83   *ibid.*
84   Holland-Rose, 254-5.
85   Pitt to Rutland, 24th Feb. 1785, *Pitt-Rutland*, 95.
86   As early as 19 January Sydney had warned Rutland of this possibility, *H.M.C. Rutland*, III, 165.
87   Dawson, 32. See also Witt Bowden, "The influence of the manufacturers on some of the early policies of William Pitt", *American Historical Review*, xxix, no. 4, July 1924.
88   *Grattan*, III, 250.
89   Sydney to Rutland, 3 March 1785, P.R.O., H.O. 100/16, ff 218-19; V.T. Harlow, *The Founding if the Second British Empire, 1763-1793* (1952), 586n.
90   Pitt to George III, 14 March 1785, A. Aspinall (ed.), *Later Correspondence of George III* (Cambridge, 1962), I, 138.
91   Orde to [Rutland], 12 March 1785, *H.M.C. Rutland*, III, 188-90.
92   Ehrman, *Younger Pitt: Years of Acclaim*, 205-9.
93   Pulteney to [Rutland], 12th March 1785, *H.M.C. Rutland*, III, 190, 191. Also Orde to [Rutland], 16 March 1785, ibid., 191. Pulteney may have been wrong in believing the cabinet to be timid. Pitt's letters to Rutland of 14 and 16 April indicate that Pitt was strategically allowing Fox to exhaust himself before proceeding. Pitt seems to have seen no danger in the delay which this would cause in Ireland.
94   Orde to [Rutland], 16 March 1785, *H.M.C. Rutland*, III, p 191.
95   Orde to [Rutland], 18 March 1785, ibid., 192.
96   Pulteney to [Rutland], 21 March [1785], ibid., 192.
97   Orde to [Rutland], 27 March 1785, ibid., 195.
98   Rutland to Sydney, 7 April 1785, P.R.O., H.O. 100/16, ff 311-15, quoting Sydney's letter.
99   Sydney to [Rutland], 2 April 1785, *H.M.C. Rutland*, III, 196.
100   Rutland to Sydney, 7 April 1785, P.R.O., H.O. 100/16, ff 311-15.
101   Sydney to Rutland, 15 April 1785, ibid., ff 317-19; Ashbourne, 122.
102   Pulteney to [Rutland], 6 April [1785], *H.M.C. Rutland*, III, 197.
103   *ibid.*
104   J.A.G. Whitlaw, "Anglo-Irish commercial relations", 146.
105   Pulteney to [Rutland], 16, 23 April [1785], *H.M.C. Rutland*, III, pp 201, 203.

106 Pulteney to [Rutland], 2 May [1785], ibid., 204.
107 Rutland to Sydney, 13 April 1785, P.R.O., H.O. 100/16, f 323.
108 Orde to Grattan, 16 April 1785, *Grattan*, III, pp 237-8; Grattan to [Orde], 16, 19, 22 April 1785, N.L.I. MS. 16,351 (Bolton Papers), ff 14, 15, 16.
109 Rutland to Sydney, 13 April 1785, P.R.O., H.O. 100/16 (enclosure), ff 325-9; Rutland to Sydney, 20 April 1785, ibid., f 328; Orde to Rose?; 10 April 1785 (incomplete), N.L.I., MS. 16,358 (Bolton Papers), 87-9.
110 *Grattan*, III, p 242.
111 Whitlaw, 164-5.
112 [Orde] to [Rose], 10 April 1785; [Orde] to Pitt, 15 April 1785, N.L.I., MS. 16,358 (Bolton Papers), 88, 93-6.
113 *Grattan*, III, 254-5.
114 Whitlaw 167.
115 Pitt to [Orde], 24 May 1785, N.L.I., MS. 16,358 (Bolton Papers), 109-11.
116 E. Burke to Sir John Tydd, 13 May [1785], *Grattan*, III, 250-2.
117 Pulteney to [Rutland], 24, 26 May [1785], *H.M.C. Rutland*, III, 208-9.
118 Rutland to Sydney, 20 May 1785, P.R.O., H.O. 100/16, f 262; Rutland to Pitt, 26 May 1785, *H.M.C. Rutland*, III, 210.
119 Rutland to Pitt, 19 May 1785; Pitt to Rutland, 21 May 1785, *H.M.C. Rutland*, III, 100-102, 103-7.
120 Orde to Pitt, 8 June 1785, N.L.I., MS. 16,358, 135; Rutland to Sydney, 11 June 1785, P.R.O., H.O. 100/16, ff 410-12.
121 Mornington to Grattan, 20 June 1785, *Grattan*, III, 253-4.
122 Pulteney to [Rutland], 23 June [1785], *H.M.C. Rutland*, III, 217.
123 Orde to Beresford, 3 July 1785, N.L.I., MS. 16,358, 161. An abridged version of this letter was published in Beresford, *I, 270-3.*
124 Rutland to Pitt, 4 July 1785, *Pitt-Rutland*, 107-8.
125 Sydney to Rutland, 20 July 1785, P.R.O., H.O. 100/17, ff 37-50; Rutland to Sydney, 8 August 1785, *H.M.C. Rutland*, III, 233. The Lords' amendment was of the third resolution "by giving a limited time during which drawbacks could be granted on foreign articles exported from Great Britain to Ireland" - Whitlaw, 171.
126 Orde to Beresford, 19 July 1785, N.L.I., MS. 16,358, p 187.
127 Orde to Beresford, 28 July 1785; Orde to Rose, 30 July 1785, ibid., 205-6, 208.
128 Orde to Beresford, 26 July 1785; Orde to Rose, 28 July 1785, ibid., 197, 202-5.
129 *ibid.*, 196-7, 205. This stratagem seems to have been designed to create in the Irish opposition 's collective mind the impression that the alterations were of their own making.
130 *ibid.*, 196, 201.
131 Orde to Nepean, 13 August 1785, P.R.O., H.O. 100/17, ff 94-5.
132 *Grattan*, III, 495.
133 *ibid.*
134 Rutland to Pitt, 13 August 1785; Pitt to Rutland, 17 August 1785, *Pitt-Rutland*, 115, 117.
135 C.B. Fergusson, "The Colonial Policy of the First Earl of Liverpool as President of the Committee for Trade, 1786-1804" (unpub. D.Phil thesis, Oxford, 1952), 13.
136 Jenkinson to Scott, 19 April 1782; Jenkinson to Col. D. Dundas, 23 April 1782, B.L. Add. MS. 38,309 (Liverpool Papers), ff 55, 56.
137 Fergusson, 29-30.
138 See Appendix 4.
139 Wraxall quoted in Fergusson, 56.
140 Liverpool to Portland, 16 Nov. 1799, B.L. Add. MS. 38,311 (Liverpool Papers), f 33. For the financial background to the Act of Union see T.R.

McCavery, "Finance and Politics in Ireland 1801-17" (unpub. Ph.D. thesis, Queen's University, Belfast, 1981).

141 Draft endorsed "1785" in pencil, B.L. Add. MS. 38,346 (Liverpool Papers), f 109.
142 *ibid.*, ff 112.
143 *Parl. Hist.*, xxv, p 679 (24 May 1785).
144 B.L. Add. MS. 38,346, f 112.
145 *ibid.*, ff 116-17.
146 Fergusson, 46.

Chapter 4

1 *Grattan*, II, 228.
2 Fitzpatrick to Fox, 17 April 1782, quoted in *Memorials of Fox*, I, 396.
3 Grattan to Fox, 18 April 1782, ibid., 408.
4 *Grattan*, II, 224.
5 *ibid.*, 305.
6 G.O. Sayles, "Contemporary sketches of the members of the Irish parliament in 1782", *Proceedings of the Royal Irish Academy*, Vol. 56 (1954), 262.
7 See the *Dictionary of National Biography* entries on Sheridan and Yelverton.
8 Portland to Shelburne, 6, 22 May 1782, P.R.O., H.O. 100/1, ff 176-7, 282-5.
9 Sayles, 249.
10 Beresford to Eden, 7 June 1782, Beresford, I, 206.
11 C.F. Sheridan to [Fitzpatrick], 23 June 1782, B.L. Add. MS. 47,582 (Fox Papers), ff 104-5.
12 Portland to Fox, 6 July 1782, B.L. Add. MS. 47,561 (Fox Papers), f 41.
13 T.M. O'Connor, "The conflict between Flood and Grattan", H.A. Cronne, T.W. Moody and D.B. Quinn (ed.), *Essays in British and Irish History in honour of James Eadie Todd* (1949), passim; also Jupp, "Earl Temple's Viceroyalty", passim.
14 Temple to Leinster, 26 July 1782; Temple to Charlemont, 26 July 1782; Temple to Conolly, 26 July 1782; Temple to Ponsonby, 13 Sept. 1782; Temple to Leinster, 28 Sept. 1782, B.L. Add. MS. 40,733 (Temple Letterbook), ff 14, 14-15, 15, 18, 20. Leinster to [Temple], 24 Sept. 1782, P.R.O.N.I., D.3078/3/4 (Leinster Papers). Shannon and Ponsonby did, however, attend the privy council meeting on 27 Sept. 1782; see the attendance list in H.O. 100/3, f 147. I believe Beresford is wrong in thinking that Leinster followed Fox in July; see Beresford to Eden, 18 July 1782, *Beresford*, I, 222-3.
15 For the best short explanation of the Mansfield affair, see Mornington to Grattan, 9 Dec. 1782, *Grattan*, III, 35-6.
16 Temple to Townshend, 30 Nov. 1782, H.O. 100/3, ff 300-305.
17 O'Connor, "Flood and Grattan", passim, and Jupp, "Earl Temple", 511.
18 "Statutes and Ordinances of the Order of St. Patrick", with details of fees, H.O. 100/8, ff 65-85; Temple to Grenville, 2 Jan. 1783, *H.M.C. Fortescue MSS*, I, pp 175-8.
19 Northington to [North], 26 June 1783; North to Northington, 2 July 1783, H.O. 100/9, ff 181-3, 193.
20 Northington to Windham, 6 Oct. 1783, B.L. Add. MS. 37,873 (*Windham Papers*, ff 77-8.
21 *ibid.*
22 *H.M.C. Charlemont* MSS, I, 107-8.
23 Windham to [Northington], 15 July 1783, B.L. Add. MS. 37,873 (Windham Papers), ff 19-21; *Windham Papers*, 36-7.
24 W. Ponsonby to [Windham], 22 July 1783; Windham to Ponsonby, 22 July

1783, B.L. Add. MS. 37,873 (Windham Papers), ff 29, 31. Windham to [Northington], B.L. Add. MS. 33,100 (Pelham Papers), ff 215-16; Windham's assertion to Northington on 27 July that he was suffering from a venereal complaint may have been genuine, B.L. Add. MS. 33,100, ff 219-20.

25 *Windham Papers*, 36-7.

26 Northington to Windham, 6 August 1783, B.L. Add. MS. 37,873 (*Windham Papers*), ff 33-4.

27 Northington to Fox, 17 Nov. 1783, *Memorials of Fox*, II, 179.

28 Northington to North, 23 Sept. 1783, H.O. 100/10, ff 106-12.

29 North to Northington, 7 Oct. 1783, ibid., ff 134-6.

30 Beresford to Townshend, 25 May 1782, *Beresford*, I, 203.

31 Northington to North, 18 July 1783; North to Northington, 27 July 1783, H.O. 100/9, ff 259-60, 261.

32 [Pelham] to Portland, [Nov. 1783], B.L. Add. MS. 33,100 (Pelham Papers), f 431.

33 For the significance of the "cabinet dinner" as an informal political institution see A. Aspinall, "The Cabinet Council, 1783-1835", *Proceedings of the British Academy*, xxxviii (1952).

34 "Abstract of a letter to Mr. Windham", 14 Sept. 1783, B.L. Add. MS. 33,100 (Pelham Papers), f 318. Pelham to Windham, 14 Sept. 1783, B.L. Add. MS. 37,873 (Windham Papers), ff 64-5.

35 Fox thought annual sessions ". . . not . . . very material"; Fox to Northington, 1 Nov. 1783, *Memorials of Fox*, II, 166.

36 Portland to Northington, 18 Sept. 1783, B.L. Add. MS. 38,716 (Northington Letterbook), f 101.

37 North to [Northington], 3 Nov. 1783, ibid., f 125.

38 North to Northington, 3 Nov. 1783, H.O. 100/10, ff 208-10.

39 Fox to Northington, 1 Nov. 1783, *Memorials of Fox*, II, 168.

40 North to Northington, 7 Oct. 1783, H.O. 100/10, ff 236-49.

41 This may have been another factor underlying the resignation of Windham; B.L. Add. MS. 37,873 (Windham Papers), ff 29, 31, 33-4.

42 Northington to Windham, 6 Oct. 1783, ibid., f 76.

43 [Pelham] to Portland, [Nov. 1783], B.L. Add. MS. 33,100 (Pelham Papers), ff 431-2.

44 *Grattan*, III, 59-60.

45 See list in ibid., 69.

46 Northington to Windham, 6 Oct. 1783, B.L. Add. MS. 37,873 (Windham Papers), ff 77-8.

47 *H.M.C. Charlemont MSS*, I, 107-8, 108n, 109-110. This was untrue at least with regard to Forbes. FitzGibbon's appointment as attorney-general was in fact carried "by the means of Pelham's persuasions and my own" against "Grattan's disinclination to it"; Northington to Windham, 6 Oct. 1783, B.L. Add. MS. 37,873 (Windham Papers), f 79. But if Charlemont believed the story as he later told it, it seems not unlikely that other councillors did also, with predictable consequences.

48 [Pelham] to Portland, [Nov. 1783], B.L. Add. MS. 33,100 (Pelham Papers), ff 432-3.

49 *ibid.*

50 *ibid.*, f 433. *Grattan*, III, 69. A possibility exists that the return of Scott to office had something to do with the latter's influence with North; "Conversations with Ld. Temple", 15 June 1783, O. Browning (ed.), *The political memoranda of Francis, Fifth Duke of Leeds* (Camden Society, 1884), pp 87-9.

51 B.L. Add. MS. 33,100 (Pelham Papers), f 433.

52　George Ponsonby to Fitzpatrick, n.d. but 1783, B.L. Add. MS. 47,582 (Fox Papers), ff 179-80. H.G. Quin to Scrope Bernard, 9 Nov. 1783, Buckinghamshire Record Office, Spencer-Bernard Papers, OI/8/11. Louisa Conolly to William Ogilvie, 24th July 1783, B. Fitzgerald (ed.), *Correspondence of Emily, Duchess of Leinster* (1957), III, 365.

53　Northington to North, 23 Sept. 1783; North to Northington, 3 Nov. 1783; North to Northington, 7 Oct. 1783, H.O. 100/10, ff 106-12, 208-15, 236-49. The explanation for Grattan's prominence may lie in Portland's advice to Northington the previous July: "I look upon Ld. C[harlemont] as magni hominis umbra, and that Grattan is the real substantial part of that connection", 6 July 1783, B.L. Add. MS. 38,716 (Northington Letterbook), f 47.

54　[Pelham] to Portland, [Nov. 1783], B.L. Add. MS. 33,100 (Pelham Papers), f 433.

55　I have excluded divisions on matters of private interest which were not clear party issues.

56　Northington to [North], 3 Dec. 1783; Northington to North, 22 Nov. 1783, H.O. 100/10, ff 343-4, 291-3.

57　*Parl. Reg.*, II, 197-204, and 213 for Grattan's absence. The third opposition victory was on a motion by Wesley Pole to reduce the size of the salary rise — *Parl. Reg.*, II, p 204.

58　*ibid.*, 205-10.

59　The speakers for the motion were Hartley, Hussey, Cavendish, Molyneux, Newenham, Brownlow, Corry, Griffith, Jones, Prime Serjeant Kelly; against the motion were the attorney-general, Beresford, FitzGibbon, Mason, Daly, John Scott, W. Ponsonby, Lodge Morres.

60　*Parl. Reg.*, II, 333-7.

61　*ibid.*, 95-107.

62　*ibid.*, 177-82.

63　*ibid.*, 45-8. 270.

64　Doyle supported the bill's introduction but stated his opposition to the bill itself.

65　*Parl. Reg.*, II, 259.

66　In forming this conclusion limited use has been made of the apparently inaccurate division list published in *Grattan*, III, 150-54n.

67　[Pelham] to Portland, 30 Nov. 1783, B.L. Add. MS. 33,100 (Pelham Papers), ff 427-30; Northington to North, 30 Nov. 1783, H.O. 100/10, ff 314-16; Northington to Fox, 30 Nov. 1783, *Grattan*, III, 157.

68　Northington stayed on good terms with Grattan; see *Grattan*, III, 177, 186.

69　*ibid.*, 148.

70　*Parl. Reg.*, II, 259.

71　Northington to North, 4 Nov. 1783; Pelham to North, 10 Nov. 1783, H.O. 100/10, ff 252-3, 263. *Parl. Reg.*, II, pp 73-85, 95-107.

72　*Parl. Reg.*, II, 85, 107, 264.

73　J. Cannon, *The Fox-North Coalition* (Cambridge, 1969), 133; L.G. Mitchell, *Charles James Fox and the Disintegration of the Whig Party* (Oxford, 1971), 73.

74　Northington to [Temple], 27 Dec. 1783; Northington to Sydney, 28 Dec. 1783; Sydney to North, 3 Jan. 1784, H.O. 100/12, ff 3-4, 5-6, 17-19. Fox to Northington, 26th Dec. 1783, *Memorials of Fox*, II, 224.

75　Sydney to Northington, 9 Jan. 1784; Northington to Sydney, 12 Jan. 1784; Sydney to Northington, 17 Jan. 1784; Pery to Sydney, 17 Jan. 1784; Northington to Sydney, 18 Jan. 1784; Northington to Sydney, 25th Jan. 1784; Northington to Sydney, 26 Jan. 1784 (two letters); Sydney to Northington, 2 Feb. 1784; Sydney to Northington, 11 Feb. 1784, H.O. 100/12, ff 24-5, 34-5, 42-3, 46, 54, 64-5, 67-9, 71-2, 90, 92.

76 *Parl. Reg.*, II, 352-6.
77 Northington to Sydney, 9 Feb. 1784, H.O. 100/12, f 94.
78 Northington to Sydney, 23 Feb. 1784, ibid., f 115.
79 Northington to [Rutland], 19 Feb. 1784, *H.M.C. Rutland MSS*, III, 75.
80 Quin to Scrope Bernard, 3 Jan. 1784, Bucks. R.O., Spencer-Bernard Papers, OI/8/16.
81 "Arrangements", [Feb. 1784?], and Northington to [Rutland], 27 Feb. 1784, *H.M.C. Rutland MSS*, III, 76.
82 Forbes to Adair, 6 Feb. 1780, B.L. Add. MS. 53,802 (Adair Papers), ff 1-6. George Ponsonby to Fitzpatrick, n.d. but 1783, B.L. Add. MS. 47,582 (Fox Papers), ff 179-80.
83 Rutland to Sydney, 27 Feb. 1784, H.O. 100/12, ff 125-9.
84 Charles Sheridan to R.B. Sheridan, 10th March 1784, Moore, *Sheridan*, I, 411.
85 *ibid.*, 413-14. Lord Clifden was reported to have deserted the opposition ranks in March 1784 because he "did not choose to work for nothing"; Beresford to Robinson, 11 April 1784, *Beresford*, I, 253.
86 Moore, *Sheridan*, I, 409.
87 Rutland to Sydney, 27 Feb. 1784, H.O. 100/12, ff 125-9.
88 *Parl. Reg.*, III, 119-20. As late as 10 March the "negotiation with the Duke of Leinster and the Ponsonbys still remains open"; [Rutland] to [Sydney], 10 March 1784, *H.M.C. Rutland MSS*, III, p. 80.
89 *ibid.*, 79-80. Rutland to Sydney, 4 March 1784, H.O. 100/12, ff 152-5.
90 *Parl. Reg.*, III, 56-9, 60-1, 61. The Register lists the speakers for the motion as Kearney, D. Browne, Newenham, Molyneux, Montgomery, Hartstonge, Day, O'Hara, Ogle, Smith, Corry, Dunn, A. Browne, Westby, Hartley, Brownlow, Rowley, Lowther, Massey, Forbes, Grattan. Against the motion were Moore, Hutchinson, Wolfe, Hayes, Doyle, Boyd, H. Cavendish, Bushe, Denis Daly; according to Rutland to Sydney, 22 March 1784, H.O. 100/12, ff 203-7, Mason, Langrishe, Hewitt, Boyle Roche and Green also spoke against the motion.
91 *Parl. Reg.*, III, 83-5.
92 See E.M. Johnston, "Members of the Irish parliament, 1784-7", *Proc. of the Royal Irish Academy*, Vol. 71 (1971), 157-8 for lists of supporters of the "great interests" at this time. By 24th March negotiations with leading figures had been all but completed by government with a high degree of success; [Rutland] to [Sydney], 24 March 1784, *H.M.C. Rutland MSS*, III, 82-4.
93 Orde to [Nepean], 21 March 1784, H.O. 100/12, f 201.
94 *Parl. Reg.*, III, 106-11.
95 Orde believed that Grattan was not "hostile" and did not intend the resolution to be an opening shot in a campaign of systematic opposition, but that having made veiled accusations of government extravagance early in the session, he was now trying to save face; Rutland to Sydney, 26 March 1784; Orde to Nepean, 28th March 1784, H.O. 100/12, ff 222-4, 242.
96 *ibid.*, and Rutland to Sydney, 29 March 1784; Rutland to Sydney, 1 April 1784, H.O. 100/12, ff 244-5, 246-7. *Parl. Reg.*, III, pp 116-17.
97 Johnston, "1784-7", 194-5.
98 *Parl. Reg.*, III, 30-4.
99 Johnston, "1784-7", 214.
100 *Parl. Reg.*, III, 130-2.
101 *ibid.*, 132-42.
102 Rutland to Sydney, 22 March 1784, H.O. 100/12, ff 203-7.
103 *Parl. Reg.*, III, 199-200.
104 *ibid.*, 206.

105   Johnston, "1784-7", 183.
106   *Parl. Reg.*, III, 202-3, 205-6, 212.
107   *ibid.*, 212.
108   Rutland to Sydney, 14 May 1784, H.O. 100/13, ff 69-70.
109   Rutland to [Sydney], 8 May 1784, *H.M.C. Rutland MSS*, III, 94.
110   Beresford to Robinson, 11 April 1784, *Beresford*, I, p 254.
111   *Parl. Reg.*, VIII (1788), 264 for instance.
112   *Beresford*, I, 253. See also the correspondence between the Duchess of Portland and Louisa Ponsonby (about ten letters), 1782-4, for evidence of informal links between British whigs and Irish "great interests"; Durham University library, Grey of Howick Papers.
113   *Parl. Reg.*, III, 201-3.
114   *ibid.*, 216-17.
115   Rutland to Sydney, 14 May 1784, H.O. 100/13, ff 69-70; Rutland to Sydney, 20 May 1784, f 75.
116   *Parl. Reg.*, III, 217-18.
117   *ibid.*, 222-3; Foster - "Let the Hon. Gentleman confine his address to . . . proper and practicable commercial relations, between this country and Great Britain, and that the interval between this session and the next may be employed in preparing them".
118   *Parl. Reg.*, III, 217-21. Johnston, "1784-7", 192, 186, 214.
119   Rutland to Sydney, 20 May 1784, H.O. 100/13, f 75.
120   The original of the "situation report" on which this estimate is based is in the Library of Congress, Vernon-Smith MSS, and is referred to briefly in *H.M.C. Vernon-Smith MSS*, p 373. I am grateful to Dr. A.P.W. Malcomson and to those involved with the History of the Irish Parliament project at P.R.O.N.I. for allowing me access to a photocopy of this document.
121   *Parl. Reg.*, III, 214. For the importance of members' seating patterns see P.D.G. Thomas, *The House of Commons in the Eighteenth Century* (1971).
122   Sydney to Rutland, 2 June 1784, H.O. 100/13, f 157; [Sydney] to Rutland, 14 August 1784; Sydney to Rutland, 22 Oct. 1784; Sydney to Rutland, 29 Nov. 1784, H.O. 100/14, ff 50, 179, 242. Sydney to Rutland, 29 Nov. 1784, *H.M.C. Rutland MSS*, III, 151.
123   Orde to [Rutland], 24 June 1784, *H.M.C. Rutland MSS*, III, 113.
124   *ibid.*, and Sydney to [Rutland], 12 August 1784, ibid., p 131.
125   Shannon to Rutland, 13 July 1784, ibid., 123.
126   Rutland to Sydney, 13 Jan. 1785, H.O. 100/16, ff 40-5.
127   "Hints and precautions to be made use of", 14 Jan. 1785, *H.M.C. Rutland MSS*, III, 164.
128   Orde to Sydney, 19 Jan. 1785, H.O. 100/16, ff 59-60.
129   [Quin] to Scrope Bernard, 20 Jan. 1785, Bucks. R.O., Spencer-Bernard Papers, OI/8/41. *The Debates and Proceedings of the House of Commons of Ireland . . . 1785* (Dublin, 1786), I, 29-30, 33, 162.
130   *Debates*, I, 27-40. Johnston, "1784-7", 178.
131   The "distinguished share" reported taken by Grattan in the 20 January debate is unrecorded in the published accounts. It is clear, however, that Grattan did support government; Orde to Grattan, 24 Jan. 1785, *Grattan*, III, 216.
132   Orde to Grattan, 18, 28 Sept. 1784, *Grattan*, III, 209-11.
133   *ibid.*, 216.
134   Foster to Grattan, 28 Jan. 1785, *Grattan*, III, 236-7.
135   *Debates*, I, 42-57.
136   *ibid.*, 409.
137   *ibid.*, II, 95, 96, 68.
138   *ibid.*, I, 73.

139 *ibid.*, 180, 410.
140 *ibid.*, 97-104.
141 *ibid.*, 147.
142 *ibid.*, 30-1, 35-6, 37, 39, 40, 154-65, 323-64, 381-94.
143 By "full" I mean vocal; it is likely that the Leinsters voted with the patriots on other issues as well, though probably for their own purposes.
144 *Debates*, I, 323-64, and 154-5 for Lord Charles Fitzgerald's contribution.
145 *ibid.*, 139-44.
146 *ibid.*, 216-17.
147 *ibid.*, II, 23-9.
148 *ibid.*, I, 168-76.
149 *ibid.*, 201-2.
150 *ibid.*, 219-27.
151 *ibid.*, 240.
152 Orde to Nepean, 12 Feb. 1785, H.O. 100/16, ff 166-8. *Debates*, I, 240.
153 *Debates*, II, 144-54.
154 Johnston, "1784-7", 191.
155 *Debates*, II, 149, 153.
156 *ibid.*, 163, 164.
157 It should be noted that even in early August Corry still regarded himself (and was regarded by the London whigs) as the leader of the patriot group. The extent to which this belief was shared by the patriots themselves is unclear but there seems to have been an understandable reluctance among them to rock the boat at this stage; Corry to R.B. Sheridan, 5, 10 August 1785, Moore, *Sheridan*, I, 432-5. See also P. Kelly, "British and Irish Politics in 1785", *English Historical Review*, July, 1975.
158 *Debates*, II, 169, 231-47.
159 *ibid.*, 390-3, 403. Rutland to Sydney, 9 Sept. 1785, H.O. 100/17, f 125. The reason for this uncharacteristic miscalculation by Grattan no doubt lies partly in the fact that he entered the Commons only after Conolly and Forbes (who had supported the address) had spoken. Conolly had already warned Grattan against any such move; Conolly to Grattan, 3 Sept. 1785, *Grattan*, III, 274.
160 *Pitt-Rutland*, 122.
161 Charlemont to Stewart, 20 August 1785, P.R.O.N.I., Stewart of Killymoon Papers, D.3167/1/18.
162 Sydney to Rutland, 18 August 1785; Orde to Rutland, 19 August 1785; S. Hamilton to [Rutland], [29 August? 1785], *H.M.C. Rutland MSS*, III, 234, 237.
163 Hamilton to [Rutland], [29 August? 1785]; Rutland to Sydney, 30 August 1785, *H.M.C. Rutland MSS*, III, 237, 238. Charlemont to Stewart, 31 August 1785, P.R.O.N.I., Stewart of Killymoon Papers, D.3167/1/19. George Ponsonby to Forbes, n.d. (two letters), T.J. Kiernan (ed.), "Forbes Letters", *Analecta Hibernica*, no. 8. (1938), 339, 339-40.
164 Rutland to [Sydney], 5 Sept. 1785, H.O. 100/17, f 111. Rutland, curiously, had tended to overestimate the strength of the Ponsonbys. In the immediate aftermath of 12 August he believed that "Their connection is very large, and would have turned the poise of the business"; *Pitt-Rutland*, 122-3. In fact the Ponsonby members were linked rather loosely, often only by marriage. They had no local power base and the county members among them tended to be swayed by the local popular feeling through which they had been elected. I am grateful to Professor L.M. Cullen for this point.
165 *Pitt-Rutland*, 118-19. Orde to Pitt, 4 Sept. 1785, P.R.O. 30/8/329 (Chatham Papers), ff 243-4.
166 Johnston, "1784-7", 158, 173.

167   *ibid.*, 165, 186.
168   Orde to [Rutland], 23 Sept. 1785; Orde to Rutland, 30 Sept. 1785, *H.M.C. Rutland MSS*, III, 243, 246.
169   Beresford to Rose, 25 August 1785, *H.M.C. Vernon-Smith MSS*, 347-50.
170   Pitt to Rutland, 28 Oct., 13 Nov. 1785, *Pitt-Rutland*, 125-31, 132. Rutland to Pitt, 6 Nov. 1785, P.R.O. 30/8/330 (Chatham Papers), ff 141-8. Before we leave 1785 it may be noted that the punishment of Lord Bellamont (and probably of the others also) arose from Ponsonby's assault on the Speakership; Orde to Pitt, 29th Jan. 1786 — "... Lord Bellamont declares in the most solemn manner that he never interfered at all in the choice of Speaker at the close of last session. The plan was moved at his house accidentally but he insists that [he?] had nothing to do with it" — Kent Archives Office, Stanhope-Pitt Papers, U.1590/S5 03/8.
171   Mornington to [Rutland], 9 Jan. 1786, *H.M.C. Rutland MSS*, III, 274.
172   With the exception of K. Boyle, "Police in Ireland before the Union", *Irish Jurist*, vii, 1972, and viii, 1973 (three articles).
173   P.R.O. 30/8/329 (Chatham Papers), ff 247-51.
174   *Parl. Reg.*, VI, 326.
175   L. Radzinovicz, *History of English Criminal Law* (1956), III, 108-23.
176   Orde to [Rutland], 9 Nov. 1785. *H.M.C. Rutland MSS*, III, 257-8.
177   *Pitt-Rutland*, 124; Johnston, "1784-7", 157-9.
178   Morres to [Rutland], 11 Dec. 1785; Lodge Morres was a Ponsonby supporter but had tried for several years to sell himself to the Castle — *H.M.C. Rutland MSS*, III, 267 (for the above letter), 321-2, 331, 417.
179   Orde to Pitt, 29 Jan. 1786, K.A.O, Stanhope-Pitt Papers, U.1590/S5 03/8.
180   The letter from Grattan to Forbes in Jan./Feb. 1786 regarding the proposed pension and place bills is perhaps the only surviving documentary evidence of patriot collusion during this session; "Forbes Letters", 330-1.
181   *Parl. Reg.*, VI, 27-8, 40-1, 54, 80-1.
182   *ibid.*, 91-3.
183   *ibid.*, 96, 97, 101-2, 103, 105-9, 110-13, 113-20.
184   *ibid.*, 124. Orde to Nepean, 9 Feb. 1786, H.O. 100/18, ff 58-9.
185   *Parl. Reg.*, VI, 155-60.
186   Orde to Pitt, 29 Jan. 1786, K.A.O, Stanhope-Pitt Papers, U.1590/S5 03/8.
187   *Parl. Reg.*, VI, 198-9.
188   Rutland to [Sydney], 22 Feb. 1786, H.O. 100/18, f 79. The pension list as an economic grievance had been attacked briefly by Newenham on 9 February but no full-scale assault on the list was made due to Blaquiere's coup on 20th February. It is likely that Forbes's decision to play the "constitution" card on 6 March was due to presure of time. See *Parl. Reg.*, VI, pp 101-2 for Newenham's remarks.
189   *Parl. Reg.*, VI, 237.
190   *ibid.*, 236-7.
191   Government's information was that Forbes's proposed legislation was based on Burke's Act of 1782; Orde to Pitt. 29 Jan. 1786, K.A.O., Stanhope-Pitt Papers, U.1590/S5 03/8.
192   *Parl. Reg.*, VI, 237-9.
193   *ibid.*, 239.
194   *ibid.*
195   Forbes was a less able tactician even than Corry. Despite Corry's embarrassingly public warning to him that he would "damn it by the procrastination", Forbes delayed the bill's introduction while he tried in vain to attract further support. These attempts merely resulted in the patriots losing two further divisions on the issue on 10 March by 128 to 67 and 128 to 75; *Parl. Reg.*, VI, pp 256-7, 264.

196 *ibid., 295.*
197 *ibid.,* 314. Orde to Nepean, 14 March 1786, H.O. 100/18, ff 136-9.
198 *Parl. Reg.,* VI, 291.
199 Orde to [Pitt], 15 March 1786, P.R.O. 30/8/329, ff 270-1.
200 Orde to Nepean, 3 April (misdated March) 1786, H.O. 100/18, f 158.
201 *Parl. Reg.,* VI, 340-1.
202 *ibid.,* 353.
203 *ibid.,* 364-5, 367, 374.
204 *ibid.,* 377. For the government's view of the debate on the police bill see
Orde to Nepean, 3 April (misdated March) 1786, H.O. 100/18, ff 158-60.
205 *Parl. Reg.,* VI, 327-8.
206 *ibid.,* 326, 336, 353, 374-86, 388-92, 394-9.
207 *ibid.,* 323-4.
208 *ibid.,* 394-5.
209 *ibid.,* 378-9.
210 *ibid.,* VII, 16-19, 26-31, 43-5.
211 *ibid.,* 45.
212 Sydney to Rutland, 12 Jan. 1787; Orde to [Nepean], 10 Jan. 1787 (misdated
1786), H.O. 100/20, ff 22, 33-4.
213 Curran, although "Prior" of the original "Monks of the Screw", owed his
seat and hence his allegiance to Richard Longfield. It was believed by the
government that Longfield's support could be bought. His asking price,
however, was for years too high; Johnston, "1784-7", 165, 191, 210, 234, 244.
214 Orde to Nepean, 19 Jan. 1787, H.O. 100/20, f 35.
215 Orde to Pitt, 29 Jan. 1787, Cambridge University Library (Chatham Papers),
MS. 6958, letter 273.
216 *Parl. Reg.,* VII, 93-103.
217 *ibid.,* 133-9.
218 *ibid.,* 160-3.
219 *ibid.,* 179-201. Orde to Nepean, 19 Feb. 1787, H.O. 100/20, f 113.
220 *Parl. Reg.,* VII, 241-50.
221 *ibid.,* 317-36.
222 Sarah Napier to Duchess of Leinster, 3 April 1787, *Corr. of Emily, Duchess
of Leinster,* II, 327.
223 Sarah Napier to Susan O'Brien, 28 March 1787, Ilchester and Stavordale
(ed.), *Life and Letters of Lady Sarah Lennox, 1745-1826* (1901), II, 61.
224 *Parl. Reg.,* VII, 339-60. It is more than possible that the refusal of several
patriots to support Grattan on this issue was due to the belief (simplified
in the following session) that to attack the tithe system was to attack the
Established Church itself. In this light the reasons for Conolly's revolt become
clearer, especially in view of his strange connection with the Bishop of Cloyne
who "was reckoned to govern Mr. Conolly in matters he took no concern
in"; Sarah Lennox to William Ogilvie, 18 Feb. 1780, *Corr. of Emily, Duchess
of Leinster,* II, 319-20. See also T. Moore, *Life and Death of Lord Edward
Fitzgerald* (1831), I, 60, for a 1787 reference to this connection.
225 Louisa Conolly to Duchess of Leinster, 9 March 1787, *Corr. of Emily, Duchess
of Leinster,* III, 400.
226 *Parl. Reg.,* VII, 377-400. Despite the fact that Grattan was allowed to propose
the motion on this issue (on 20 March) it is clear that Corry was still the
leader as it was he who first called upon the Commons (on 16 March) to consider
the bill carefully; *Parl. Reg.,* VII, 369-70. Also, the facts that the patriots
did not oppose the bill in toto, but instead moved cautious amendments to
it, suggest that they had come to terms with the necessity to define Ireland's
position in the Empire in maritime terms. They would also have accepted

(as did the Commons) that, removed from its 1785 context, the lone fourth proposition was largely robbed of its previous significance.

227 *Parl. Reg.*, VII, 431-40.
228 *ibid.*, 447.
229 *ibid.*, 445-51.
230 *ibid.*, 459-76.
231 Buckingham to Grenville, 10 Jan. 1788, *H.M.C. Fortescue MSS*, I, 297.
232 Forbes to Grattan, 26 Nov. 1787, *Grattan*, III, 314-15. Sir Gilbert Elliot to Lady Elliot, 8 Dec. 1787, *Life and Letters of Sir Gilbert Elliot, First Earl of Minto* (1874), I, 175.
233 R. Longfield to Buckingham, 21 Jan. 1788, Buckingham and Chandos, *Memoirs of the courts and cabinets of George III* (1853-5), I, 343-6. Scrope Bernard to Grenville, 19 May 1788, *H.M.C. Fortescue MSS*, I, 330. The only apparent explanation for this rise is that a number of "bought" Castle supporters may have been alienated in Buckingham's drive to satisfy the Duke of Leinster; Buckingham to Grenville, 17 Jan. 1788, ibid., 298. Leinster himself proved a most unreliable ally to the Castle throughout the session; Buckingham to Grenville, 14, 16 March, 11 April 1788, ibid., 309, 310, 320.
234 *Parl. Reg.*, VIII, 21-7.
235 *ibid.*, 353-6. Scrope Bernard to Grenville, 29 Feb. 1788, *H.M.C. Fortescue MSS*, I, 306-7. Buckingham referred to the pension as "that great cheval de battaile, which always carries many with the opposition who usually vote with us, and leaves many shabby fellows out of either list of voters"; Buckingham to Grenville, 2 March 1788, ibid., p 308.
236 *Parl. Reg.*, VIII, 305-6, 334-43.
237 This was the Castle's proposal to renew the 1769 augmentation of the army. Grattan and Conolly complained of irregular procedure and queried the expense, but Corry explicitly refused to support them and took up a diametrically opposite stance; *Parl. Reg.*, VIII, 84-6.
238 *ibid.*, 215-17.
239 *ibid.*, 233-4, 237. Scrope Bernard to Grenville, 15 Feb. 1788: "Above twenty members were shut out in the coffee-room, among whom were Mr. Beresford senior, and Mr. Sackville-Hamilton, and the others chiefly Government men. Of the leading interests late in opposition, the Duke of Leinster's, Mr. Conolly's, and Longfield's men were on our side, except Burgh of Old Town, and Curran, who has emancipated himself from Longfield. None with the late Administration crossed over" — *H.M.C. Fortescue MSS*, I, 303. Buckingham to Grenville, 18 Feb. 1788: "From the same causes the continuation of the Provost's Compensation Bill has been a work of much labour and discussion; and you will laugh to read that we were forced to adjourn on Saturday night, having only gone through half the Bill, because all the Crown servants (most of whom had spoken early in favour of the Bill) had got drunk at the coffee-house, and, at midnight, were loud in every part of the House abusing it" - ibid., 305.
240 The government, whose members clearly had not taken the trouble to attend the enquiry, barely won this division (56 to 49). The division was followed by an unprecedented occurrence: Fitzherbert declared that the enquiry "had made some strong impressions on his mind" and moved that it be allowed to continue; *Parl. Reg.*, VIII, 305-6.
241 *ibid.*, 395.
242 *ibid.*, 400 (Stewart), 406 (Grattan).
243 R.B. Sheridan to Charles Sheridan, [Feb. 1784], *Letters of Sheridan*, I, 158. Charles Sheridan to R.B. Sheridan, 10 March 1784, Moore, *Sheridan*, I, 409.
244 Corry to R.B. Sheridan, 5 August 1785, Moore, *Sheridan*, I, and 10, 12 August

1785, 432-5. Sheridan to Stratford Canning, [20 July 1785], [26 July 1785]; R.B. Sheridan to Charles Sheridan[early August? 1785]; R.B. Sheridan to Eden, [19 August 1785], *Letters of Sheridan*, I, 162-5. For Eden's role see P. Kelly, "British and Irish Politics in 1785", passim.

245   Mrs R.B. Sheridan to R.B.'s sister, Lissy, 16 August [1784], Moore, *Sheridan*, Ii, 148.

246   Hardy to Forbes, 30 May 1786, "Forbes Letters", 332.

247   *Grattan*, III, 337.

248   Grattan to Day, 5 Dec. 1788, ibid., 341.

249   33 Hen. VIII, c.1.

250   Yelverton to Forbes, 6 Dec. 1788, N.L.I. (Forbes Papers), MS. 10,713.

251   Hardy to Forbes, 19 Dec. 1788, "Forbes Letters", 348.

252   Charlemont to Forbes, 18 Dec. 1788, *H.M.C. Charlemont MSS*, II, 84-5.

253   Denis Kennedy, "The Irish Whigs 1789-1793" (unpub. Ph.D. thesis, Toronto, 1791). His argument is conveniently summarised in his article, "The Irish Whigs, administrative reform, and responsible government 1782-1800", *Eire-Ireland*, VIII, no. 4 (1973).

254   *Parl. Reg.*, IX, 260. The references to the original programme in the 6 February debate were made in the context of a personal attack on Buckingham and no attempt was made to bring forward resolutions on any of the issues; ibid., 10-14. Grattan's promise to the gallery on 7 February that he would repeal the police act and limit pensions similarly was not followed through; Buckingham to Grenville, 7 Feb. 1789, *H.M.C. Fortescue MSS*, I, 410. The lapse was noticed by Molyneux — "He wondered how gentlemen who had so long cried out against pensions, should now when they had an opportunity of restraining them, pass by that opportunity, and talk of doing it by a subsequent act. Did this prove the sincerity of their former declarations?" — *Parl. Reg.*, IX, 44.

255   J. Derry, *The Regency Crisis and the Whigs, 1788-9* (Cambridge, 1963), 188.

256   "Forbes Letters", 351-8.

257   Portland to Forbes, 9 Jan., 2, 22 Feb. 1789; Charles[?] Sheridan to Forbes, 1 Dec. 1788; Richard Sheridan to Forbes, 9 Dec. 1788, N.L.I. (Forbes Papers), MS. 10,713. Pelham to Grattan, 19 Feb. 1789; Portland to Grattan, 21 Feb. 1789; Burke to Grattan, 19 March 1789, Grattan, III, 372-6.

258   *Parl. Reg.*, IX, 193.

259   Buckingham to Grenville, 21 Feb. 1789 (enclosure), *H.M.C. Fortescue MSS*, I, 419.

260   Buckingham to Grenville, 25 Feb. [1789], ibid., 422.

261   *Grattan*, III, 383-4.

262   Buckingham to Grenville, 21 Feb. 1789, *H.M.C. Fortescue MSS*, I, 418.

263   Buckingham to Grenville, 25 Feb. [1789], ibid., 421-2.

264   *Grattan*, III, 389-90.

265   *Parl. Reg.*, X, 330-1, 406.

266   *ibid.*, 18.

267   *ibid.*, 102, 349.

268   Hobart to [Nepean], 12 Feb. 1790, H.O. 100/29, ff 61-2.

269   *Parl. Reg.*, X, 7-22, 25-8.

270   *ibid.*, 383.

271   *ibid.*, 383-5.

272   Hobart to [Nepean], 6 March 1790, H.O. 100/29, ff 99-100. A printed copy of the responsibility bill survives in H.O. 100/32, ff 166-71.

273   *Parl. Reg.*, X, 402-4. Hamilton to [Scrope Bernard[, 6 March 1790, H.O. 100/29, f 102.

274   *Dublin Evening Post* quoted in Kennedy (thesis), 317.

275 Abercorn list quoted in Kennedy (thesis), 302.
276 *Parl. Reg.*, XI, 247.
277 Kennedy (thesis), 300-301.
278 *Parl. Reg.*, XI, 128-44, 154-88, 262-6, 313-29, 347-52. See also H.O. 100/32, ff 57-8, 163-4.
279 *Parl. Reg.*, XI, 326-7.
280 *ibid.*, 192-6.
281 *ibid.*, 198-203.
282 *ibid.*, 199, 221-2. See also H.O. 100/32, ff 60-1, 71-3.
283 Hobart to Nepean, 22 Feb. 1791, H.O. 100/32, f 76.
284 *Parl. Reg.*, XI, 203, 247. H.O. 100/32, f 73 gives the division figures as 144 to 83.
285 "3rd — The East India Trade — Observations and Remarks", National Library of Scotland (Dundas-Melville Papers), MS. 65, ff 6, 9, 10-11. See also Cooke to Scrope Bernard, 11 March, 2 April 1791, Bucks. R.O., Spencer-Bernard Papers, published in *Eighteenth-Century Irish Official Papers* in *Great Britain* (Belfast, 1973), I, 207-12. (Note: In the latter volume the document referred to in this footnote as N.L.S. MS. 65 is incorrectly listed as MS. 68).
286 Westmorland to Pitt, 4 April 1792, P.R.O. 30/8/331 (Chatham Papers), f 77.
287 E. O'Flaherty, "The Catholic Question in Ireland 1774-1793" (unpub. M.A. thesis, University College, Dublin, 1981), 115.
288 *Parl. Reg.*, XII, 41-2, 116-19.
289 Hobart to Scrope Bernard, 20 Feb. 1792, H.O. 100/36, ff 283-9. *Parl. Reg.*, XII, 124-79.
290 Hobart to Scrope Bernard, 20 Feb. 1792, B.L. Add. MS. 35,933 (Hardwicke Papers), ff 46-7.
291 *Parl. Reg.*, XII, 182-231. Hobart to Scrope Bernard, 21 Feb. 1792, H.O. 100/36, ff 295-7 gives the minority as 25. The extent to which the Castle exploited the split (if they did so at all) is unclear from the debate itself. What is clear is that the nature of the split was known by the Castle in advance; see Cooke to Scrope Bernard, 21st Jan. 1792, H.O. 100/36, f 137 — "Ld. Shannon I hear will not support any relaxation and I suppose the Ponsonbys will take the same line".
292 The government opposed this but there appears to have been no division.
293 *Parl. Reg.*, XII, 65-77, 85-112. Cooke to Scrope Bernard, 9 Feb. 1792, H.O. 100/36, f 244.
294 *Parl. Reg.*, XII, 270-81.
295 *ibid.*, 294-7. The Register did not record that the government lowered the curtain on this debate by carrying an adjournment 124 to 53; Hobart to Scrope Bernard, 19 March 1792, H.O. 100/37, f 36.
296 *Parl. Reg.*, XII, 282, 284-8.
297 Pitt to Westmorland, 10 Nov. 1792, H.O. 100/38, f 374.
298 Dundas to Westmorland, 17 Dec. 1792, ibid., ff 157-60.
299 Westmorland to Dundas, 29 Dec. 1792, H.O. 100/ 42, f 3. See Westmorland to Pitt, 18 Jan. 1793, for evidence of Westmorland's vacillating optimism in this matter; Cambridge University Library (Pitt Papers), MS. 6958, letter 1199.
300 *Parl. Reg.*, XII, 231.
301 Loughborough to Grattan, 30 Jan., 21 Feb. 1793, *Grattan*, IV, 107-110.
302 *Parl. Reg.*, XIII, 72-6, 150-2, 51-63, 159-88.
303 *ibid.*, 52.
304 *ibid.*, 51-63.
305 *ibid.*, 145-9.
306 *ibid.*, 372-83.

307 *ibid.*, 395, 412, 416-17.

308 Westmorland to Pitt, 30 March 1793, P.R.O. 30/8/331 (Chatham Papers), ff 119-120.

309 The details of this machinery may be found in Volumes 1 and 2 of the Glenbervie Papers at the Advocates Library, Edinburgh, MS. 4.1.2.

310 *Parl. Reg.*, XIII, 431-2, 438.

311 Copies of the Melville list (N.L.I. MS. 54, ff 19-20) and of the Westmorland list (Irish State Paper Office, MS. 202) were made available to me courtesy of the History of the Irish Parliament project.

312 *Parl. Reg.*, XIII, 432, 466, 539. It is possible that the extraordinary duration of the session had something to do with the division figures. The government's figures were also reduced and the Commons had to be adjourned on 17 June because only 40 members were present — see *Parl. Reg.*, XIII, 447.

313 *Parl. Reg.*, XIV, 16. Westmorland suspected in January 1794 that the opposition were "very angry with Grattan"; Westmorland to Pitt, 29 Jan. 1794, P.R.O. 30/8/331, f 193.

314 *Parl. Reg.*, XIV, 49-53, 62-108.

315 Fitzwilliam to Grattan, 23 August 1794, *Grattan*, IV, pp 173-4.

316 On 2 March 1795; *Parl. Reg.*, XV, 142.

317 Duquery's avowed opposition to the war had a somewhat hollow ring; *Parl. Reg.*, XV, 12, 82.

318 *ibid.*, 77.

319 *ibid.*, 91-3.

320 *ibid.*, 104, 105-7, 109-110.

321 The genuineness of the document among the Fitzwilliam-Grattan Papers in the Hull University Library dated 15 Nov. 1794 specifying the terms on which Grattan and the Ponsonbys would support the Castle is a trifle doubtful.

322 *Grattan*, IV, 176.

323 *Parl. reg.*, XV, 121, 130-1.

324 *ibid.*, 133-6.

325 *ibid.*, 141-52.

326 *ibid.*, 157, 163.

327 *ibid.*, 168-93. Camden to Pitt, 22 April 1795, P.R.O. 30/8/326 (Chatham papers), ff 6-7. Camden to Portland, 22 April 1795, K.A.O., Pratt Papers, U1 968/017.

328 *Parl. Reg.*, XV, 195-6. It will have been noticed that reference to Grattan's intended Catholic bill has been avoided. The lack of evidence as to the Ponsonbys' view of this matter obscures the reasons why Grattan insisted on bringing it forward. In view of the Ponsonbys' stated views of Catholic emancipation in 1793 the possibility cannot be ignored that they intended not to support Grattan and to force him to abandon the bill. George Ponsonby arose to support the bill only towards the close of the long debate of 4 May, by which time the Commons had already shown itself to be opposed to the measure. The bill was lost by 155 to 84; *Parl. reg.*, XV, 354-7, 361. Camden to Portland, 5 May 1795, K.A.O., Pratt Papers, U1 968/032.

329 *Parl. Reg.*, XV, 195-6, 361.

330 Camden to Portland, 26 May 1795, K.AA.O., Pratt Papers, U1 968/046.

331 *Parl. Reg.*, XV, 205-6.

332 Resolutions of the Whig Club, 8 Dec. 1795, K.A.O., Pratt Papers, U1 968/0124/3.

333 Summary of first sitting, 21 Jan. 1796, ibid., U1 968/0145/2.

334 Camden to Portland, 26 Feb. 1796, ibid., U1 968/0157.

335 Camden to Pitt, 27 July 1796, P.R.O. 30/8/326 (Chatham Papers), f 84.

336 *Grattan*, IV, 242.

337   *ibid.*, 245.
338   *ibid.*, 242-58. *Report of Debates in the House of Commons of Ireland, session 1796-7* (Dublin, 1797), 13-14, 37-40, 72-80, 120-1.
339   *Report*, 71.
340   "that the admissibility of persons professing the Roman Catholic religion to seats in parliament, is consistent with the safety of the crown, and the connection of Ireland with Great Britain" — ibid., 80.
341   Camden to Portland, 18 Oct. 1796, K.A.O., Pratt Papers, U1 968/0257.
342   *Report*, 158.
343   Fox to Grattan, 7 April 1797, *Grattan*, IV, 314-16. "Observations on the affairs of Ireland, received May 30 1797 from Carlton House, for the perusal of the Cabinet", initialed by the Prince of Wales; this document, which criticises the government's coercion policy and anti-Catholic attitude as counter-productive and dangerous, is in B.L. Add. MS. 38,103 ("Letters relating to Irish Affairs 1782-1837", ff 11-16. See also Dundas to Lord Keith, 17 Feb [1797], Scottish Record Office, Melville Papers, MS. GD 51 I, no. 325/1, in which Dundas bluntly refuses to discuss Irish affairs with any representative of the Prince of Wales.
344   *Grattan*, IV, 287.
345   Lord President to Rutland, August 1785, P.R.O., P.C.1/43/A148, P.C.1/31/78.
346   Sydney to Buckingham, 12 April 1788; Buckingham to Sydney, 17 April 1788, H.O. 100/23, ff 224-7, 238.
347   Buckingham to Sydney, 11 March 1789; Fitzherbert to Nepean, 11 March 1789; Sydney to Buckingham, 19 March 1789, H.O. 100/26, ff 223, 227, 231-3.
348   H. Grattan, *A letter on the nature and tendency of the Whig Club and of the Irish Party* (Dublin, 1797 — oddly misdated 1791), 19.
349   Johnston, *Great Britain and Ireland*, 102.
350   Buckingham to Grenville, 2 April 1788, *H.M.C. Fortescue MSS*, I, 315.

Chapter 5

1   Derry, *Regency Crisis*, 25. Buckingham to Grenville, 3 Nov. 1788, *H.M.C. Fortescue MSS*, I, 360.
2   *ibid.* See also P.N. Meenan, "The Regency Crisis in Ireland" (unpub. M.A. thesis, University College, Dublin, 1971), Chapter 1, passim.
3   Derry, *Regency Crisis*, 45-7.
4   Grenville to Buckingham, 7 Nov. 1788, *Courts and Cabinets*, I, 436.
5   Meenan, 16. Buckingham to Grenville, 11 Nov. 1788, *H.M.C. Fortescue MSS*, I, 363. Buckingham to Sydney, 29 Oct. 1788, H.O. 100/23, f 350.
6   Buckingham to Grenville, 12 Nov. 1788, *H.M.C. Fortescue MSS*, I, 364-5.
7   Buckingham to Grenville, 13 Nov. 1788, ibid., 366.
8   Grenville to Buckingham, 13 Nov. 1788, *Courts and Cabinets*, I, 453-4.
9   Buckingham to Grenville, 13 Nov. 1788, *H.M.C. Fortescue MSS*, I, 367.
10   Buckingham to Grenville, 15, 18 Nov. 1788, ibid., 369, 372.
11   Buckingham to Grenville, 12, 23 Nov. 1788, ibid., 365, 374-5.
12   Buckingham to Grenville, 2 Dec. 1788, ibid., 378-80.
13   Buckingham to Grenville, 23 Nov. 1788, ibid., 374-5.
14   Grenville to Buckingham, 10 Dec. 1788, *Courts and Cabinets*, II, 44.
15   Grenville to Buckingham, 9, 10 Dec. 1788, ibid., 41-2, 46.
16   Buckingham to Grenville, 13 Dec. 1788, *H.M.C. Fortescue MSS*, I, 384.
17   *ibid.*, 385. Buckingham to Sydney, 23 Nov. 1788, Cambridge University Library, Pitt Papers, MS. 6958, letter 604.
18   *Courts and Cabinets*, II, 60, 65.

19 Buckingham to Grenville, 22 Dec., 18 Dec. 1788, *H.M.C. Fortescue*, I, 391, 388.
20 Grenville to Buckingham, 25 Dec. 1788, *Courts and Cabinets*, II, 76-8.
21 Buckingham to Grenville, 22 Dec. 1788, *H.M.C. Fortescue MSS*, I, 389.
22 Buckingham to Grenville, 3 Jan. 1789, *ibid.*, 395-6.
23 Buckingham to Grenville, 3, 8 Jan. 1789, *ibid.*, 396, 396-7.
24 Mornington to Buckingham, 6 Jan. 1789, *Courts and Cabinets*, II, 89-90, and Grenville to Buckingham, 12 Jan. 1789, *ibid.*, 92-3.
25 Buckingham to Grenville, 22 Dec. 1788, *H.M.C. Fortescue MSS*, I, 391.
26 Buckingham to Sydney, 18 Jan. 1789, H.O. 100/26, ff 30-3.
27 Fitzherbert to [Nepean], 18 Jan. [1789], *ibid.*, f 37.
28 [Sydney] to Buckingham, 25, 31 Jan. 1789, *ibid.*, ff 40, 47.
29 Buckingham to Sydney, 29 Jan. 1789, *ibid.*, ff 52-4.
30 Buckingham to Grenville, 27 Jan. 1789, *H.M.C. Fortescue MSS*, I, 404-6.
¯31 Buckingham to Grenville, 5 Feb. 1789, *ibid.*, 406.
32 *Parl. Reg.*, IX, 6-7.
33 Buckingham to Sydney, 7 Feb. 1789, H.O. 100/26, ff 75-6.
34 *Parl. Reg.*, IX, 26.
35 Derry, *Regency Crisis*, 188.
36 *Parl. Reg.*, IX, 28-32.
37 *ibid.*, 35.
38 *ibid.*, 40.
39 *ibid.*, 71-2.
40 *ibid.*, 36-9.
41 *ibid.*, 40.
42 *ibid.*, 44.
43 *ibid.*, 48-9, 52.
44 *ibid.*, 60.
45 Fitzherbert to Nepean, 13 Feb. 1789, H.O. 100/26, f 99.
46 *Parl. Reg.*, IX, 75.
47 *ibid.*, 88. Buckingham to Sydney, 12 Feb. 1789; Fitzherbert to Nepean, 13 Feb. 1789, H.O. 100/26, ff 85-7, 97-100.
48 Buckingham to Sydney, 7 Feb. 1789; Fitzherbert to Nepean, 7 Feb. 1789; Buckingham to Sydney, 12 Feb. 1789; Fitzherbert to Nepean, 13 Feb. 1789, H.O. 100/26, ff 75-7, 79-81, 85-7, 97-100.
49 Grenville to Buckingham, 7 Feb. 1789, *Courts and Cabinets*, II, 104.
50 Pitt to Buckingham, 15 Feb. 1789, *ibid.*, 111-12. Buckingham to Grenville, [8 Feb. 1789?], *H.M.C. Fortescue MSS*, I, 411.
52 *Courts and Cabinets*, II, 108-11. Buckingham to Sydney, [?] Feb. 1789, *H.M.C. Fortescue MSS*, I, 411.
53 *Courts and Cabinets*, II, 109, 110-11.
54 *Parl. Reg.*, IX, 116.
55 Fitzherbert to Nepean, 13 Feb. 1789, H.O. 100/26, ff 97-8.
56 Buckingham to Sydney, 14 Feb. 1789; [Sydney] to Buckingham, 21 Feb. 1789, *ibid.*, ff 107, 121-2.
57 Pitt to Buckingham, 15 Feb. 1789, *Courts and Cabinets*, II, 111-12.
58 Buckingham to Grenville, 5 Feb. 1789, *H.M.C. Fortescue*, I, 407.
59 *Parl. Reg.*, IX, 119.
60 In the actual refusal issued at the presentation these words were changed to "Under the impressions which I feel of my official duty, and of the oath which I have taken as chief governor of Ireland, I am obliged to decline . . .."; *Parl. Reg.*, IX, 119.
61 Buckingham to Grenville, 5, 14 Feb. 1789, *H.M.C. Fortescue*, I, 407, 414. Buckingham to Sydney, 19 Feb. 1789, H.O. 100/26, ff 127-30.

62 Sydney to Buckingham, 17 Feb. 1789, ibid., f 102.
63 These are Buckingham's own words; there is no indication that any announcement was made by the Speaker. Buckingham to Grenville, 21 Feb. 1789, *H.M.C. Fortescue MSS*, I, 417.
64 *Parl. Reg.*, IX, 120-53.
65 *ibid.*, 142.
66 *ibid.*, 163-4.
67 Leinster, Charlemont, Conolly, John O'Neill, W.B. Ponsonby and J. Stewart.
68 Buckingham to Sydney, 21 Feb. 1789 gives the minority as 71; H.O. 100/26, f 142.
69 *Parl. Reg.*, IX, 153-4.
70 *ibid.*, 155.
71 Buckingham to Grenville, 21 Feb. 1789, *H.M.C. Fortescue MSS*, I, p 417.
72 Buckingham to Sydney, 21 Feb. 1789, H.O. 100/26, f 143.
73 *Parl. Reg.*, IX, 336.
74 *ibid.*, 388, 424.

Chapter 6

1 R. Reilly, *Pitt the Younger* (1978), 2.
2 Ehrman, *Younger Pitt: Years of Acclaim*, 323-4.
3 Despite several lengthy conversations with Pitt on Irish matters, the incoming chief secretary in 1794, Sylvester Douglas, was less than clear as to what was expected of him. His account of briefings included: "His plan seems to be . ." and "I had two conferences with Mr. Pitt . . . and two with Mr. Dundas, before I left London. They were very general". See F. Bickley (ed.), *The Diaries of Sylvester Douglas* (1928), I, 35-6.
4 Westmorland to Pitt, 18 April 1793, P.R.O. 30/8/331 (Chatham Papers), f 124.
5 Camden to Pitt, 7 May 1796: "I believe, as you candidly acknowledged to me before I came hither that Ireland occupies little of your thoughts . . ."; P.R.O. 30/8/326, ff 76-7.
6 Daly to Grattan, 15 Dec. 1782, *Grattan*, III, 17.
7 Lord Pembroke to Lord Carmarthen, [2nd to 11 August 1781]; Pembroke to Rev. W. Coxe, 8 August 1782, Lord Herbert (ed.), *Pembroke Papers* (1780-1794) (1950), 206, 208.
8 Grenville to Temple, 15 Dec. 1782, *Courts and Cabinets*, I, 88.
9 Temple to Lord Devlin, 26 July 1782, B.L. Add. MS. 40,733 (Temple Letterbook), f 13.
10 Memo., 22 June 1782; Portland to Townshend, 18 July 1782, H.O. 100/2, ff 149, 236-40.
11 Portland to Townshend, 9, 29 August, 14 Sept. 1782, H.O. 100/3, ff 36-8, 65-6, 98-9.
12 McBride to Grenville, 5 Oct. 1782; Townshend to Burgoyne, 8 Oct. 1782, H.O. 100/3, ff 176-8, 199-200.
13 Louisa Conolly to Sarah Lennox, 6 Oct. 1782, West Suffolk Record Office, Bunbury MSS, E18/750/2/17, 5-6 (paginated letterbook).
014 C. Sheridan to Fitzpatrick, 30 Dec. 1782, B.L. Add. MS. 47,582 (Fox Papers), ff 142-3.
15 Temple to Lord Viscount Valentia, 5 Dec. 1782, B.L. Add. MS. 40,733 (Temple Letterbook), f 31.
16 Temple to Sydney, 4 April 1783, H.O. 100/8, ff 271-2.
17 [Pelham] to Portland, 24 Oct. 1783, B.L. Add. MS. 33,100 (Pelham Papers), f 374.
18 Fox to Northington, 1 Nov 1783, *Grattan*, III, 106.

19   Northington to North, 4 Nov. 1783; Pelham to North, 10 Nov. 1783, H.O. 100/10, ff 252-3, 263.
20   Quin to [Scrope Bernard], 9 Nov. 1783, Bucks. R.O., Spencer-Bernard Papers, O1/8/11.
21   Northington to North, 30 Nov. 1783, H.O. 100/10, ff 314-16.
22   *Grattan*, III, 14.
23   Pelham to his father, 30 Nov. 1783, B.L. Add. MS. 33,128 (Pelham Papers), f 237.
24   Eden to [Northington], 10 Dec. 1783, B.L. Add. MS. 33,100 (Pelham Papers), f 452.
25   Orde to Nepean, 24 April 1784, H.O. 100/12, ff 377-80; Orde to [Nepean?], 20 May 1784, H.O. 100/13, f 73; Rutland to [Sydney], 8 May 1784, *H.M.C. Rutland MSS*, III, 93.
26   Rutland to Sydney, 19, 24 May 1784, H.O. 100/13, ff 79-80, 81-2.
27   Rutland to Sydney, 2 June 1784, H.O. 100/13, f 97; Rutland to [Sydney], 29 May 1784, *H.M.C. Rutland MSS*, III, 99.
28   Hillsborough to [Rutland], 15 July 1784, *H.M.C. Rutland MSS*, III, 124.
29   Orde to Rutland, 9 June 1784; General W.A. Pitt to Rutland, 17 June 1784, ibid., 104, 109.
30   Sydney to Rutland, 6 August 1784, ibid., 130. Rutland to Pitt, 16 June, 24 July 1784, *Pitt-Rutland*, 18, 2 Sydney to Rutland, 6 August 1784, ibid., 130. Rutland to Pitt, 16 June, 24 July 1784, *Pitt-Rutland*, 18, 24, 26.
31   Rutland to Sydney, 7 Oct. 1784, *H.M.C. Rutland MSS*, III, 141.
32   Orde to [Pitt], 24 Oct. 1784, P.R.O. 30/8/329, ff 170-1. [Rutland] to Sydney, 25 Oct. 1784, *H.M.C. Rutland MSS*, III, 145.
33   Pitt to Rutland, 4 Nov. 1784, *Pitt-Rutland*, 49. Rutland to Pitt, 11 Nov. 1784, *H.M.C. Rutland MSS*, III, 148.
34   Rutland to Sydney, 22 Nov. 1784, *H.M.C. Rutland MSS*, III, p 150.
35   Orde to [Rutland], 30 Nov. 1784, ibid., 152.
36   Orde to [Rutland], 6, 14 Dec. 1784, ibid., 157, 158.
37   Rutland to Pitt, [Nov. 1784], ibid., 154.
38   Rutland to Pitt, 18 Dec. 1785, *Pitt-Rutland*, 134-5.
39   Pitt to Rutland, 4 Nov. 1784, ibid., 49.
40   Minutes of cabinet meeting, 10 Jan. 1785, N.L.I., MS. 52 (Sydney Papers), P/4. Sydney to Rutland, 11 Jan. 1785, *H.M.C. Rutland MSS*, III, 161. [Sydney] to Rutland, 11 Jan. 1785, H.O. 100/16, f 8.
41   Pitt to Rutland, 11th Jan. 1785, *Pitt-Rutland*, 81.
42   Rutland to Sydney, 24 Jan. 1785, *H.M.C. Rutland MSS*, III, 167.
43   *Grattan*, III, 227.
44   *Parl. Reg.*, IV, 220-38. Rutland to Sydney, 15 Feb. 1785, H.O. 100/16, ff 170-2.
45   *ibid.*, Rutland to Sydney, 15 Feb. 1785, *H.M.C. Rutland MSS*, III, 180-1.
46   Rutland to Sydney, 19 Feb. 1785, H.O. 100/16, ff 183-5.
47   Copy in H.O. 100/17, ff 163-9.
48   Minute of conversation between Pitt and Orde on probable issues of the approaching 1786 session, P.R.O. 30/8/329, ff 250-1.
49   Orde to [Rose?], 27 Feb. 1785, N.L.I., MS. 16,358 (Bolton Papers), 86 (paginated letterbook).
50   Rutland to Pitt, 6 Nov. 1785, P.R.O. 30/8/330, ff 147-8. Rutland to (Sydney), 29 Jan. 1786, H.O. 100/18, f 47.
51   See the articles on the fortunes of local Volunteer units by P. Ó Snodaigh in *Jnl. of the Kerry Arch. and Hist. Society* (1971) and in the *Irish Sword* (1971).
52   Pitt to Lt. Col. Sharman, 11 August 1783, P.R.O., 30/8/325, f 54.
53   Ehrman, 58-76.

54 McDowell, *Ireland in the Age*, 310.
55 Rutland to Sydney, 4 March 1784, H.O. 100/12, ff 152-5.
56 Rutland to Sydney, 17 March 1784, ibid., ff 192-6. Sydney to (Rutland) 9 March 1784, *H.M.C. Rutland MSS*, III, 79.
57 Pitt to (Orde), 19 Sept. 1784, N.L.I. MS. 16,358, 5.
58 Rutland to Sydney, 22 March 1784, 100/12, ff 203-7. McDowell, *Ireland in the Age*, 310-11.
59 Rutland had been a supporter of English reform; see I.R. Christie, *Wilkes, Wyvill and Reform* (1962), 194.
60 Rutland to Pitt, 16 June 1784, *Pitt-Rutland*, 17-18.
61 Orde to Rutland, 3, 9, 17 June 1784, *H.M.C. Rutland MSS*, III, 101, 104, 110.
62 Pulteney to (Rutland), 17 June 1784, *ibid.*, 111-12.
63 *Pitt-Rutland*, 62.
64 Orde to Pitt, 16 August 1784, P.R.O. 30/8/329, f 103.
65 Rutland to Pitt, 24 July 1784, *Pitt-Rutland*, 25. Rutland to Sydney, 19 August 1784, H.O. 100/14, ff 56-9. Sydney to (Rutland), 16 Sept. 1784, *H.M.C. Rutland MSS*, III, 140
66 Orde to (Pitt), 4 Oct. 1784, P.R.O. 30/8/329, ff 151-4.
67 Pitt to Rutland, 7 Oct. 1784. *Pitt-Rutland*, 43-4.
68 Orde to Pitt, 4 Oct. 1784. N.L.I. MS. 16,358, 28-9.
69 Orde to (Rutland), 6 Dec. 1784, *H.M.C. Rutland MSS*, III, 157.
70 Orde to (Rutland), 30 Nov., 14 Dec. 1784, *ibid.*, 153, 159.
71 Pitt to Rutland, 4 Dec. 1784, *Pitt-Rutland*, 52.
72 Pitt to Rutland, 14 Dec. 1784, *ibid.*, 54. Also *H.M.C. Rutland MSS*, III, 159.
73 Sydney to Rutland, 11 Jan. 1785, *H.M.C. Rutland MSS*, III, 161. Pitt to Rutland, 9 Oct. 1784, *Pitt-Rutland*, 45. McDowell, *Ireland in the Age*, 320-1. Pitt to Rutland, 28 July 1784, P.R.O., 30/8/325, ff 47-9.
74 *H.M.C. Rutland MSS*, III, 161. McDowell, *Irish Public Opinion*, 111. Ashbourne, *Pitt*, 123. Pitt to Rutland, 11 Jan. 1785, *Pitt-Rutland*, 76-9. N.L.I. MS. 52, P/4.
75 Pitt to Rutland, 11 Jan. 1785, *Pitt-Rutland*, 81. Richmond to Pitt, 24 Dec. 1784, P.R.O., 30/8/330, f 48.
76 *Pitt-Rutland*, 81.
77 Bolton, *Passing of Irish Act of Union*, 7, 14, 54n2.
78 Johnston, *Ireland in the eighteenth century* (Dublin, 1973) 175.
79 Reprinted in *English Historical Documents, 1783-1832* (1969), ed. A. Aspinall and E.A. Smith, 158.
80 See R.E. Willis, "Cabinet politics and executive policy-making procedures, 1794-1901", in *Albion*, 1975, 1-23.
81 Pitt, *Speeches*.
82 It is referred to only by Christie in *Wilkes*.
83 The only account of this English bill is in L. Radzinovicz, *History of English Criminal Law* (1965), Vol. III.
84 The only account (very incomplete) is in B. Ward, *The Dawn of the Catholic Revival in England, 1781-1803* (1909), Vol. I.
85 *Pitt-Rutland*, 24-6. *H.M.C. Rutland MSS*, III, 104, 113, 148. Orde to (Pitt), 24 Oct. 1784. P.R.O., 30/8/329, ff 168-9.
86 *H.M.C. Rutland MSS*, III, p 117. Newenham to Mon. B. Folsch, 13 Oct. 1784, P.R.O. 30/8/329, f 52.
87 See note 47 above.
88 Information provided by Mr E. O'Flaherty.
89 Petre to (Mitford), 24 May 1787, Gloucestershire R.O. (Redesdale Papers), D 2002/c5. The relevant cause of the 1786 treaty was:"In matters of religion, the subjects of the two crowns shall enjoy perfect liberty. They shall not

be compelled to attend divine service, whether in the churches or elsewhere; but on the contrary, they shall be permitted, without any molestation, to perform the exercises of their religion privately in their own houses, and in their own way";*Annual Register*, 1786, 269.

90   See Ward, 126-315 for details of this memorial.
91   Fermor to (Grenville), 5 May 1788, B.L. Add. MS. 59,264 (Dropmore Papers), ff 5-6.
92   Fermor to (Grenville), 28 July 1788, P.R.O. 30/8/135 (Chatham Papers), ff 73-4.
93   J. Cantaur to (Mitford), 16 June 1789, Glouc. R.O. (Redesdale Papers), D 2002/c5.
94   Grenville to Mitford, 16 June 1789, B.L. Add.MS. 59,264 (Dropmore Papers), f 10.J. Cantaur to (Mitford), 16 March 1790, Glouc. R.O. (Redesdale Papers), D 2002/c5, 8.
95   Petre to (Mitford), 8 March 1790, ibid., D 2002/c5, 7-8.
96   Mitford to Grenville, 1 Dec. 1790, Mitford to Grenville, 10 Jan. 1791, Grenville to Mitford, 16 Jan. 1791, B.L. Add. MS. 59,264 (Dropmore Papers), ff 14, 16-17, 18.
97   Fermor to Grenville, 17 April 1796, ibid., f 34. It is not clear why Petre was not allowed to share this information but it may have been related to the split in the English Catholic Committee which had been caused (partly) by the required oath.
98   "Resolutions of the General Committee of the Catholics of Ireland", endorsed 18 Feb. 1791, Irish State Paper Office (Fane Papers), Carton I, f 12.
99   Grenville to Westmoreland, 24 March 1791, ibid., f 13.
100   E. O'Flaherty, "The Catholic Question", vii, 35, 57.
101   Westmoreland to Pitt, 24 Oct. 1790, P.R.O., 30/8/331, f 26.
102   (Westmoreland) to Dundas, 12 July 1791, I.S.P.O. (Fane Papers), f 16.
103   O'Flaherty, 114-15.
104   P.R.O., 30/8/331. f 26.
105   Dundas to Westmoreland, 26 Dec. 1791, I.S.P.O. (Fane Papers), f 27.
106   *Pitt-Rutland* 19.
107   See 187-9 above.
108   H.O. 100/2, quoted in O'Flaherty, viii.
109   O'Flaherty, 127-8. Westmoreland to Pitt, 30 Nov. 1791, 1 Jan. 1792, 18 Feb. 1792, P.R.O., 30/8/331, ff 65-72.
110   Dundas to Westmoreland, 26 Dec. 1791, I.S.P.O. (Fane Papers) f 29.
111   Westmoreland to Pitt, 13 Nov. 1792, P.R.O.30/8/331, ff 94-5.
112   Pitt to Westmoreland, 18 Nov. 1792, I.S.P.O. (Fane Papers), f 71.
113   Westmoreland to Pitt, 28 Nov. 1792, Camb. Univ. Library MS. 6959, no. 1156 (Pitt Papers).
114   Hobart to (Westmoreland) 25 June 1792, I.S.P.O. (Fane Papers), f 57.
115   Memo., N.L.I. MS. 54A (Dundas/Melville Papers), f 74.
116   Westmoreland to Pitt, 18 April 1793, P.R.O., 30/8/331, f 125.
117   *Diaries of S. Douglas*, Vol. I, 34-6.
118   E.A. Smith, *Whig principles and party politics* (Manchester, 1975), 175-219.
119   Johnston, *Ireland in the eighteenth century*, 192.
120   Westmoreland to Pitt, 18 April 1793, P.R.O. 30/8/331, f 125.
121   This was Mr. Johnson of Redemmon, near Ballynahinch, "the neighbour and friend of Lord Moira, who very much relies upon his judgment, in his opinions on the affairs of Ireland"; N.L.I. MS. 54A (Dundas/Melville Papers), f 111 (12).

Conclusion

1 S.A. Cummins, "Opposition and the Irish Parliament (1759-1771)" (Unpub. M.A. Thesis, St Patricks's College, Maynooth, 1978).
2 *Parl. Reg.*, XII (1792), 163. The topic was the Catholic Relief Bill and the speaker was Grattan.

Bibliography

A. *Manuscript Sources*

Advocates Library, Edinburgh
Glenbervie Letterbooks, Vols. 1 & 2, MS. 4.1.2.
(Photocopies in the Public Record Office of Northern Ireland, T.3294).

British Library
Adair Papers, Add. MSS. 53,802-7.
Auckland Papers, Add. MSS. 34,417-19.
Dropmore Papers, Add. MSS. 59,251-4, 59,264, 59,407.
Flood Letterbook, Add. MS. 22,930.
Fox Papers, Add. MSS. 47,561, 47,579-82.
Hardwicke Papers, Add. MS. 35,933.
"Letters relating to Irish affairs 1782-1837", Add. MS. 38,103.
Liverpool Papers, Add. MSS. 38,309, 38,311, 38, 346.
Northington Letterbook, Add. MS. 38,716.
Pelham Papers, Add. MSS. 33,100-02, 33,118, 33,128.
Temple Letterbooks, Add. MSS. 40,177, 40,733.
Windham Papers, Add. MS. 37,873.

Buckinghamshire Record Office
Hobart Papers
Spencer Bernard Papers

Cambridge University Library
Pitt Papers, MS. 6958.

Durham University Library
Grey of Howick Papers (Photocopies in P.R.O.N.I., T.3393).

Gloucestershire Record Office
Redesdale papers, MS. D 2002/c5 (Photocopies in P.R.O.N.I., T.3030).

Hull University Library
Fitzwilliam-Langdale Papers, MS. DDLA/39/1-4 (P.R.O.N.I., Microfilm 71)

Irish State Paper Office
Fane (Westmoreland) Papers

Keele University Paper
Sneyd Papers

Kent Archives Office
Pratt Papers, MSS. U.480, U1 968
Stanhope-Pitt Papers

Leeds University Library
Sydney Papers (Brotherton Coll.)

National Library of Ireland
Bolton (Orde) Papers, MS. 16,352, 16,358.
Forbes Papers, MSS. 978, 10,713.
Dundas/Melville Papers, MSS. 54, 54A.
Sydney Papers, MSS. 51-2.

National Library of Scotland
Melville Papers, MS. 65.

Nottingham University Library
Portland Papers

Public Record Office
S.P. 63/468-80.
H.O. 100/1-100.
P.C. 1/43/148, 1/12/29, 1/31/78.
Chatham Papers, P.R.O., 30/8/135, 30/8/321, 30/8/325-31.

Public Record Office of Northern Ireland
Abercorn Papers, T.2541.
Rosse Papers (numbering incomplete at time of consultation).
Shannon Papers, D2707.
Stewart (Killymoon) Papers, D3167.
Leinster Papers, D3078.
Working Papers of the History of the Irish Parliament, 1692-1800.

Scottish Record Office
Melville Papers, MS. GD 51 I.

Sheffield City Library
Rockingham Papers
Fitzwilliam Papers

West Suffolk Record Office
Bunbury (Conolly) Papers, vols. 1-34.
MS. Diary of the Third Duke of Grafton, 1782, H.A. 513/4/3.

B. Contemporary Printed Sources

An Anglo-Irish dialogue: a calendar of the correspondence between John Foster
    and Lord Sheffield 1774-1821 (Belfast, 1975)
Journal and correspondence of William Eden, first Lord Auckland, 4 vols.
    (1861).
The correspondence of the Rt. Hon. John Beresford, 2 vols. (1854), ed. Rt.
    Hon. William Beresford.
Buckingham and Chandos, Memoirs of the courts and cabinets of George III,
    4 vols. (1853-5).
Correspondence of Edmund Burke and William Windham, ed. J.P. Gilson
    (Cambridge, 1910).
The Drennan Letters, ed. D.A. Chart (Belfast, 1931).
(Curran, J.P.), A letter to the Rt. Hon. Edmund Burke on the present state
    of Ireland (Dublin, 1795).
216

The diaries of Sylvester Douglas, ed. Francis Bickley, 2 vols. (1928).

Eighteenth century Irish official papers in Great Britain vol. I (Belfast, 1973).

English historical documents, 1783-1932, vol. II, ed. A. Aspinall & E.A. Smith (1969).

Moore, T., *The life and death of Lord Edward Fitzgerald*, 2 vols. (1831).

Flood, W., *Memoirs of the life and correspondence of the Rt. Hon. Henry Flood* (Dublin, 1838).

Original letters . . . to the Rt. Hon. Henry Flood, ed. T. Rodd (1820).

Memorials and correspondence of Charles James Fox, 4 vols., ed. Lord John Russell (1853-7)

The correspondence of King George III, vols. 5 & 6, ed. J. Fortescue (1928)

The later correspondence of King George III, 5 vols., ed. A. Aspinall (Cambridge, 1962-71).

Grattan, H., *A letter on the nature and tendency of the Whig Club and of the Irish Party* (Dublin, 1797 — misdated 1791).

Grattan, H., *Miscellaneous Works* (1822).

Grattan, H., *Observations on the Mutiny Bill* (Dublin & London, 1781).

Grattan, H. (Jnr.), *Memoirs of the life and times of the Rt. Hon. Henry Grattan*, 5 vols. (1839-46).

The political memoranda of Francis, Fifth Duke of Leeds, ed.O. Browning (Camden Soc., 1884).

Correspondence of Emily, Duchess of Leinster, 3 vols. (Dublin, 1953).

Life and letters of Lady Sarah Lennox, 1745-1826, 2 vols., ed. Ilchester and Stavordale (1901).

MacDougall, H., *Sketches of Irish political characters* (1799).

Life and letters of Sir Gilbert Elliot, First Earl of Minto from 1751 to 1806, 2 vols., ed. Countess of Minto (1874).

O'Regan, W., *Memoirs of the legal, literary, and political life of the late Rt. Hon. John Philpot Curran* (1817).

Parsons, Sir L. *Thoughts on Liberty and Equality* (1793).

Pembroke Papers (1780-1794), ed. Lord Herbert (1950).

Correspondence between the Rt. Hon. William Pitt and Charles, Duke of Rutland, 1781-1787, ed. John, Duke of Rutland (Edinburgh and London, 1890).

Memoirs of the Marquis of Rockingham and his contemporaries, 2 vols., ed. Earl of Albemarle (1852).

Diaries and correspondence of the Rt. Hon. George Rose, 2 vols., ed. L.V. Harcourt (1860).

Life of William, Earl of Shelburne, 3 vols., ed. Lord E. Fitzmaurice (1876).

Lord Shannon's letters to his son, ed. E. Hewitt (Belfast, 1982).

Betsy Sheridan's Journal, ed. W. LeFanu (1960).

Sheridan, C.F., *Observations on the doctrine laid down by Sir William Blackstone, respecting the extent of the power of the British Parliament, particularly with relation to Ireland* (Dublin, 1779).

(Sheridan, C.F.), *A review of the three great national questions relative to a Declaration of Right, Poynings' Law, and the Mutiny Bill* Dublin & London, 1781).

Sheridan, C.F., *The Roman Catholic claim to the elective franchise discussed in an essay upon the true principles of civil liberty and of free government* (Dublin, 1793).

217

The letters of Richard Brinsley Sheridan, 3 vols., ed. C. Price (Oxford, 1966).
Moore, T., *Memoirs of the life of the Rt. Hon. R.B. Sheridan*, 2 vols. (1825).
Correspondence of Adam Smith, ed. E.C. Mossner & I.A. Simpson (Oxford, 1977).
The last journals of Horace Walpole, 2 vols.(1910).
The Windham Papers, 2 vols. (1913).
Wraxall, Sir N.W., *Historical memoirs of my own times*, 2 vols. (1815).
Wraxall, Sir N.W., *Posthumous memoirs of his own time*, 3 vols. (1836).

C. *Publications of the Historical Manuscripts Commission*

Abergavenny MSS (MSS. of John Robinson), *10th Report, Appendix vi*.
Carlisle MSS (MSS. of 5th Earl of Carlisle as Lord Lieutenant, 1780-2), *15th Report, Appendix vi*.
Donoughmore MSS (MSS. of John Hely-Hutchinson, Secretary of State, 1777-94), *12th Report, Appendix ix*.
Fortescue MSS (MSS. of William Grenville), vol. I, *13th Report, Appendix iii*.
Emly MSS (MSS. of E.S. Pery, Speaker of the Irish House of Commons, 1771-85), *8th Report, Appendix i*, and *14th Report, Appendix ix*.
Lothian MSS (MSS. of 2nd Earl of Buckinghamshire as Lord Lieutenant, 1776-80).
Rutland MSS (MSS. of the 4th Duke of Rutland as Lord Lieutenant, 1784-7), *14th Report, Appendix i*, vol. 3.
Stopford-Sackville MSS (MSS. of Lord George Germain), vol. 1.
Vernon-Smith MSS (MSS. of Philip Vernon-Smith, Pitt's private secreatry from 1787), *12th Report, Appendix ix*.

D. *Parliamentary Proceedings, Speeches and Statutes*

Debates in the House of Commons of Ireland on a Motion whether the King's most excellent Majesty, and the Lords and Commons of Ireland, are the only powers competent to bind or enact laws in this kingdom. By a Gentleman (Dublin, 1780).
The Parliamentary Register, or History of the Proceedings and Debates of the House of Commons, 1781-97 (Dublin, 1782-1801).
The Parliamentary History of England from the Norman Conquest to 1803 (1806-20).
The Debates and Proceedings of the House of Commons of Ireland . . . 1785, 2 vols. (Dublin, 1786).
The whole of the debates in both Houses of Parliament, on a Bill to prevent tumultuous risings and assemblies (Dublin, 1787).
Speeches of the Rt. Hon. Charles Fox in the House of Commons, 6 vols. (1815).
Speeches of the Rt. Hon. Henry Grattan, with prefatory observations (Dublin, 1811).
The speeches of the Rt. Hon. Richard Brinsley Sheridan, 5 vols.(1842), ed. "A Constitutional Friend".
Burtchaell, G.D., *Genealogical memoirs of the Members of Parliament for the County and City of Kilkenny* (1888).
Journals of the House of Commons of the Kingdom of Ireland, 1613-1800, 19 vols. (Dublin 1796-1800).

The Statutes at Large passed in the parliaments held in fIreland, 1310-1800,
20 vols. (Dublin, 1789-1800).

E. *Secondary Sources*

Aspinall, A., "The Cabinet Council, 1783-1835", *Proc. of the British Academy,* xxxviii, 1952.

Beckett, J.C., *Confrontations* (1972).

Beckett, J.C., "The Irish parliament in the eighteenth century", *Proc. of the Belfast Natural History and Philosophical Society,* 2nd series, IV, 1951.

Beckett, J.C., *The making of modern Ireland, 1693-1923* (1966).

Bingham, M., *Sheridan: the track of a comet* (1972).

Bolton, G.C., *The passing of the Irish Act of Union* (Oxford, 1966).

Boulton, J.T., *Arbitrary power: an eighteenth-century obsession* (Nottingham, 1966).

Boulton, J.T., *The language of politics in the age of Wilkes and Burke* (1963).

Bowden, W., "The influence of the manufacturers on some of the early policies of William Pitt", *American Historical Review,* xxix, no. 4, July 1924.

Boyce, D.G., *Nationalism in Ireland* (London, Canberra & Dublin, 1982).

Boylan, H., *A dictionary of Irish biography* (Dublin, 1978).

Boyle, K., "Police in Ireland before the Union", *Irish Jurist,* vii, 1972; viii, 1973.

Willis, R.E., "Cabinet politics and executive policy-making procedures, 1794-1801", *Albion,* 1975.

Burns, R.E., "Parsons, priests and the people: the rise of Irish anti-clericalism, 1785-1789", *Church History,* xxxi, no. 2, June 1962.

Cannon, J., *The Fox-North Coalition* (Cambridge, 1969).

Cannon, J., *Lord North: the noble lord in the blue ribbon* (1970).

Christie, I.R., *Crisis of Empire: Great Britain and the American Colonies 1754-1783)* (1966).

Christie, I.R., & Labaree, B.W., *Empire or Independence 1760-1776* (Oxford, 1976).

Christie, I.R., *The end of North's ministry 1780-1782* (1958).

Christie, I.R., *Myth and reality in late eighteenth century British politics* (Berkeley & Los Angeles, 1970).

Connell, B., *Portrait of a Whig Peer* (1957).

Craig, M., *Dublin 1660-1860* (1953).

Cullen, L.M., *An economic history of Ireland since 1660* (1972).

Cullen, L.M. "The 1798 rebellion in its eighteenth century context", a paper read at the 16th conference of Irish historians, 1983.

Derry, J., *Castlereagh* (1976).

Derry, J., *Charles James Fox* (1974).

Derry, J., *English politics and the American Revolution* (1976).

Derry, J., *The Regency Crisis and the Whigs 1788-9* (Cambridge, 1863).

Derry, J., *William Pitt* (1962).

Dickinson, H.T., *Liberty and property* (1977).

Edwards, O.D. "Ireland", *Celtic Nationalism,* by O.D. Edwards et al.

Edwards, R.D., "The minute book of the Catholic Committee, 1773-92", *Archivium Hibernicum,* ix, 1942.

Ehrman, J., *The Younger Pitt: the years of acclaim* (1969).
Ehrman, J., *The Younger Pitt: the reluctant transition* (1983).
Elliott, M., *Partners in revolution* (New Haven & London, 1982).
Ferguson, K.P., "The Volunteer Movement and the Government, 1778-1793", *The Irish Sword*, 1971.
Fothergill, B., *The mitred earl* (1974).
Goodwin, A., *The Friends of Liberty* (1979).
Gwynn, S., *Henry Grattan and his times* (Dublin, 1939).
Hand, G.J., "The constitutional position of the Irish military establishment from the Restoration to the Union: an introductory note", *Irish Jurist*, iii, 1968.
Harlow, V.T., *The founding of the Second British Empire 1763-1793* (1952).
Hobhouse, C., *Fox* (1934).
Hoffman, R., *The Marquis: a study of Charles Watson Wentworth, Marquis of Rockingham* (1973).
Hunt, Rev. W., *The Irish Parliament 1775* (1907).
Inglis, B., *The freedom of the press in Ireland 1784-1841* (1954).
James, F.G., *Ireland in the Empire 1688-1770* (Harvard, 1973).
Johnston, E.M., *Great Britain and Ireland 1760-1800* (Edinburgh & London, 1963).
Johnston, E.M., *Ireland in the eighteenth century* (Dublin, 1974).
Johnston, E.M., "Members of the Irish Parliament, 1784-7", *Proc. of the Royal Irish Academy*, vol. 71, sec. C, no. 5, 1971.
Jupp, P., "The aims and achievements of Lord Grenville", *Essays presented to Michael Roberts*, ed. J. Bossy & P. Jupp (Belfast, 1976).
Jupp, P., *Lord Grenville (1759-1834)* (Oxford, 1985).
Jupp, P., "Earl Temple's viceroyalty and the question of Renunciation", *Irish Historical Studies*, xvii, 1971.
Kelly, P., "British and Irish politics in 1785", *English Historical Review*, July 1975.
Kennedy, D., "The Irish Whigs, administrative reform, and responsible government 1782-1800", *Eire-Ireland*, VIII, 4, 1973.
Kiernan, T.J. "Forbes Letters", *Analecta Hibernica*, no. 8, 1938.
Kieran, T.J., *History of the financial administration of Ireland to 1817* (1930).
Koebner, R., "The early speeches of Henry Grattan", *Bull. of the Institute of Historical Research*, vol. 30, 1957.
Koebner, R., *Empire* (Cambridge, 1961).
Lambert, S., *Bills and Acts: legislative procedure in eighteenth century England* (Cambridge, 1971).
Lansdowne, Marquis of, *Glanerought and the Petty-Fitzmaurices* (Oxford, 1937).
Lecky, W.E.H., *History of Ireland in the eighteenth century*, 5 vols. (1892).
Lee, J., "Grattan's Parliament", *The Irish parliamentary tradition*, ed. B. Farrell (Dublin & New York, 1973).
Litton Falkiner, C., "Lord Clare", *Studies in Irish history and biography* (1902).
Macalpine, I., & Hunter, R., *George III and the mad-business* (1969).
McCracken, J.L., *The Irish parliament in the eighteenth century* (Dundalk, 1971).

MacDonagh, O., *The Inspector-General* (1981).

McDowell, R.B., *Ireland in the age of imperialism and revolution 1760-1801* (Oxford, 1979).

McDowell, R.B., *Irish public opinion, 1750-1800* (1944).

McDowell, R.B. "Some Fitzgibbon letters from the Sneyd Muniments in the John Rylands Library', *Bull. of the John Rylands Library*, vol. 34, 1952.

MacMadden, A.F., "The imperial machinery of the Younger Pitt", *Essays in British History*, ed. H.R. Trevor-Roper (1964).

Mackesy, P., *The war for America 1775-1783* (1964).

Malcomson, A.P.W., "The Gentle Laviathan: Arthur Hill, 2nd Marquess of Downshire, 1753-1801", *Plantation to Partition* ed. P.Roebuck (Belfast, 1981).

Malcomson, A.P.W., *Isaac Corry 1755-1813* (Belfast, 1974).

Malcomson, A.P.W., *John Foster: the politics of the Anglo-Irish ascendancy* (Oxford, 1978).

Malcomson, A.P.W., "The Politics of the 'natural right'; the Abercorn family and Strabane borough, 1692-1800", *Historical Studies X*, ed. G.A. Hayes-McCoy (Galway, 1976).

Malcomson, A.P.W., "Speaker Pery and the Pery Papers", *North Munster Antiquarian Journal*, vol. XVI, 1973-4.

Maxwell, C., *Country and town in Ireland under the Georges* (1940).

Maxwell, C., *Dublin under the Georges, 1714-1830* (1936).

Essays in eighteenth century history, ed. R. Mitchinson (1966).

Mitchell, L.G., *Charles James Fox and the disintegration of the Whig Party 1782-1794* (Oxford, 1971).

Murray, A.E., *A history of the commercial and financial Jrelations between England and Ireland from the period of the Restoration* (1903).

Namier, Sir L., & Brooke, J., *The House of Commons, 1754-90*, 3 vols. (1964).

Namier, Sir L., *Crossroads of power* (1964).

Namier, Sir L., *The structure of politics at the accession of George III* (2nd ed. 1957).

Norris, J., *Shelburne and reform* (1963).

O'Brien, G., "The Grattan Mystique", *Eighteenth-century Ireland*, vol. 1 (1986).

O'Brien, G., "An account of a debate in the Irish Parliament, 1787", *Analecta Hibernica* (1986).

O'Connell, M.R., "Daniel O'Connell and the Irish eighteenth century", *Studies in eighteenth century culture*, vol. 5, ed. R.C. Rosbottom (Wisconsin, 1976).

O'Connell, M.R., *Irish Politics and social conflict in the age of the American Revolution* (Philadelphia, 1965).

O'Connell, M.R., "The political background to the establishment of Maynooth College", *Irish Ecclesiastical Record*, vol. 35, May-June 1956.

O'Connor, T.M., "The conflict between Flood and Grattan", *Essays in British and Irish history in honour of James Eadie Todd*, ed. H.A. Cronne, T.W. Moody & D.B. Quinn (1949).

O'Donoghue, P., "The Holy See and Ireland, 1780-1803", *Archivium Hibernicum*, xxiv, 1976-7.

O'Gorman, F., *The rise of party in England: the Rockingham Whigs 1760-82* (1975).

O'Gorman, F., *The Whig Party and the French Revolution* (1967).

Olsen, A.G., *The Radical Duke* (Oxford, 1961).

Ó Snodaigh, P., "Notes on the Volunteers, Yeomanry and Fencibles of Kerry", *Journal of the Kerry Historical and Archaeological Society*, no. 4, 1971.

Packenham, T., *The year of liberty*, (1969).

Pares, R., *George III and the politicians* (Oxford, 1953).

Pares, R., *Limited monarchy in Great Britain in the eighteenth century* (1957).

Pares, R., *Politics and Personality 1760-1827*, ed. M.J. Barnes (1967).

Reid, J.P., *In a defiant stance* (Pennsylvania, 1977).

Reid, L., *Charles James Fox* (1969).

Reid, L. "Speaking in the eighteenth century House of Commons", *Speech Monographs*, vol. XVI, 1949.

Reilly, R., *Pitt the Younger* (1978).

Roxby, P.M., *Henry Grattan* (1902).

Sainty, J.C., "The secretariart of the chief governors of Ireland, 1690-1800", *Proc. of the Royal Irish Academy*, vol. 77, sec. C, no. 1, 1977.

Sayles, G.O., "Contemporary sketches of the members of the Irish parliament in 1782", *Proc. of the Royal Irish Academy*, vol. 56, sec.C, no. 3, 1954.

Schwoerer, L.G., *No standing armies* (Baltimore & JLondon, 1974).

Simms, J.G., *The Treaty of Limerick* (Dundalk, 1966).

Simms, J.G., *The Williamite Confiscation in Ireland 1691-1703* (1956).

Smyth, P.D.H., "The Volunteers and parliament 1779-84", *Penal era and golden age*, ed. T. Bartlett & D.W. Hayton (Belfast, 1979).

Snoddy, O., "Notes on the Volunteers, Militia Yeomanry, Orangement and Fencibles of Co. Limerick", *The Irish Sword*, vol. X, no. 39, 1971.

Syndergaard, R., "The Fitzwilliam crisis and Irish nationalism", *Eire-Ireland*, VI, 3, 1971.

Smith, E.A., *Whig principles and party politics* (Manchester, 1974).

Thomas, P.D.G., *Lord North* (1976).

Thomas, P.D.G., *The House of Commons in the eighteenth century* (Oxford, 1971).

Tyler, J.E., "A letter from the Marquis of Rockingham to Sir William Mayne on the proposed absentee tax of 1773", *Irish Historical Studies*, viii, 1953.

Ward, B., *The dawn of the Catholic revival in England, 1781-1803*, 2 vols. (1909).

Western, J.R., *The English militia in the eighteenth century* (London & Toronto, 1965).

Willcox, W.B., "Lord Lansdowne on the French Revolution and the Irish Rebellion", *Journal of Modern History*, XVII, no. 1 (March, 1945).

Zimmern, A.E., *Henry Grattan* (London & Oxford, 1902).

F. *Theses and unpublished material*

Barrett, R.J., "A comparative study of imperial constitutional theory in Ireland and America in the age of the American Revolution" (Ph.D., Univ. of Dublin, 1958).

T. Bartlett, "The Townshend Viceroyalty, 1767-72" (Ph.D. Q.U.B., 1976).

Callen, R.V., "The structure of Anglo-Irish poltics during the American Revolution: Cavendish's diary of the Irish Parliament, October 12, 1779 to September 2, 1780; Edition of the partial text and a critical essay" (Ph.D., Notre Dame, 1973).

Clune, M.E., "The Irish Parliament, 1776-83" (M.A., U.C.D. 1943).

Cummins, S.A., "Opposition and the Irish Parliament (1759-1771)" (M.A., St Patrick's College, Maynooth, 1978).

Dawson, J., "Pitt and Ireland" (unpub. research paper).

Donaldson, A.G., "The application in Ireland of English and British legislation made before 1801" (Ph.D., Q.U.B., 1952).

Fergusson, C.B., "The colonial policy of the First Earl of Liverpool as President of the Committee for Trade, 1786-1804" (D.Phil., Oxford, 1952).

Griffin, J., "Parliamentary Politics in Ireland during the reign of George I" (M.A. U.C.D., 1977).

Griffin, W.D. "John FitzGibbon, Earl of Clare" (Ph.D., Fordham, 1962).

Hayton, D.W., "Ireland and the English Ministers, 1707-1716" (D.Phil., Oxford, 1975).

Kelly, P., "The establishment of Pitt's administration, 1783-6" (D.Phil., Oxford, 1971).

Kennedy, D., "The Irish Whigs, 1789-1793" (Ph.D., Toronto, 1971).

Lammey, D., "A study of Anglo-Irish relations between 1772 and 1782, with particular reference to the 'Free Trade' movement" (Ph.D., Q.U.B., 1984).

McCavery, T.R., "Finance and politics in Ireland 1801-17" (Ph.D., Q.U.B., 1981).

Meenan, P.N., "The Regency Crisis in Ireland" (M.A., U.C.D., 1971).

O'Flaherty, E., "The Catholic Question in Ireland, 1774-1793" (M.A., U.C.D. 1981).

Victory, I.L., "Colonial Nationalism in Ireland, 1692-1725: From Common Law to Natural Right" (Ph.D., T.C.D., 1985).

Whitlaw, J.A.G., "Anglo-Irish commercial relations, 1779-85" (M.A., Q.U.B., 1958).

Index

231